AP

Advanced Placement

MACROECONOMICS/ MICROECONOMICS

Michael Taillard

XAMonline

Melrose, MA

XAMonline, Inc.

21 Orient Avenue
Melrose, MA 02176
Toll Free: 1-800-509-4128
Email: info@xamonline.com

Web: www.xamonline.com
Fax: 1-617-583-5552

Library of Congress Cataloging-in-Publication Data

Wynne, Sharon

AP Macroeconomics/Microeconomics / Michael Taillard

ISBN: 978-1-60787-633-5

1. Advanced Placement   2. Study Guides   3. Macroeconomics

4. Microeconomics

Disclaimer:

The opinions expressed in this publication are the sole works of XAMonline and were created independently from the College Board, or other testing affiliates. Between the time of publication and printing, specific test standards as well as testing formats and website information may change that are not included in part or in whole within this product. XAMonline develops sample test questions, and they reflect similar content as on real tests; however, they are not former tests. XAMonline assembles content that aligns with test standards but makes no claims nor guarantees candidates a passing score.

Cover photo provided by ©Can Stock Photo Inc./robwilson39; ©Can Stock Photo Inc./labamba; ©Can Stock Photo Inc./karenr; ©Can Stock Photo Inc./radiantskies; ©Can Stock Photo Inc./Bialasiewicz

Printed in the United States of America

AP Macroeconomics/Microeconomics

ISBN: 978-1-60787-633-5

Table of Contents

About the Author

Michael Taillard is a freelance research experimentalist and an Adjunct Professor of Economics at Bellevue University, USA. He received his PhD in Financial Economics and has an academic background that includes degrees in International Economics as well as International Finance, and military training at the Army Transportation Corps in Ft. Eustis, VA. His work includes economic research projects for The American Red Cross, theoretical study for the United States Strategic Command (STRATCOM) on which this book is based, and consulting panels given at horror movie industry expos who ve since dubbed him The Econozombist for his work helping to build an accurate representation of the world after the zombie apocalypse. His interest in the military applications of economics stems from the time he spent as a United States Army Reservist and seeing the untapped tactical potential.

About the Exam

The AP Program offers two separate exams in economics: one in microeconomics and one in macroeconomics. Each exam is intended for qualified students who wish to complete studies in secondary school equivalent to a one-semester college introductory course. Each exam presumes at least one semester of college-level preparation. Students may take one or both exams in a given year. A separate score is reported for each.

The material included in the Course Descriptions and in the two exams has been selected by economists who serve as members of the AP Macroeconomics Development Committee and AP Microeconomics Development Committee. In establishing the courses and exams, the committees surveyed the economics departments of more than 200 institutions receiving the most AP scores in economics. Using the information obtained about the content of typical introductory college courses, the committees developed the course outlines and had the multiple-choice questions covering the outlines pretested on college students enrolled in the appropriate economics courses.

The AP Course Descriptions and exams are thus representative of college courses and are, therefore, considered appropriate for the measurement of skills and knowledge in the fields of introductory microeconomics and macroeconomics. Inclusion of the content, ideas, and values expressed in the material is not intended as an endorsement of them by the College Board or ETS.

How the Exam is Scored

The multiple choice part of the test is scored by machine and the free response portion is scored by hand (every summer hundreds of professors, content specialists, and AP Economics teachers meet to grade the 300,000+ exams that are taken). Once both scores have been tallied, they are combined and scaled. This raw score is then changed into a composite score ranging from 1 – 5.

The College Board proposes the following qualifications for each of the potential score:

Exam Grade	Recommendation
5	Extremely Well Qualified
4	Well Qualified
3	Qualified
2	Possibly Qualified
1	No recommendation

The minimum score required for college credit to be granted is a 3. As mentioned above, many schools require scores of 4 or 5 in order to grant credit.

For comparison, the College Board makes the equivalents of the AP Exam scores at follows:

AP Exam Grade	Letter Grade Equivalant
5	A
4	A-, B+, B
3	B-, C+, C
2	None
1	None

Specifics of AP Economics Tests

The AP Microeconomics Exam and the AP Macroeconomics Exam are each a little over 2 hours long. Each exam consists of a 70-minute multiple-choice section and a 60-minute free-response section. The multiple-choice section accounts for two-thirds of the student's exam score and the free-response section for the remaining one-third.

Part I – 80 Multiple Choice Questions, 70 minutes, 66% of your total score

Part II – Free Response, 50 minutes + 10 minute reading period, 33% of total score

    A 1 Very Long Question
    B 2 Shorter Questions

Many questions in both the multiple-choice and free response parts of the exam will require graphical analysis and use of mathematical calculations.

In the free-response section of the exam, students have a 10-minute reading period and 50 minutes to answer one long and two short free-response questions. These questions generally require students to interrelate different content areas and may ask them to analyze a given economic situation and to set forth and evaluate general microeconomics principles.

Students are expected to show both analytical and organizational skills in writing their responses and to incorporate explanatory diagrams that clarify their analyses. Some questions will require students to interpret graphs that are provided as part of the questions; other questions will require students to draw their own graphs as part of their answers. All graphs should be clearly labeled. A correctly labeled diagram must have all axes and curves clearly labeled and must show directional changes.

The longer free-response question will generally require students to interrelate several content areas; the two shorter questions will typically focus on a specific topic in a given content area.

When answering the AP Economics free-response questions, you should respond clearly and concisely. Including paragraph or even full-sentence responses is not always necessary; however, it is important to address the verb prompts appropriately (as explained below). A written response that presents conflicting answers is likely to lead to the loss of points. Definitions of the following terms that are frequently used as prompts in free-response questions are:

- "Show" means to use a diagram to illustrate your answer. Correct labeling of all elements including the axes of the diagram is necessary to receive full credit.
- "Explain" means to take the reader through all of the steps or linkages in the line of economic reasoning. Graphs and symbols are acceptable as part of the explanation.
- "Identify" means to provide a specific answer that might be a list or a label on a graph, without any explanation or elaboration.
- "Calculate" means to use mathematical operations to determine a specific numerical response, along with providing your work.

Hints for Taking the Test

Part I – Multiple Choice Questions (70 minutes)

Multiple choice questions can be tricky. A lot of times it is possible to eliminate one or two of the answers right away, but then get stuck with the others. On the AP Economics exams, there is no penalty for incorrect answers, so be sure to record an answer for every question, even if it is a complete guess.

It is also very important to know what the question is asking of you. The College Board is notorious for saying things like, "All of the following are examples, EXCEPT…"

or, "Which of these is NOT…" These words can change the entire meaning of the sentence. Be on alert for qualifiers like this.

You will be using a number 2 pencil to bubble in your answers on an answer sheet. At this stage your academic career you have taken enough tests of this type that hopefully you know how to properly fill in the circles. If you need to erase an answer, be sure to do it completely.

Remember your timing. Sure, 80 questions in 70 minutes sounds easy enough. But remember, many of the questions will take longer to answer than you think. They will require you to calculate economic formulas, draw your own diagrams, and consider the implications of policy decisions.

Many times multiple choice questions will have a visual that relates to several questions. The directions may say, "Use the diagram to answer questions 42-44." Be aware of this.

Use #2 pencil.

Part II – Free Response (50 minutes + 10 minute preparation)

The free response questions are usually the items that give students the most difficulty. The problem usually results from not organizing one's thoughts sufficiently and then getting them down on paper fast enough. The score on the long question will account for one-half of the student's total free-response score; the scores on the shorter questions will each account for one-quarter of the student's total free-response score. It is suggested that you spend approximately half your time on the first question and divide the remaining time equally between the next two questions.

Be certain your answers are in essay form. These are not short-answer questions intended to show that you know the basics of economic mechanics. Instead, these questions are intended to show your ability to think critically and apply economic principles to real-world situations. In other words, when answering free response questions, showing the process you used to find the answer is more important than the answer itself.

Like the multiple choice, you do not lose credit for presenting incorrect information. However, you do lose time. Other things the readers do not care about include: spelling, grammar, and penmanship. Obviously, if a reader in unable to determine what is was you wrote, they cannot grade it, but they do their best to interpret a student's "chicken scratch."

Be aware of what you are writing. You do not want to say one thing in the first paragraph and then say the complete opposite in the second paragraph. If you do this, you will not get any credit, even if one of them is correct. This is because the reader does not know if you knew which was correct or just took a guess and got lucky.

It is expected that you'll include diagrams or graphs in your answers. Be sure to properly number the visual so the reader knows to which question and part of the question it belongs. Additionally, make certain to label everything!! The last thing you want is not receive points because your beautifully constructed graph or data table was missing a title.

Use a blue or black pen.

What to Expect in this Book

As you move forward through these next pages, you will find 2 separate sample tests for both AP Macroeconomics and AP Microeconomics. While these do not necessarily include the same questions you will see on the AP Economics exams, they cover the same material with each topic area discussed in roughly the same proportions. Each begins with sample multiple choice question, and then move-on to sample free response questions. In this book you'll also find the answers to the multiple choice questions, and sample answers for the free response questions.

Economic Principles

Economics is a field of behavioral science which studies the manner in which people distribute resources. Economists utilize the scientific method to perform research that advances our understanding of how people function, organize themselves into firms such as businesses or governments, and how they behave collectively together. In a lot of ways, economics has been a way to quantify psychology to measuring human behavior in various ways in order to determine how people will respond to changes in resource availability, the amount to which people value given resources, how they cooperate and compete with each other for resources, how they make decisions, and so forth. This research is then applied by businesses, governments, investors, and others to help them better manage people and resources. It helps companies to maximize the productive efficiency of their employees, invest in the best production methods, meet the needs of potential customers and attract their attention, and more. Governments utilize this information to develop better policy in order to increase total national economic growth, maximize peoples' quality of life, ensure resources are utilized in a sustainable way, and otherwise ensure a bright future for the people within that nation.

There is one basic assumption that permeates all the introductory material of economics: ceteris paribus. This means "all other things remaining the same." Given that economics is the study of people, and people are a very dynamic thing, at any given point there's a lot of things which can be influencing the situation (in sciencey-speak, there are multiple independent variables determining the behavior of the dependent variable). So, in order to illustrate specific points, we just assume that everything not being discussed is being held constant. It's not that these things don't change, but we're not interested in them at the moment because we want to focus on just one thing at a time. So, before you start shouting "But anything could happen in that time!" remember that this is already taken into consideration. You need to understand how each of those things influences the outcome individually, before you can start looking at them in combination.

The organization of this portion of the book is exactly as outlined by the official AP tests in economics, with 1 exception. Both the tests on microeconomics and macroeconomics include a portion on Basic Economic Concepts, and it's the exact same material. Since basic economics (and common sense) says that you don't want to pay for redundant material repeated over and over again in repetition, I just included it as a unique section, by itself.

Regarding the nature of this book, all the content you'll see on the test is in this book, but not all the content in this book will be seen on the test. Some of it is provided either to offer context for the information you need to know, to provide some basics required before you can understand the points being made, or to offer additional information which will help you to understand these principles through the ways in which they fit with other mechanisms in economics. Have you ever walked into a conversation halfway through, after a minute think you know what's happening, only to be informed that you clearly do not? It's the same thing here. You don't want to get just enough information that you think you know what you're doing only to find-out that you would've understood better if given some information on the context of things.

Basic Economic Concepts

The entirety of economics extends from a single problem: **scarcity**. Scarcity is merely the principle that states that at any given moment in time, there is not enough resources necessary to meet every desire. For example, when you go to a new town for work or leisure, you must choose at which restaurant you want to eat. You can choose to go to a chain you've visited before, which has moderately good food at a moderately good price. You could also choose to go to a local place about which you know nothing; you might get a mouthful of disappointment in every bite you take, or you find that it's your new favorite place to eat. Clearly you can't eat at both since you only have $10, so you must choose the manner in which you'll use the scarce resources available to you with the goal of picking the option with the greatest value. People, companies, government, charities, and even plants and animals must all choose the way in which to utilize the resources available to them. A company might need to choose what materials to buy, which machine to invest in, how much of each product to make, who to hire, and so forth. Making a **choice** between competing options, including the option to refrain from doing anything, is the basis for each economic decision we make.

There is a cost associated with each choice. In our example, you decide to go to the new restaurant. You eat and the bill is $10, which is what you would have paid at the chain restaurant. That amount is your **accounting cost**, which is the amount of money you pay for something. In economics, we're also concerned with the **opportunity cost**, though. The opportunity cost is the benefits of the option you didn't choose. In our example, your opportunity cost would be the amount of benefit you would have received at the chain restaurant. If the new restaurant is worse, then your opportunity cost is above the benefits you received, putting you at an economic loss. If the new restaurant is better, then you've generated economic value added in the amount that the new restaurant was better than the chain.

Consider the following:

Investment A Investment B
Price: $100 $100
End Value: $300 $200
Profit: $200 $100

No matter which investment you choose, the accounting cost will be $100. In choosing investment A your opportunity cost is $100, because that's how much benefit you would have received had you chosen investment B. By contrast, the opportunity cost of investment B would have been $200.

When you combine accounting and opportunity costs together, you get your **economic cost**. The economic cost of investment A is $200, and the economic cost of investment B is $300. It is the goal of economic decision to maximize the amount of **economic value added** created over the economic cost, not just the accounting cost, which means making choices that maximize the amount of benefit created over the economic cost.

Since you must choose how to allocate your limited resources, when choosing what to produce you must consider how many of a given item you're able to produce using an equal number of resources. Given the option of choosing to produce pizza or beer, you could focus all your resources on just one or the other, or produce some combination of both. The range of possible combinations is called a **production possibilities curve** (PPC), as shown:

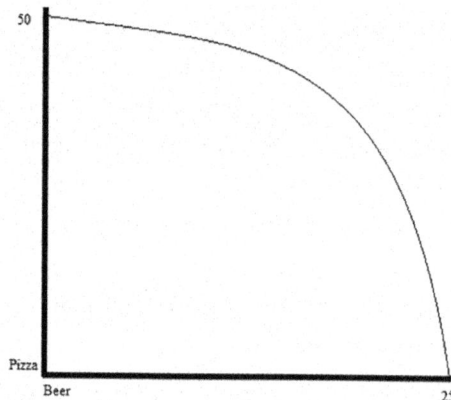

It is possible to produce anywhere along the edge, known as the **production possibilities frontier** (PPF), or anywhere inside the curve, although that would be an inefficient use of resources. The entire area outside the curve, however, represents production combinations which are impossible using the current availability of resources and technology.

Using the same volume of resources, you can produce either 50 pizzas, or 25 beers, or some combination of both. To avoid getting too complicated, let's say that the rate of exchange between pizza and beer remains the same, in which case you'd have to give-up 2 pizzas for each beer you produce. In other words, your opportunity cost of each beer is 2 pizzas; conversely your opportunity cost for producing each pizza is 0.5 beers. The problem is that even though you're a lot better at producing pizza than you are at producing beer, there is demand for both. Instead of trying to produce something at which you're not very efficient, instead we opt for **trade**.

The brewers making beer could try to grow their own hops and barley, build their own brew kettle with steel they smelted themselves from iron ore, and so forth. They could do that, but they would get very little accomplished, since there would by many different skills they'd have to know and they'd never get a chance to get very good at any of them. Instead, people focus on one type of job – a narrow skill set – and become extremely good at it, so that they can produce a lot using very few resources, in what is known as the **specialization of labor**. So, the brewers produce far more beer than they need, and then sell most of it so that they then might purchase those things which they never learned to make. As everyone works within their area of specialization and trade for the other things they need, each becomes very good at their job and can produce much greater volume using fewer resources, and so together they are able to produce more total stuff than they would be able to if they didn't trade. This increased economic value added is known as the **gains from trade**.

As people around the world trade with each other, the people in a particular nation will tend to specialize in a broad type of skill set, and trade with a nation whose people specializes in a different type of skill set. For example, over the past few decades China has specialized in the unskilled and semi-skilled mass manufacturing of consumer and industrial goods, which they then sell all over the world, including to the US. In exchange, the US has specialized in agricultural goods and skilled services, which it sells to China, in addition to a variety of other nations. The trade between nations is made of the trade between individual people, just as if you went to the store for pizza instead of making your own, but on a much larger scale. An entire nation isn't going to specialize in a single type of labor, though, so instead of the specialization of labor experienced by individual people, nations have more generalized specializations known as a **comparative advantage**. The people in China haven't all specialized in one type of job, but the population has specialized in ways that create an industry based on mass manufacturing, which includes a wide range of jobs and skills. At the same time, people in the US don't all work in the same industry, but certain industries tend to dominate in the US especially as compared to other nations in the world, such as advanced computer tech, and industrial agriculture.

Think of it like this: In the specialization of labor, people get good at a particular thing and sell it to others in exchange for other things. These people sometimes start businesses in order to make their things to more people, and when several companies offer the same thing, the one that does it best as a **competitive advantage**. As businesses trade with businesses in other nations, sometimes the foreign businesses are better and people stop buying from local companies. This causes broad specializations between nations, as the individual competitive advantages of these businesses start to appear as national trends known as comparative advantages. In other words, when the businesses of one nation can produce equal value utilizing fewer resources than the businesses in another country, then as those businesses increase in popularity and size, comprising a bigger percentage of the country's total output, the nation itself forms a specialization.

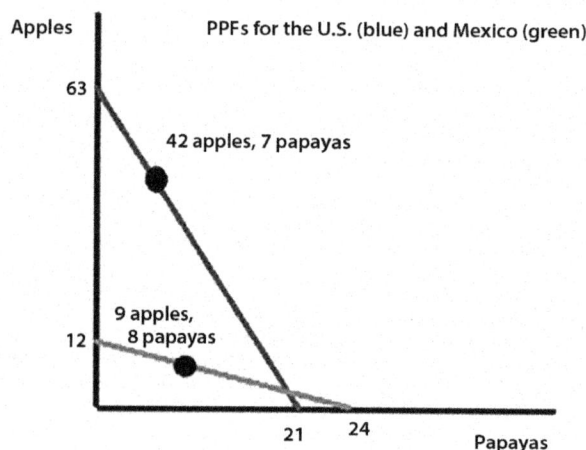

Apples   PPFs for the U.S. (blue) and Mexico (green)

63

42 apples, 7 papayas

9 apples,
12   8 papayas

21   24   Papayas

The above chart is a typical comparison of production possibilities curves between nations, showing the relative opportunity costs each nation faces. In the graph, the US has an absolute advantage, able to produce more total stuff, but it also has a higher opportunity cost in producing papayas – it must forego more apples than it would be able to produce papayas. Mexico, on the other hand, has a higher opportunity cost in apples. The opportunity cost can be quantified by dividing the volume of one item being produced by the volume of the item foregone as a result. In the graph above, Mexico could produce 24 papayas, but if they wanted to produce 1 apple they would have to give up 2 papayas. So, for 1 apple, the opportunity cost is 2 papayas, giving them an opportunity cost in apples of 1/2, or 0.5. This means they are producing 50% as much value by focusing on apples as they would by focusing on papayas, actually decreasing the total amount of stuff they can produce.

Consider this example:

No Trade   **Nation A**   **Nation B**
Pizza: 26   10
Beer: 12   10
Total: 38   20

Trade   **Nation A**   **Nation B**
Pizza: 50   0
Beer: 0   40
Total: 50   40

Nation A, as in our previous example, must give-up 2 pizzas for every beer it makes. Nation B has a 3/1 ratio favoring beer, which means it must give-up 3 beer for each pizza it makes. If each nation tries to fulfil the demands of their own nation without trading, they're going to end-up allocating resources toward things with a high opportunity cost. Together, the two nation will produce 58 total units. If each nation focuses just on producing those things in which it has the lowest opportunity cost, and then trade with the other, then together they'll have more total stuff, achieving a full 90 total units.

Nation A has greater total production capacity, making it able to produce more total units. This is what's known as an **absolute advantage**. If it tries to produce everything, though, its resources will be used less efficiently, and the increased resource consumption will force its prices to increase so that it can't trade in anything. So, nations instead trade on their comparative advantages, creating gains from trade.

The way in which a nation manages these gains from trade, whether earned in trade between individuals or between nations, depends partly on the type of economic system each nation uses. There are two theoretical extremes of economic systems, while the reality always falls somewhere in the middle of a spectrum between the two. At the one end there's **planned economies**, and at the other end there's **free market economies**. A fully planned economy would be one wherein the entirety of resource distribution is managed through a centralized organization of some sort. Everything is decided by this organization: production volume, product types, prices, distribution, and so forth. Economies emphasizing planning tend to be very inefficient and lack responsiveness to changes in demand thereby creating shortages, but they also tend to be less volatile and are able to focus long-term goals without being hindered by the need for short-term profits. By contrast, a fully free market economy would be one wherein each exchange is decided on a case-by-case basis, in which there is no type of intervention at all. A fully free market economy, by necessity, has no government, because there would be no taxation and no tax revenues with which to fund government operations. Economies emphasizing the free market tend to be more responsive to market forces and are more efficient, but also tend to be more volatile, lack protections, and advances in science and art are hampered by the need to generate constant, short-term profits.

It is because there are pros and cons to both planned and free market economies that every nation and community throughout history combine elements of both, in what's known as a **mixed economy**. Even the most planned economies have elements of barter and trade, and even primal communities with no formal government include planning in terms of preparing for the winter/drought seasons, and interacting with other communities. Within a single business, there is competition between departments for resources, and between people for status, but the functions and goals of the company are decided by management. Communities and nations which move too far in either direction are always doomed to fail.

Introductory economics makes the assumption that firms all behave rationally. It assumes that the decisions people and companies make is based entirely upon a logical attempt to maximize utility and economic value added. There are times you'll be tempted to say "That's not how it works every time!" You'll even read news headlines from time to time talking about how some new study disproves economics by showing people aren't rational. The reality, though, is that economists have already known people aren't rational since the very beginning of economics as a field of scientific research. The assumption of rationality is only used as a starting-point. By understanding how things function under optimal conditions and then using that as a reference point, it's possible to then identify the reasons which we deviate from rational decision making, and the degree to which we deviate. A great example of this is the work by Kahneman and Tversky which showed that people make risky decisions based more on the presentation of information provided rather than the information,

One of the issues that arises from the economic system being used is that of property rights – the right to ownership. A government which oversteps its planning may try to take ownership of the entirety of a nation's resources, as with North Korea, but a government which does not concern itself at all with property rights will not be able to enforce ownership laws which prevent activities such as counterfeiting goods. The market for HIV drugs once became the center of the debate on property rights, as companies which incurred all the costs of researching and developing these drugs would lose money if they weren't allowed to protect their ownership of the drugs, making them unable to pursue the production of these drugs within a free market system. The problem is that the majority of people who needed HIV drugs were people completely incapable of affording them, especially if prices were kept high by preventing companies from counterfeiting them, allowing the counterfeiters to avoid the costs of development and thereby giving them the opportunity to sell the drugs more cheaply. The question became how to properly apply economic planning in a way that both put the drugs in the hands of those who needed it while simultaneously maintaining the **incentive** for companies to pursue research and development into improved drugs.

As a final point of basic economic principles, the matter of marginal analysis applies. The word **marginal** is one which has unique meaning in economics, and refers to +1. The marginal benefit of beer means the amount of benefit received from drinking one more beer. Marginal cost refers to the cost associated with buying or producing one additional unit of something. This plays an important role, as values never stay the same with additional units. As you buy more of something, eventually each marginal unit will increase in price as supply runs-out and you need to resort to more expensive suppliers. As you produce more, you'll eventually need to reduce price as there will be fewer people willing to pay the same price for each marginal unit. This also relates to a principle known as the **law of diminishing marginal returns**. Even though you're buying or producing more units of the same product, you're getting less benefit relative to the amount of money spent. This is very closely related to the **law of diminishing marginal utility**. If you're really hungry, that first slice of pizza will be the best, and every slice after that might be good, but less and less good until you eat so much you make yourself sick. These laws both illustrate the nature of marginality in economics, which states that a there will be less economic value added for each marginal unit in most cases.

Microeconomics

Microeconomics is a specific field of economics which studies the individual firm. A firm is any collection of people and resources come together for a mutual goal. That includes businesses, non-profits, individual households, and even individual people. This also includes governments, but only in the respect of their internal operations, rather than national policy. The point is that whereas other fields of economics might be concerned with entire nations or other large groups of firms, microeconomics deals specifically with the individual players within an economy.

Firms act in consistent, predictable ways in response to the availability of resources and the manner in which those resources are utilized. Regardless of the type of organization or the industry in which they operate, the relationship that firms have with society remains consistent. They require people and resources in order to operate, and they must provide more value than they consume in order to earn money either from customers, or in the case of non-profit organizations, attract donors. As a result, the manner in which each firm manages their resources and people is fundamentally the same. It is the field of microeconomics which seeks to identify, measure, and develop ways to accurately predict the behaviors that firms exhibit.

The nature and function of product markets. _____

The two base economic forces are **supply** and **demand**. Demand refers to the amount of something that people have the ability to acquire and the willingness to incur a given cost to acquire it. Supply refers to the amount of something which is available and the willingness to provide it to others at a given rate of exchange. An exchange takes place when someone who has demand and someone who has supply agree on the terms of the exchange. If that definition is a little odd, it's because not all exchanges take place using money. Consider the simple example of a butcher and a brewer: the brewer gets hungry and wants meat from the butcher, and offers the butcher a volume of beer in exchange for some amount of meat. If the butcher wants beer but does not agree to the rate of exchange, then another rate of exchange might be suggested in a counteroffer. It goes-on like this until the two either come to an agreement, or give-up their attempts at the exchange. Of course, bartering in this fashion is difficult, particularly if one party to an exchange doesn't want what the other has to offer. If the butcher doesn't want beer, then the brewer can sell beer to the baker in exchange for a voucher for bread, which the brewer can then give to the butcher in exchange for meat. The brewer gets meat, the butcher gets a voucher for bread, and the baker gets beer. When everyone starts using the same kind of voucher to make these exchanges, then they've invented money.

Since money is just a measurement of resource value that is owed to you through exchanges, it is easiest to think of these exchanges in terms of money. So, from this point forward in the book, all exchanges will be measured in terms of **price**. Price refers to any volume of money within the context of exchange. As the price of a good increases, the demand will decrease because fewer people will be willing or able to pay the price; whereas if price decreases demand increases. By contrast, as price increases the supply will go up because more producers will be able and willing to offer greater volume at the higher prices.

itself. The study was later replicated by Gonzalez et al. using a brain-scanner (fMRI), showing that the brain actually responds to risk potential and reward potential in different ways. This isn't just idle phenomenon, either. We can quantitatively measure these deviations from rationality. Go to the store sometime when you're very hungry and see how much you spend, then at some later time go to the store after you've already eaten and see how much you spend. The total cost difference between them is the degree to which hunger influences your purchasing decisions, once accounting for any changes in the price you pay for things.

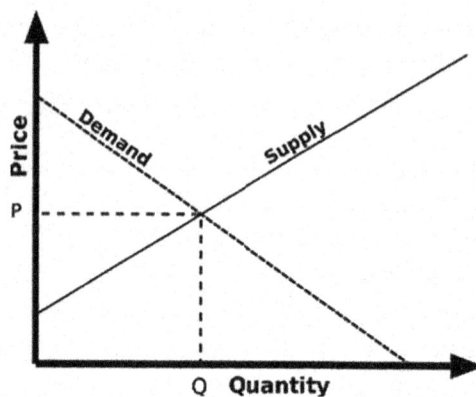

Note in the image how the demand and supply of a good changes in quantity as price goes up or down. The point at which supply and demand meet is called **equilibrium**. The equilibrium is the amount of a good that will be exchanged and the price at which it will be exchanged. There are many things which can shift equilibrium, though. For example, a drought one year might force farmers to buy more water. Since the farmers' costs increase, they must charge a higher price for their food. On the supply and demand graph above, this will cause the supply curve to move straight upward, while the demand line stays the same. The result will be that the new equilibrium will have a higher price and lower quantity.

There is a variety of things which determine demand, and things which determine supply. Demand is largely influenced by population, income, consumer preferences, availability of competing/substitution options from which to choose, and confidence about future economic trends. Things which influence supply include things like technological advances, size and skills of labor force, availability of competitors and substitutes, cost and availability of raw materials, and expectations about future economic trends. Supply and demand curves are only depicted as straight lines for simplicity purposes, however. They are actually curvilinear like this:

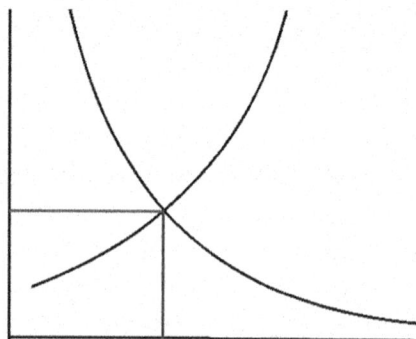

This plays an important role in both measuring and planning, as measures of elasticity are included. **Elasticity** measures the percentage by which one thing changes in response to a percentage change in another thing. **Price elasticity of demand** (PED) calculates the percentage change in quantity demanded to a percentage change in price: $\Delta D/\Delta P$. That triangle is called delta, and it only means "percentage change". So, if price increases by 2% and demand decreases by 1%, then PED would be -1/2. **Price elasticity of supply** (PES) measures how much the quantity supplied changes in response to a change in price. If price increases by 1% and supply increases by 2%, then PES would be 2/1 or just 2, as calculated using the formula $\Delta S/\Delta P$. **Cross elasticity of demand** (CED) measures how much that demand in one product changes in response to changes in price of a competitor. If demand for Coca Cola goes up 1% in response to a 1% increase in the price of Pepsi, then CED = 1/1 or just 1 ($\Delta D_A/\Delta P_B$). **Income elasticity of demand** is a formula showing how much demand changes in response to a change in income: $\Delta D/\Delta Y$ (Income is denoted as Y). You can use these basic calculation for just about anything. For example, if you increase how much a baby drinks before bed by 1%, what will be the change in wet diapers you need to change throughout the night? You can build a model for this as: $\Delta Diaper/\Delta Milk$.

Here are some definitions –

Elastic: >1. When response is greater than cause. In PED this would mean that demand changes faster than price.

Inelastic: <1. When response is less than cause. In PED this would mean that price changes faster than demand.

Unit Elastic: =1. When response and cause change at the same rate.

Perfectly Elastic: ∞. Any change in cause results in a response directly to 0. In PED this would mean that any change in price causes demand to drop to nothing.

Perfectly Inelastic: 0. There is no response to a change in cause. In PED this would mean that any change in price will not change demand, at all.

Note that both the demand and supply curve have parts on them which are elastic, inelastic, and unit elastic. This has a strong influence of business strategy and consumer choice, such as whether a company will charge low prices to maximize the quantity sold, or whether they'll charge a high price to maximize the amount of money they earn per unit sold. Not all goods even follow the basic laws of demand. For most goods, as price increases, demand should decrease.

There are some things which violate this law, though.

Giffen Goods: These are considered **inferior goods**. They are lower quality or otherwise off-brand goods with lower prices. Demand for these goes up as overall pricing increases relative to the amount of income being made. During the 2008 recession, demand at discount stores like Dollar Tree and Family Dollar increased quite a lot, for example. By contrast, **superior goods** will follow the traditional laws of demand.

Veblen Goods: These are goods which increase in demand with higher prices because they are considered **ostentatious goods**. In other words, part of the reason people buy them is simply because they are expensive. They are not only status symbols, but people do take greater pleasure from them simply because they paid more. In studies it was shown that when people are drinking cheap wine but are told it's expensive, they enjoy it more.

Investments: These are goods whose value is expected to increase over time. This makes investing unique from consumption in that consumption implies a decrease in the value of the goods over time, whereas investing comes, at least, with the expectation of an increase in value.

When discussing the amount of benefit received by consumers or producers, these are measured in terms of surpluses. Refer to this image:

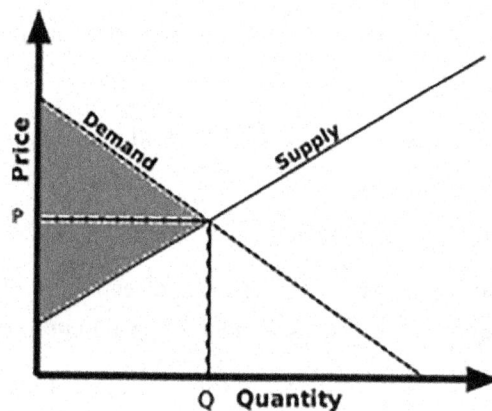

Under normal conditions, both sides of every transaction benefit. The seller gets more value from the money they receive than keeping the goods they sell, and the buyer gets more value from the goods they buy than keeping their money. The amount of benefit that you get from buying something in excess of the benefit you receive from keeping the money is called the **consumer surplus**. The consumer surplus is the area shaded in green. The **producer surplus** is the amount of benefit received by the seller in any transaction in excess of the benefits of keeping their things (typically measured as profit), and is the area shaded in blue.

More times than not, there is some kind of government intervention in pricing. In fact, it is inherently necessary for the government to intervene in economic markets in some way, otherwise no government would exist. In order to fund government operations, they must raise revenues, and this is typically done through taxation, taxation being a type of government intervention. It's not necessarily a bad thing, just a necessary fact.

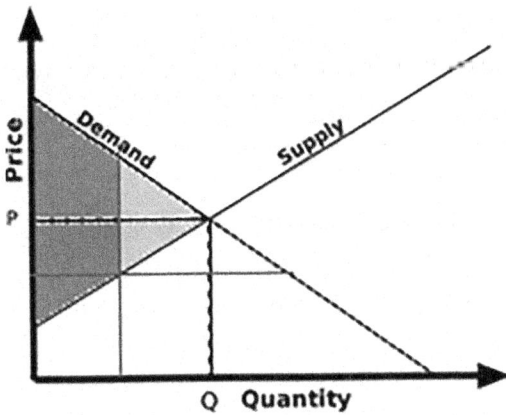

This example shows a price control known as a **price ceiling**, which is an economic policy that prevents sellers from raising prices above a specified threshold. The red lines show the points at which the government set the price floor, and the quantity supplied at that price. Note that demand is above supply at this point, which means there is a shortage at that price level. The area shaded in orange is **deadweight loss**, which is value that has been prevented from being achieved by that policy.

Other price controls include **price floors**, which prevent sellers from dropping price below a given threshold. Minimum wages are a common form of this, and laws which prevent producers from selling at a price below the cost of production are also typically banned as a form of predatory pricing. The most common form of price intervention is taxation. Taxes inherently increase the price of a transaction; the difference between equilibrium price and actual sales price is the amount of tax revenues collected in that transaction. There are also controls on quantity, known as **quotas**, which dictates either a minimum or (most commonly) a maximum volume of production.

It is worth knowing that although these principles in price controls are the way they will be presented on the AP test, they are woefully insufficient. For example, an increase in minimum wage does not actually cause a deadweight loss, but rather a decrease in producer surplus, with equilibrium price and quantity remaining mostly constant. The response to this change comes in the form of inflationary pressure.

Measuring the benefits of a transaction for a business is simple because it's all measured in terms of money. Measuring the benefits of a transaction for the consumer is a bit more complicated, because it's difficult to assess exactly how much enjoyment or usefulness a person gets from their purchase. To estimate this, we rely on an abstract concept known as **utility**. Utility is defined as the state of being useful. A thing has utility when it is useful to the owner or user in any way, even if that usefulness is just the pleasure that a person gets from owning it.

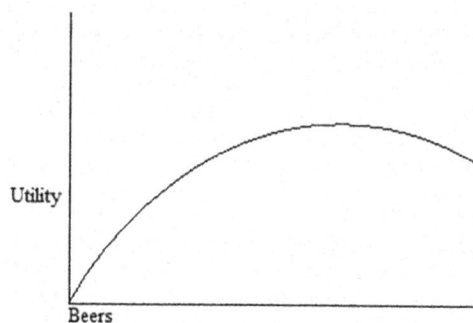

This graph demonstrates the amount of utility derived from drinking beer. The first beer has the most utility – it quenches your thirst and is quite satisfying. The second will also have utility, but less utility than the first. The third even less, and so forth, until you drink too many and you get sick at which point the beers actually provide you with negative utility. This behavior is typical of nearly everything. As you consume more units of something, each additional unit may provide positive utility but it will be less than the previous unit. This is what's known as the law of diminishing marginal utility. Remember that marginal means +1, so **marginal utility** is the utility derived from consuming one more unit. Looking at the graph, it shows that drinking more beers will increase **total utility**, but that marginal utility will decrease, so that the rate at which total utility increases slows with each unit.

In attempting to maximize their utility, consumers must consider the manner in which to use their money.

Money = $25
$5 Pizza = 10U-2n
$5 Beer = 20U-5n

In this problem, you have decided to go out to dinner and have $25 to spend. Both pizza and beer are $5 each. The utility you receive for the first pizza is 10 which diminishes by 2 marginally. The utility you receive for the first beer is 20 which diminishes by 5 marginally. By stating 20U-5n, it means that the first unit of beer has 20 utility, and that you subtract 5 for each unit consumed (e.g.: for the 3rd beer the equation would state 20-5(3) which equals 20-15, which is 5.). Your goal is to maximize your total utility. To do this, your first purchase will be beer, and then beer again, at which point choosing either beer or pizza will give you the same amount of utility, so if you drink a 3rd beer then you'd be obligated to buy some pizza, as shown:

Money	Beer	Pizza	Marginal Utility	Total Utility
$25	**20**	10	20	20
$20	**15**	10	15	35
$15	10	**10**	10	45
$10	**10**	8	10	55
$5	5	**8**	8	63

This process of maximizing utility is known as **equalizing marginal utility per dollar**.

Although your demand for beer is 3 when priced at $5 per unit, another person might have a different demand, each of you contributing to market demand. In a market of two, it might be:

Unit Price	Person A Demand	Person B Demand	Total Demand
$5	3	2	5
$3	6	5	11
$1	10	8	18

Although these demand curves between individuals and the market might change. The **income effect** says that as incomes rise relative to prices, demand will also rise, particularly for high-end goods. By contrast, the **substitution effect** says that as prices rise relative to income that people will find inferior alternatives which are cheaper to their typical purchases. This should not be confused with the **marginal rate of substitution**, which measures the rate at which one good can be a substitute for another. In other words, it may initially take 3 beers to equal the same utility of 1 pizza, which is the rate of substitution, but with every beer consumed it will take marginally more units of beer to equal a single unit of pizza.

As for what consumers must pay in order to receive this utility, it is primarily determined by the production function of the supplier. This refers to the amount of output produced per unit of input. There are 4 broad categories of inputs, known as the factors of production: Land, Labor, Capital, and Entrepreneurship. **Land** includes the physical land being used, and its production potential, such as with agriculture. **Labor** includes any direct human effort that goes into production, or the operations which support production. **Capital** is stuff – all the stuff – generally referring to larger things of significance such as machines, vehicles, computers, and money; but technically also including furniture, stationary, window cleaner, and so forth. **Entrepreneurship** is an abstract concept which refers to the willingness of a person to risk their own resources in order to acquire more resources. For a person to start a business, they must acquire startup capital from somewhere, and whether that comes from themselves or some investor/debtor, there is a person who must be willing to spend their own money to get things started.

It can be a little difficult to grasp the idea of entrepreneurship. It's a little strange because the purpose of entrepreneurship is to raise money or other capital in order to start or expand a business, but money and capital itself is not entrepreneurship. It doesn't help that anyone who starts a business or goes self-employed is colloquially referred to as an entrepreneur. So just what is this madness?

There's this thing called the accounting equation which says: Assets = Debt + Equity

You don't need to know that for the AP econ test, but it helps to illustrate who is or isn't technically an entrepreneur. It says that everything a company owns is funded either by debt or equity. In order to start a business, or expand a business, then you must acquire assets, which means you need to use either debt or equity. Not necessarily your own debt and equity, but someone's. That person who provides that debt or equity is an entrepreneur.

If you use your own money to buy things for the business, then you're an entrepreneur because the

For each unit of any of these factors of production which are consumed, some number of units, or fractions of a unit, of output are produced. The amount of output produced per unit of input is called the **marginal product**.

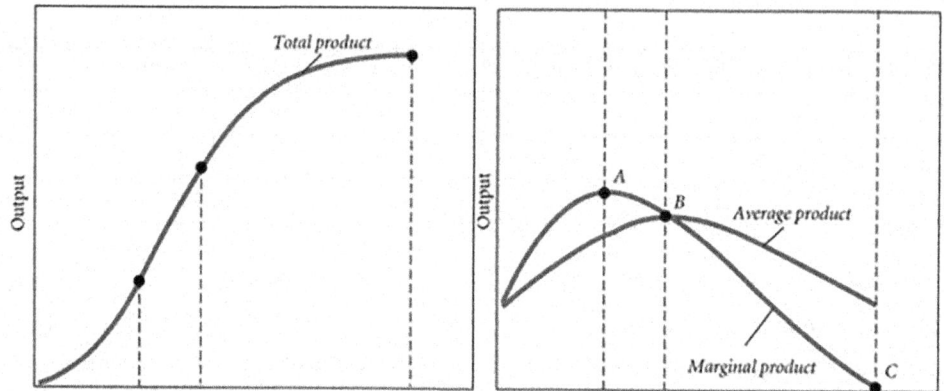

These graphs illustrate the behavior of output to input in production. Note that after point A, each unit produces marginally less output, and that once marginal product decreases, and that once marginal product drops below the average, the rate of increase in total production per unit begins to slow, as well. This is the result of the law of diminishing marginal returns. This is of particular importance in regards to efficiency, because as less output is produced per unit of input, the per-unit cost of production is going to increase.

For each unit of any of these factors of production which are consumed in the production of some good/service, a cost is incurred. It is the goal of a business to use those inputs to produce something of greater value than the cost of the inputs. There are primarily 5 types of costs relevant to introductory economics. You've already been introduced to the first: marginal cost. That's the cost of producing one additional unit.

Output	Total Cost
0	$13
1	20
2	25
3	28
4	32
5	43
6	60

In the above data, the total cost of producing 4 units is $32, which is $4 more than it costs to produce 3 units. As a result the marginal cost of the 4th unit is $4. By contrast, the marginal cost of the 1st unit is $7. Note that even when producing nothing, there is a total cost of $13. This brings us to the remaining types of costs.

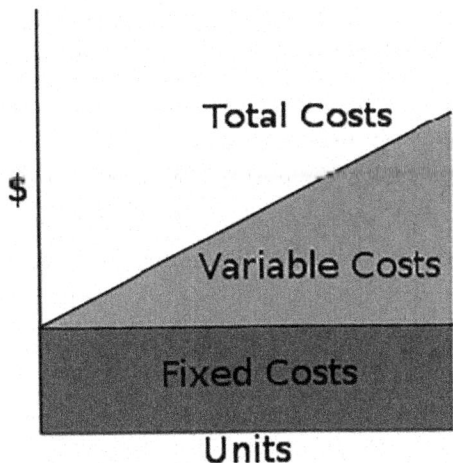

Total Costs

$

Variable Costs

Fixed Costs

Units

Fixed costs (FC) are those which do not change with the volume of production. In colloquial terms this is often called the overhead. In accounting terms, fixed costs are typically included in the general and administrative expense portion of the income statement. Fixed costs include such things as rent on a building, the wages of supporting operations, and anything else which will incur a cost even if operations remain stagnant. Variable costs, by contrast, are those which increase with volume. **Variable costs** (VC) will be $0 with no production volume, but will increase with each unit of volume produced. This relates to marginal costs in that variable costs increase marginally, and marginal costs are all variable. Variable costs include such things as raw materials used to make stuff, the labor required to make and sell things, depreciation on equipment (reduction in the useful life of expensive equipment), and anything other expense which is only incurred with active production. Total cost is variable cost plus fixed cost, stated in the formula: $TC = FC+VC$, or $TC = x+y(n)$, where n is the number of units produced. The final type of cost discussed is average cost.

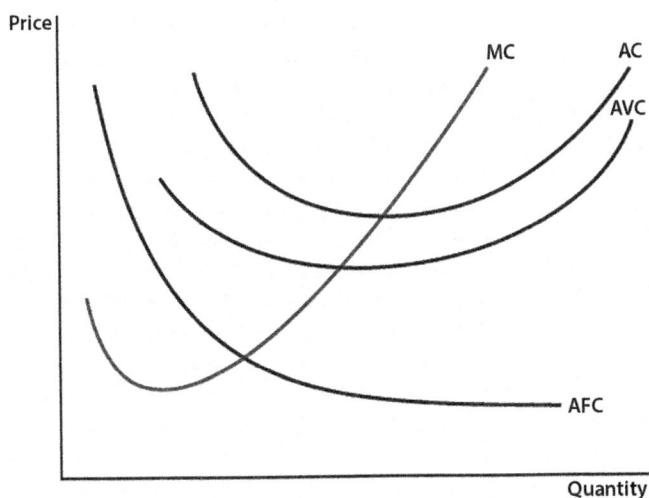

Price

MC   AC

AVC

AFC

Quantity

things you bought are yours to own, meaning you have put equity in your business. If you get the money from a venture capitalist or angel investor, then they are the entrepreneurs and you are labor. If you get a loan from a bank, friend, the mob, or anywhere else, then you're both entrepreneurs. The lender because they're offering their own assets, and yourself because you now have to repay that loan. It can even be the assets being offered instead of money.

The point is that there is no guarantee that the business will succeed, but whoever provided the assets was willing to accept that risk. It was their goal to get more assets in return, by earning the interest you pay, or a percentage of your earnings equal to their ownership stake in your business. That is the nature of entrepreneurship.

To calculate **average cost** (AC), divide total cost by the number of units of production. More specifically, this refers to **average total cost** (ATC), but anytime the term "average cost" is used, it refers to ATC. Other costs can also be averaged, but they are referred to more specifically. **Average variable cost** (AVC) is the total sum of variable costs divided by the number of units produced. **Average fixed cost** (AFC) includes is fixed cost divided by the number of units produced.

Note the behavior of each of the costs. AFC continuously decreases with increasing production volume, since fixed cost does not change with volume. That means as production volume increases, the fixed cost is divided over an ever-greater number of units. This influences AC by causing it to decrease more sharply than AVC at lower volumes of production. AC will continue to decrease until the point that MC exceeds AC. The reason for this is simply that as each additional unit costs less to produce than average, the average will decrease, but the average will increase again once MC surpasses the average. The reason marginal cost increases is because of decreasing returns on marginal product. As more resources must be consumed to produce each additional unit, it will become more expensive to do so, thereby increasing marginal cost. Since MC is variable, AVC will decrease until the point that MC surpasses AVC, at which point AVC will increase again.

Revenue refers to money earned for the sale of a product. **Marginal revenue** (MR), equal to price, is the amount of money a company earns for the same of the next unit of production. **Total revenue** (TR) is the total amount of money earned for sales. **Average revenue** (AR) is total revenue divided by the number of units produced. So long as TR is higher than TC, the company will earn an accounting **profit**. Profit is the total amount of revenue earned which exceeds the amount of cost. This is expressed in a simple formula:

$$\text{Profit} = \text{Total Revenue} - \text{Total Cost}$$

This formula is one which calculates the total amount of **accounting profit** earned by a company in a period (e.g.: annually, quarterly, monthly, etc.). This is in contrast to other forms of profit. Recall that economic profit starts with the accounting profit and then subtracts the profits that would have been earned if pursuing the next best option. This addresses the amount of unique economic value added by the operation as opposed to that which would have otherwise been produced.

$$\text{Economic Profit} = \text{Accounting Profit} - \text{Accounting Profit of Plan B}$$

Marginal profit is the amount of profits earned by each unit produced. Since the amount by which each unit produced contributes to total revenues or total costs will change, as previously described, the marginal profit is measured as the amount by which the next unit produced will contribute to total profits.

$$\text{Marginal Profit} = \text{Marginal Revenue} - \text{Marginal Cost}$$

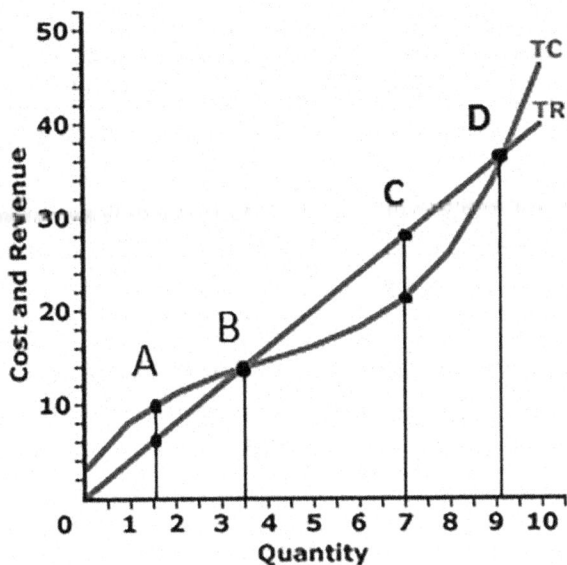

Look at the graph above. The black line at the bottom measures the amount of total profits earned by any given company. The point at which **profit margin** is highest is the point where TC is most below TR. The profit margin is equivalent to the average marginal profit. In other words, the average amount by which revenue generated exceeds production costs.

Marginal Profit/Number of Units Produced

A company will continue to make profits past that point, but the amount of marginal profits will decrease until the point that costs finally start to exceed revenues. When that happens, it means the company is operating at a **loss**. Losses are generally a bad thing, being the point where a company is spending more money than it makes, but it is very common within the first few years a company begins operating, while demand for their products is still being developed (i.e.: growing their customers base).

Profit maximization occurs at TC=TR. If TR drops below TC, then a company will lose money for each unit produced. It is still worth staying in business, however, if MR is above MC. Considering that a company will have to pay FC even if they produce nothing, a company should continue to produce more volume as long as the revenue they earn exceeds their variable costs, so that they can minimize their losses on TC. It is only when MR<MC that a company should stop operating. This is known as the **shutdown point**. In the long-run, if MR<AC, then a company will exit the market entirely, known as the **market exit point**.

At this point, it must be noted that average cost behaves differently in the long-run compared to the short-run. In order to understand why this is, first we must define the time period for these terms. It is not a fixed period, as the difference between short- and long-run will be different for each company. The **short-run** is defined as any period of time shorter than necessary for a company to replace any piece of capital. In other words, if the market has a sudden change which requires a company to change its production volume or operations, then that company must change the factors of production it owns. Whatever factor of production takes the longest to replace defines short-run, and the period of time in which it takes to replace that factor of production is the length of short-run. The reason for this is that short-run is defined by a company's ability to respond to changes in the market. This is true of individuals and even nations, too: in the short-run, it may not be possible to properly respond to some change in the market. In the long-run, however, it is possible to respond to any market change. **Long-run** is any period of time greater than it takes to replace any factor of production. As a result, average costs will be different depending on whether you're talking about short-run or long-run time periods because of the ability to change the factors of production being used as inputs.

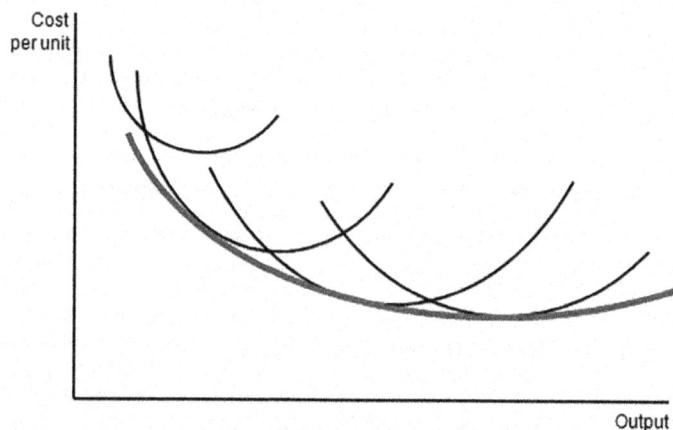

In this image, the small black curves are various **short-run average cost** (SRAC) curves, while the large red curve is **long-run average cost** (LRAC). In the short-run, the minimum average cost is limited. A firm can produce until MC=AC, which is the cost-minimization point, but using the factors of production available, MC will be higher than might be possible. In the long-run, a company might have access to more efficient factors of production. For example, a manufacturing facility which is successful might find that demand is so high that they are producing beyond their cost-minimization point, so they decide to buy a larger piece of machinery which produces things more efficiently, allowing them to decrease AC even further. Each time this company gets larger, they are able to improve and become more efficient, allowing them to decrease their MC and, as a result, their AC. This decrease in AC is known as **economies of scale**. Think of it like a bulk-discount; if you produce things in larger numbers, the per-unit cost gets cheaper. Economies of scale is just a fancy way of saying bulk-discount. This is in contrast to economies of agglomeration, which is a decrease in cost associated with geographic clustering of companies with their suppliers and customers.

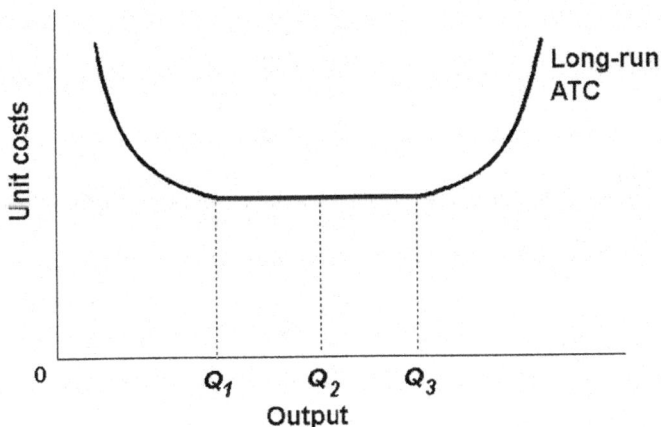

In looking at SRAC or LRAC, there are three portions with different **returns to scale**. There is the portion in which average cost decreases with increased volume. This process is known as **increasing returns to scale** (IRS). This is a reference to the marginal product; if a company is experiencing IRS, then one unit of input creates more than one unit of output. On the graph above, the portion between 0 and Q_1 demonstrates IRS. If one unit of input produces one unit of output, then the company is experiencing **constant returns to scale** (CRS), as shown in the graph between points Q_1 and Q_3. On the graph, the portion after Q_3 illustrates AC when a company is producing less than one unit of output for each additional unit of input, known as **decreasing returns to scale** (DRS). So long as a company continues to experience increasing returns to scale, they will continue to increase their economies of scale. Once a company starts producing so much that they are experiencing decreasing returns to scale, then they will start to have **diseconomies of scale**, in which average cost increases with greater volume.

In attempting to maximize their returns to scale, a company must find the proper combination of inputs which maximizes their productive efficiency. In other words, by maximizing Output/Input, the company will have reached their maximum economies of scale, which means they have found the combination of factors of production that will create the maximum amount of output possible per unit of input. Generally speaking, finding the **cost-minimizing input combination** means balancing labor and capital. This is achieved by balancing the cost of each, as illustrated in the formula:

$$MP_L/w = MP_K/r$$

Where:

MP = marginal product

L = Labor

W = Wages

K = Capital

r = Rent (or otherwise the cost of capital divided by number of units produced over the life of the capital)

Formally, this states that the cost-minimizing input combination is achieved when the average cost of the marginal product of labor is equal to the average cost of the marginal product of capital.

Production typically includes inputs by both labor and capital, and for any given function a company might have a choice between the two. In minimizing cost, a company will pick whichever is cheaper on average. That is to say, a company will pick either labor or capital depending on which produces the most amount of output for the cost incurred. The company will continue to rely on the cheaper one until its cost equals or exceeds the cost of the other. Ideally the cost of labor and cost of capital will be equal per unit produced at a given production level and, if not, the company will attempt to change their factors of production until they are equalized. This behavior is typical of any firm attempting to minimize costs.

The decisions any firm will make – collectively, the behaviors they exhibit – is determined largely by the type of market in which they operate. There are 4 broad categories of markets: Perfect Competition, Monopoly, Oligopoly, and Monopolistic Competition. There are a variety of other markets as well, such as Bertrand Competition and Cournot Competition, but these are more specific variations on the 4 primary types of markets, and are not typical of introductory economics material.

All firms, regardless of market, share a few key traits. First, they seek to earn a profit. Even "non-profit" firms must earn more money than it spends if it wants to continue operating. In doing so, they have earned **accounting profits**, which is all the money earned in excess of the money spent. **Economic profits**, by contrast, includes accounting profits minus the opportunity cost. Recall that economic profits are also called economic value added. Another way to look at it is, this is the amount of accounting profit which must be made in order to at least be equivalent to the accounting profits earned from the next best alternative. This is considered the **normal profit**, which refers to the minimum amount a firm must earn in order to make it worth continuing operations. This is a little different than earning an accounting profit, which a firm must earn in order to avoid losing money, because normal profit also considers that the value of a firm could be used to earn money in some other way. It is for this reason normal profit includes accounting profit plus opportunity cost. Whether or not a firm can exceed normal profits depends on the type of market in which they operate.

Total profits are always highest at the point that marginal cost equal marginal revenue.

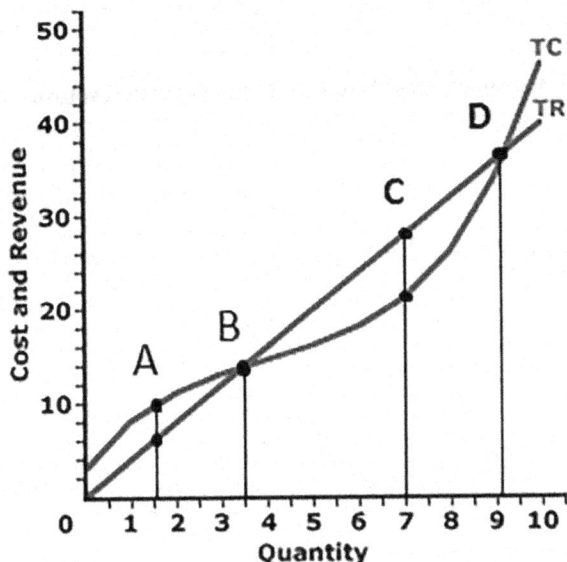

Point C indicates the point where firms attempt reach, because a firm will continue to make marginal profits until that point. The reason is that a firm will continue to incur increasing marginal costs until the point that marginal costs equal marginal revenues. As MC continues to be below MR, TC will continue to deviate further from TR. Once MC exceeds MR, the gap between TC and TR will start to close. In other words, once MC exceeds MR each unit will incur a marginal loss. So it is at point C that marginal profits are maximized. This is known as the **MR=MC Rule**, and is the point where profits of maximized. Still, some firms prefer to produce at point D, particularly inferior goods or cost-leader firms like Wal-Mart. Although such firms could potentially greater profits, it is their goal to generate extremely small profit margins and instead seek to expand their market with high levels of production and instead maximize revenues. Point B is the **breakeven point**, wherein the company has sold just enough to avoid losing money, but isn't yet making a profit. Breaking-even is typically one of the first goal set by new entrants, who are just happy to start turning a profit instead of continuing to incur losses. Point A isn't really anything except a potential test option which you can easily eliminate.

Industries which function in perfectly competitive markets include agriculture, mining goods, energy, and most other commodities. As with all markets, **perfect competition** has some very specific traits. In perfect competition there are many sellers, and they all sell a **homogeneous product** (meaning all suppliers are selling a product indistinguishable from each other), which implies that the inputs to create that product are also homogeneous. Also, **market information** is spread nearly instantly. Together, that makes each of the suppliers a **price taker** and the buyers the

price maker, which means the buyers largely dictate price while the suppliers merely accept that price, so long as it is at least meeting normal profits. If any supplier increases price, then the buyer will just go to another to get the exact same product cheaper, meaning that perfectly competitive markets have near-perfect price elasticity of demand. If any seller decreases price, all sellers would do so almost instantly, giving none of them incentive to drop price, but since buyers have near perfect information price is always at the lowest point, anyways.

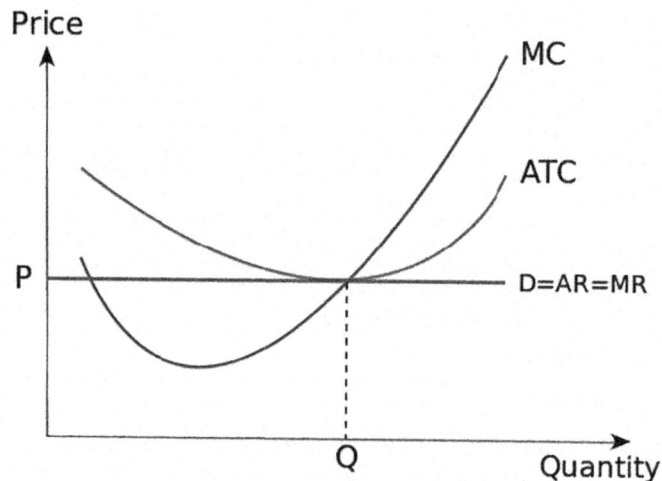

The above graph illustrates the behavior of a firm operating in a perfect competition market. Notice that equilibrium is exactly at the point where MR=MC, which implies that AC will always be at its lowest point, meaning that consumers always get the lowest price possible within that market without firms losing money. This means that firms in perfectly competitive markets have extremely high **productive efficiency** (operating at the lowest possible AC). Since there is so much competition, all selling exactly the same thing and with information spreading so quickly, the buyers are sure to get the lowest price. This also means that firms maximize their profits at the point where MC = MR, at Since companies cannot distinguish themselves from each other, they will frequently advertise as an industry, such as campaigns like "Where's the Beef" and "Got Milk?" When the industry coordinates its efforts in such a campaign or in an effort to secure government subsidies, it is possible to make abnormal profits in the long-run but these circumstances will either provide incentive for one firm to drop prices in order to increase demand dramatically (extremely high PED) or when new entrants are attracted by the potential for prospect of extremely high sales volume. This means that perfectly competitive markets have extremely high **allocative efficiency** (producing at the exact price and quantity that optimizes market benefit and the consumption of resources).

Extremely different than perfect competition, but not a polar opposite as popularly believed, monopolies are a unique type of market in which there is only one supplier but many consumers. Since the defining feature of a monopoly market is the control of supply by a single producer, the implication is that the producer is the price maker, while consumers are price takers. The price elasticity of demand in monopoly markets tend to be low, but can still vary depending on how badly the thing being supplied is needed/wanted. The single-seller nature of monopolies also necessitates **product differentiation** within the market, meaning that the product being sold is highly different than its competitors and substitutes. Granted, in monopoly markets there are no competitors or substitutes, so differentiation is more of an absolute than a comparison.

Monopolies markets exist as a result of the **barriers to entry** in a particular market (things which make it very difficult for new firms to enter the market). There may be legal barriers such as patents on a particular type of new medicine, or it may require access to resources available only to the current seller. The market may have extremely high startups costs, or necessitate the use of highly-advanced technologies inaccessible to most people. There may be no serious competitors because of the **network effect**, wherein functionality of a product depends on everyone using the same product. For example, I am currently using MS Word to write this study guide largely to maintain compatibility in the saved file between myself and the publisher, XAMOnline.

One source of market power held by monopoly firms is **predatory behavior**. Now, remember that many predatory business practices are technically illegal, but also remember that monopoly firms have the resources to win court cases which dispute their actions. In fact, that's one type of predatory behavior monopolies use: filing frivolous lawsuits too expensive for new, smaller firms to afford. Sometimes the monopoly firm will buy new entrants, or the patents on new innovations, paying large sums of money so that they can keep control of the market. If the monopoly firm has new entrants because prices are too high, then it may temporarily lower prices, even to the point of operating at a loss, in order to push-out competition (a practice called **dumping**), and then raise prices again.

There is a special type of monopoly whose source of market power is the nature of the market, itself. This is called a **natural monopoly**, and these form in markets with no decreasing returns to scale – no diseconomies of scale. In other words, as the firm expands more and more, the per-unit cost continues to drop so that the larger a firm gets, the more competitive they get, like this:

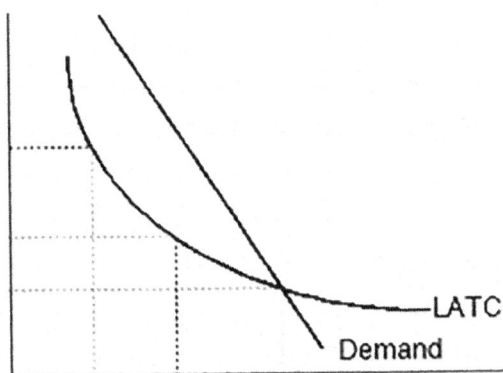

Utility companies and railroads are generally considered to be types of natural monopolies, due to the high degree of infrastructure reliance required within these markets.

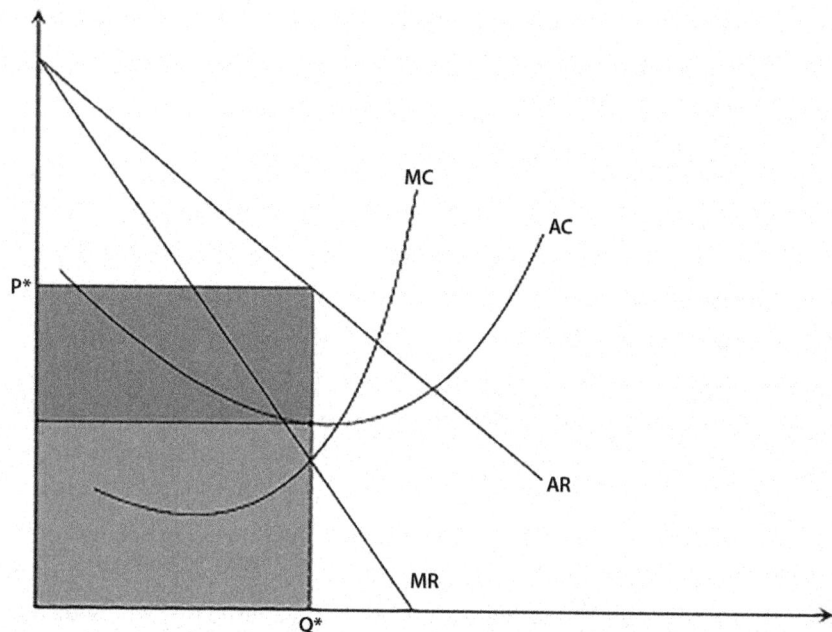

Like most firms, a monopoly maximizes its profitability at the point that MC=MR. The difference, though, is that AC is below average revenue at this point. Without any competition, a monopoly is able to make **supernormal,** or **monopolistic profits**. While it's been argued that this greater profitability can be used to fund new research, the lack of competitions leaves little incentive to allocate resources in that manner. As a result, monopolies tend to be inefficient. By keeping prices high, they are limiting output as demand is lower than it could be, meaning that there is unmet demand which could be met more efficiently by lowering price. Productively, this means that the monopoly firm is not minimizing average cost – it could lower its per-unit cost by increasing production levels, but at the prices necessary to create supernormal profits, this would create surplus supply.

There is much disapproval of monopolies. The inefficient operations of monopoly firms is frowned upon, but it was the broad use of predatory behavior which caused a strong anti-monopoly movement during the late-19th century. At the time, these firms were called **Trusts,** and these were largely broken-up by several laws intended to increase market competition within markets that severely lacked it. One of the most sweeping of these laws was the **Sherman Antitrust Act**, passed by Benjamin Harrison. Teddy Roosevelt came to be known as the Trust Buster; besides passing several more minor antitrust laws such as the Elkins Act and Hepburn Act, the federal government under the Roosevelt administration brought 44 lawsuits intended to breakup these trusts, or otherwise limit their predatory behaviors. The exact legal definition of what makes a firm a monopoly isn't very clear, though. There is no threshold for the percentage of control a firm must have over the market which clearly defines a monopoly, so it often comes down to "you know one when you see it." In other words, if a particular firm has enough influence over a market that they are able to abuse that influence, and have the willingness to do so, then antitrust suits will come into play. In the modern era, it is more common to hear of antitrust laws being cited when preventing mergers of large firms, rather than to breakup large firms.

Despite popular belief that perfect competition is the opposite of a monopoly, the true opposite of a monopoly is called a monopsony. In a monopsony there is only 1 buyer, and many sellers. Examples include such industries as national defense, and manufacturing plants which open in otherwise rural areas. We won't be going into detail about that in this book, though, because it's not a part of the AP test.

The end-result of an **oligopoly** is a market which functions quite similarly to a monopoly, but the internal workings of an oligopoly are entirely unique to any other market. An oligopoly is a market with a few firms – more than one, but not a ton – and these firms sell a homogeneous product. Oligopoly markets have the same barriers to entry as monopoly firms, and the firms do earn supernormal profits. What makes them interesting, though, is that only a few firms control the market of a product which those firms cannot distinguish from the others. This leads to a simple **game** of strategy between the firms.

	Strategy 1	Strategy 2
Strategy 1	**A** $1,000 \ $1,000	**B** $1,200 \ $600
Strategy 2	**C** $600 \ $1,200	**D** $800 \ $800

Let's say there a two-firm oligopoly consists of Company A and Company B. They each start-out making $1,000 per year using Strategy 1. Then Company A decides it wants to take customers from Company B, and switches to Strategy 2. Now Company A is making $1,200 per year, and Company B is making $600 per year. Well, Company B doesn't like that very much, and so to get back as many customers as possible, Company B also switches to Strategy 2. Now both companies are making $800 per year. These companies then figure-out that if they both just use Strategy 1 cooperatively, then they'll both be making more money, rather than being stuck competing against each other. This causes oligopoly firms to have an unusual, kinked demand curve.

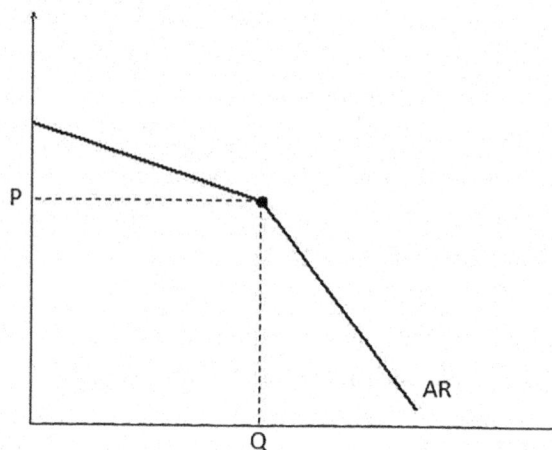

The reason for this unusual shape is the reaction of competitors to a change in price. Above the kind, demand is relatively elastic – as price increases, demand will drop quite sharply since consumers will go to the competitors. Below the kink, demand is relatively inelastic – since the other firms will also decrease their prices in response, each firm has to drop their prices quite a lot to increase revenues at all. This game that firms play in an oligopoly market is called The Prisoner's Dilemma, which is a common introductory game when learning **game theory**. Game theory, commonly used in economics as well as other fields, uses mathematical models in order to study the interactions between people or firms, assuming those people seek to make rational decision. In game theory, **Nash Equilibrium** is the point at which all players in the game are using their optimal strategy, given the strategies of other players. In an oligopoly, Nash equilibrium is the point at the kink.

As firms shift from competing to cooperating, oftentimes they'll create a formal organization with membership including those firms which are a part of the market. These organizations, intended to facilitate the cooperation between firms, is called a **cartel**. Yes, the word cartel has been associated with criminal organizations such as those connected to the global drug trade, but in economics the word is much more benign. **OPEC**, the organization for petroleum exporting countries, is a cartel made-up of some of the world's leading oil producing nations, and De Beers is a cartel in the diamond industry. De Beers once functioned as a cartel, and the companies Unilever and Proctor & Gamble once functioned together as a cartel, but both of these cartels have since ended due to political, legal, and social backlash. Needless to say, cartels are not popular, so forming an official cartel is considered a bad idea, but that doesn't stop firms from operating unofficially in cartel-like ways. There have been accusations that firms within the US telecom industry function as a cartel, just as there've been accusations at the global banking industry. Like oligopoly firms, though, it's difficult to specifically identify the point at which firms become a cartel, especially when the cooperation is kept at an informal level.

Despite the tendency to function in a predatory manner, the word cartel refers to nothing more than the cooperation of firms within an oligopoly market. Rather than anything inherently sinister, the defining features of a cartel are **collusion** and **interdependence**. Collusion is the word used to describe firms cooperating in what would ideally be a competitive market, and interdependence means that the firms are dependent upon one another in order to maintain supernormal profits. Since this does lead to market inefficiencies, oligopolies are subject to stiff competition in the wake of new technologies. The music industry is often accused of being a cartel, but with the advent of popularized digital media peer-to-peer (P2P) file-sharing, new competitors quickly entered the market. With improvements in the resources, information, and infrastructure available to brewers, the beer industry is quickly shifting from an oligopoly to monopolistic competition.

Monopolistic competition is the final major type of economic market that will be discussed. Probably the majority of brands you can name exist in a monopolistically competitive market. The traits shared by these markets include containing many buyers and many sellers supplying a differentiated product. Since each seller within a single market can provide products with different features, or qualities, or branding; and there are many buyers, each firm makes its own pricing and output decisions. The barriers to entry can vary greatly, but remain much lower than monopolies or oligopolies.

Monopolistic competition is similar to both perfect competition and monopolies, hence the name. It's similar to perfect competition in that they can achieve supernormal profits only in the short run, despite having a demand curve unique from perfect competition.

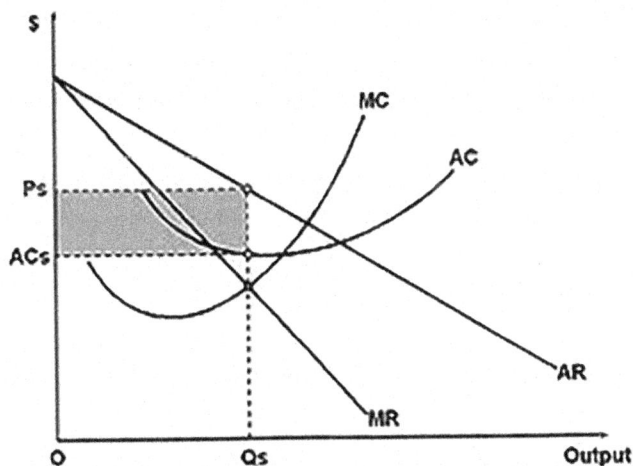

Note that in the short-run, firms in these markets operate quite similarly to monopolies, but with a lower amount of supernormal profits, since competitors and substitutes do exist, even if they are differentiated. The amount of supernormal profits varies widely, however, depending on the type of product, the type of differentiation included, and the market/pricing strategy utilized.

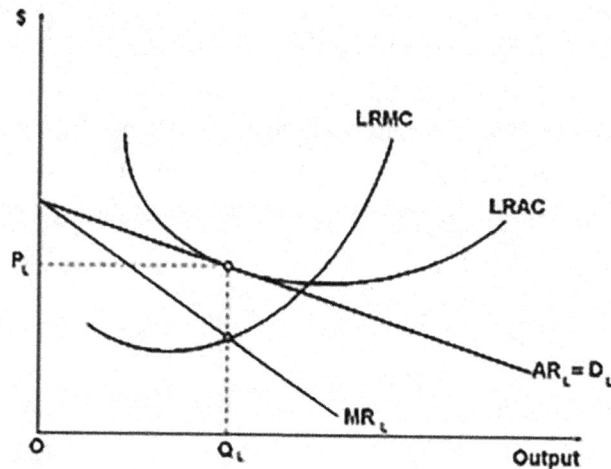

In the long-run, though, these firms will return to normal profits. Despite this achieving allocative efficiency, that the firm is still not productively efficient. This is because firms in monopolistic have difficulty fully utilizing their capital through mass production, so there tends to be a degree of excess production capacity and slightly higher marginal costs.

It is the goal of firms in monopolistic competition to continue evolving in order to maintain supernormal profits. Recall that long-run refers to the period of time it takes for a firm to respond to changes in the market, so if a firm is achieving supernormal profits and does not attempt to maintain that state through constant evolution, then the low barriers to entry will allow competitors or new entrants to overtake them. It is for this reason that firms in these markets come out with new models or designs every year or ever few years, change their image, expand into new markets, and so forth. Consider a firm that is highly successful with a new product, and then all their competitors come out with a similar product just as the original firm is coming-out with a new design.

The use of advertising is also most common in monopolistic competition. Advertising is a cost which adds no value to the product itself, which contributes to allocative inefficiencies in that the higher costs add to the selling price with no additional benefits gained by the consumer. **Advertising** is used in order to create distinctions between sellers; it is a manner by which sellers communicate to buyers in order to provide information about product features, benefits, and branding. There is a strong behavioral element to advertising in that the management of a brand uses words and imagery which anthropomorphizes the product, giving the product and the company human-like traits of ideas and behaviors shared by the target market. This helps people identify to the company and its products, shaping that individual's buying behaviors – exciting the buyers and instilling brand loyalty. Advertisements tend to target the irrational behaviors in people, attempting to convince them to buy their own product rather than facilitating rational decisions. That delves into behavioral economics, though, which you probably won't see until you're a grad student. For now, the AP test will assume people make rational decisions to help you better understand the fundamentals.

Factor markets.

When discussing factor markets, we're referring to the factors of production: land, labor, capital, and entrepreneurship. Recall that land includes the physical land and its productive capabilities, labor refers to human efforts, capital refers to tangible items including money, and entrepreneurship refers to the willing to risk one's assets to acquire more assets. That being said, within the context of broadly saying "factor markets", people are almost always talking specifically about labor and capital, and the relative balance of each in a productive environment. It's not that land and entrepreneurship are any less important or interesting, but their cost, and sometimes even quantity, tend to be fixed, whereas capital and labor consumption vary with the volume of production. So, for the purposes of introductory microeconomics within a context of understanding the nature of production (and because it's what is on the AP exam), let's focus on labor and capital.

The demand for factors of production is what's known as a **derived demand**. Derived demand means that the demand for a thing is dependent entirely on the demand for something else. If there's no demand for a company's product, then that company will not have any demand for labor. If the demand for a company's products suddenly increases, then the company's demand for labor will also increase. This doesn't just apply to factor markets, either. The demand for a video game console (e.g.: Nintendo, Playstation) is derived from the demand to play games available on that console – if not for the games, then the console would be worthless. That's why it's so important to console companies to ensure they have a strong game selection when they release a new console, or soon afterward, when interest in that particular console is at its highest. In terms of capital, demand for raw materials is derived from the demand for the things which can be made with them. Iron ore, by itself, isn't very useful except that it can be used to make steel and iron products.

Probably the most significant period of human history in terms changing derived demand was the **Industrial Revolution**. It was during this time that automation began to become common in the production of goods. To illustrate this, let's look at agriculture. Farming is the single most important activity to human civilization, and for roughly 12,000 years until 16th century AD, every aspect of farming was performed by hand, sometimes with the assistance of domesticated animals. During this period of human history, the volume of production per person which could be achieved was static – there was an upper limit that had been reached, and the only real way to increase total agricultural production was to increase the size of the population, or the proportion of a given population dedicated to farming. With the inventions of automation which became widespread in the 1700s, there was suddenly a huge increase in the production volume possible per person by utilizing machinery to supplement human efforts. This is shown in the following graph from the US Federal Reserve.

Figure 2
World Population and Production

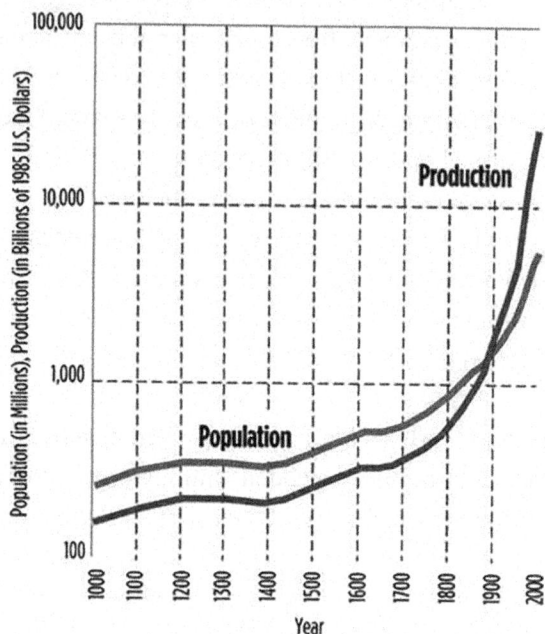

Note in the graph above how the population and production levels between the year 1,000AD and the mid-1700s are identical in their change over time; production increased only as the population size increased. Then in the mid-1700s production began to increase at an exponential rate, and shortly after the global population began to see an increase in the rate of growth, but nowhere near the rate of increase as global production. This means that the amount of production per person increased dramatically – either machines supplemented human efforts, or humans changed their efforts to running machines, increasing their total production potential to that which can be accomplished mechanically. As technology continues to advance, a greater range of work has been automated, and the rate at which our automation can produce goods has increased, to the point that even functions once thought to be uniquely human, such as logic and creativity, can be performed by computers.

This is the difference between a **labor-based economy** and a **capital-based economy**, or **industrial economy**. Labor-based economies are ones in which the majority of all production is performed by people, while an economy in which a majority of all production is performed or facilitated by capital has become to be known as an industrial economy. More recently, with the increasing importance of computers and the internet both as a means of production and a medium for distribution of products and services which exist exclusively in the digital world, the term "**information age**" has been used to describe a **knowledge-based economy**. Largely service-based, a knowledge-based economy is one in which production is dependent largely on intellectual property, highly-skilled/specialized workers, and the set of knowledge people have to offer others for a fee. For example, in writing this book I was contracted by XAMOnline as an author through a website for freelancers. They purchased my time and expertise and I provided them with a product which was created and delivered entirely by digital means. All the editing was done digitally, as well, purchased as a service offered by someone else with the expertise to do so. It is only once the product was ready to be sent to bookstores that any physical representation of all this work was put into print. These types of arrangements have become extremely common and now account for a notable percentage of production within the US.

In another example which has become very common, software as a service (SaaS) includes software programs which are hosted by the provider and used via the internet by customers on a subscription basis, or for free with advertising. This is distinct from traditionally-purchased software because purchased software is not a service being provided, but rather a product that is purchased.

Clearly technology hasn't completely replaced the need for labor, as jobs still exist. The difference is that companies now face a question about whether to use labor or capital. This is done by using a measure called the **marginal revenue product**.

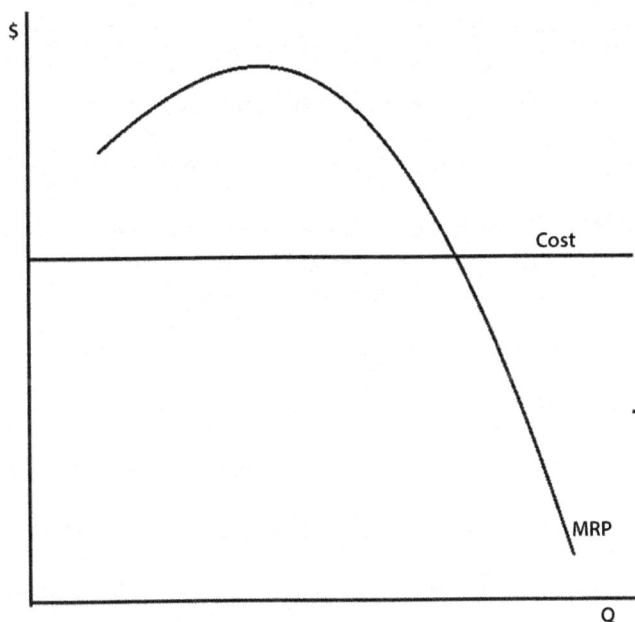

The marginal revenue product is a term that refers to the amount of revenue generated by adding one additional unit of some factor of production. In other words, if you hire another worker or buy a piece of capital, how much revenue will you earn from the increased amount of production created? The graph above shows a simplified but typical relationship between the cost of production and the marginal revenue product. Assuming that a single company is not consuming so much of any single factor of production that they are single-handedly changing the market price, the cost of labor for a particular job will remain roughly equivalent with each new person hired; the cost of buying and operating machinery will remain roughly equal for each new piece of the same type purchased. The marginal revenue product, on the other hand, has a very distinct shape. Initially it will increase, as specialization of labor takes-over, allowing people to work collaboratively rather than too few people trying to do everything on their own. It gets to the point, though, that each additional unit of a particular factor of production will earn a smaller amount of money. This is due to the decreased efficiency which results from having too many units of any factor of production, causing them to decrease their respective productivity levels, as one would expect given the law of decreasing marginal returns. Theoretically, companies will continue to consume a given factor of production until the marginal revenue product equals the marginal cost. That's because up until that point, each additional unit is still generating revenues higher than costs, creating profits, but once the marginal revenue product drops below the cost of that factor of production, then that particular asset is going to cost the company more than they are contributing to their revenues. As we discussed earlier, though, very rarely are markets efficient, and they will tend to either maintain production capacity that is too high, or otherwise underutilize the resources available to them, creating production and allocative inefficiencies.

When companies are deciding whether to use capital or labor in order to complete their production, they try to balance the costs and benefits of each. How much marginal revenue will be generated by hiring a person, and how much will that person be paid in wages? How much marginal revenue will be generated by purchasing a piece of capital, and what will it cost to buy and operate that piece of capital? In calculating the answer to these questions, a company can then compare the two to determine whether capital or labor will produce the most marginal profits. Recall from before that this comparison is also used to determine the cost-minimizing input combination, as follows:

$$MP_L/w = MP_K/r$$

Where:
MP = marginal product
L = Labor
W = Wages
K = Capital
r = Rent (or otherwise the cost of capital divided by number of units produced over the life of the capital)

Once a company has determined the relative profitability to pursuing capital or labor, they will choose the most profitable option every time. As they increasingly pursue one option, its marginal profitability will decrease, however until the point that the other option becomes the more profitable to pursue. A company will continue to balance these two things in this manner until either MR=MC, or until demand has been met.

Market failure and the role of government. _____

Despite what some would have you believe, the free market is not perfect. Depending on how you categorize them, there are between 8 and 12 specific ways in which the market fails to be the most effective mechanism for resource distribution, called **market failures**. Before you get all Friedman/Rand on me, let me give you a simple example. You're in an ambulance having a heart attack going to the nearest hospital. Clearly you don't have the opportunity to shop around for the best price, or tell the ambulance driver "Don't go to this one. The one across town has better prices." In this manner you have eliminated both competition and consumer choice – two main tenants of the free market. In fact, you likely wouldn't even have the option of whether or not to consume the product, as any onlookers will be legally and morally obligated to call emergency services on your behalf. This is a clear example of a time in which free market mechanisms have not functioned as they should, requiring that we engineer a mechanism that fixes this failure in the market.

Before getting into the role of government in economics, it's important to distinguish between economics and politics. We put politicians in charge of our economic policy, but that does not mean that politicians know anything about economics. If that were the case, we'd be electing economists instead of lawyers and inheritance recipients. Quite to the contrary, our economic policy is created almost exclusively in a manner that is politically beneficial for the politicians passing the law and the people who fund their political campaigns. There's even a dumb little joke about it in the field. "The first law of economics is that there's not enough stuff to meet everyone's wants and needs. The first rule of politics is to ignore the first law of economics." So, as we move forward, remember that the content of this guide, and the AP tests, refer to the ideal role of government from an economics perspective, whereas the real world tends to be more concerned with the ideal role of economics from a political perspective.

With that in mind, it is the **role of government** to facilitate the free market. This is accomplished as the government engineers and uses economic mechanisms which fix the different market failures. Think of the economy as an engine – it's only useful when it's moving, but it has a tendency to break-down, so it's the job of the government to keep all the parts repaired, keep it well oiled, and ensure it continues to move smoothly. This is done in the form of economic policies, which manage the manner in which resources are distributed. This topic has more to do with macroeconomics, though, so there will be more on economic policy in that part of the guide.

Out of the various market failures, the AP test focuses on 4. Quite frankly, I don't really know why they picked these 4, especially considering that one of them falls more into the realm of macroeconomic than microeconomics, but that's what they wanted. These include externalities, public goods, monopolies, and the income disparity (the last of these being the macroeconomics issue).

The first market failure usually discussed in any economics course is called **externalities**, which includes any added benefit or cost experienced by people other than the buyer which are not accounted for in the selling price. There are two types of externalities: positive and negative. When you buy something with a **positive externality**, the people around you benefit from your purchase despite not paying anything for the value they receive. For example, vaccinations are a good with a positive externality. Not only do you protect yourself from disease, the good for which you're paying, but the people around you are also less likely to get sick then, too. It's a thing called herd immunity, wherein any one person is even less likely to get sick if the people around them are not likely to get sick, which is particularly important for those who medically cannot get vaccinated.

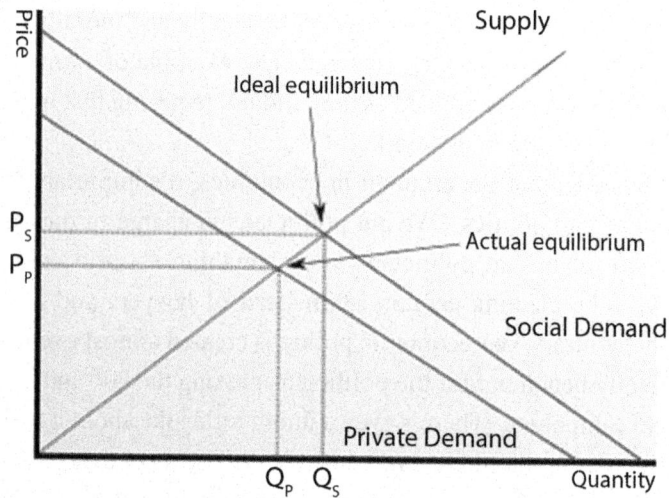

This graph illustrates the supply and demand of positive externalities. The actual equilibrium is the price and quantity actually consumed on the market, but other people also benefit. The number of people which benefit from the positive externality at the current market price is the point on the social demand curve directly to the right of actual equilibrium. Since price will increase with higher quantities, though, the ideal equilibrium is at a price and quantity which, together, encompass the total value of the externalities benefits. Depending on how you look at it, this means you're either overpaying for vaccinations because you're providing benefit to others without them compensating you, or underpaying because the seller is giving more value than they're receiving.

By contrast, **negative externalities** are things you buy which harm the people around you. The consumption of fuel, for example, pumps toxins into the air which the people around you breathe. In recent years, China has been having a particularly bad time with air pollution, as is India. Before them, though, much of Europe and North America went through the same thing during the Industrial Revolution, when people would systematically contract a pollution-related disease called "black lung". Although, the negative externalities of fuel consumption have decreased a bit ever since lead was removed from the formula, it is still clear that there is a harmful element included in our purchases creating negative value. Again, depending on how you look at it, you're either overpaying for gas because the total amount of value is less than what you paid for once accounting for the harm done, or underpaying because you're providing negative value to the people around you without compensating them.

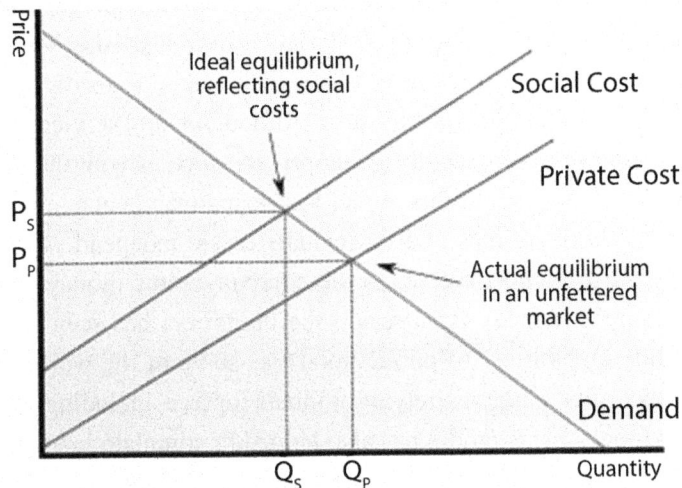

The graph above shows the price and quantity of the actual market equilibrium. Note how the ideal equilibrium puts the actual price higher, so that you're paying for the harm your consumption is causing the people around you, and since the price is higher the quantity demanded will go down.

The manner of dealing with externalities generally recommended include the implementation of a tax on negative externalities, the revenues of which are used to fix the harm caused, or a subsidy on positive externalities, paid for with tax revenues from a community benefitting from the market. Again, note the difference between economics and politics – even though there is a tax on fuel, the companies which sell it also get huge subsidies. If that seems counterproductive to you, considering the cost of implementing and processing taxes and subsidies, then you're not alone. Still, in a healthy economy, the solution is pretty simple, as described.

The second type of market failure listed is known as **public goods**. Public goods are things which are non-excludable and non-rivalrous. Non-excludability means that it is not possible to prevent people from receiving value from the existence of that particular good, while non-rivalrous means that there is no competition to receive the benefits of that good since it costs nothing for everyone to reap those benefits once they are already available. For example, national defense is a service for which the people of a nation pay, but it is impossible to provide that service to one group without providing it to everyone, and once the service is made available everyone benefits equally without competing over the cost of it. The air we breathe is a public good, being impossible to control consumption or distribution of it. Pubic infrastructure such as roads are considered a public good, as well.

The nature of public goods have inspired unique methods of raising revenues. Since there is no way to stop people from accessing radio and television broadcasts, or charging them for it, they are considered a public good. That being said, the content on these stations are privately owned, so the broadcast companies are responsible for raising their own revenues, rather than relying on tax dollars, like road systems. Since the suppliers can't control who receives broadcast content, instead the suppliers took control over the content being broadcast by including paid advertising – other pay the broadcast companies to have their own messages included periodically within the content of the station, giving them public exposure. Although many services typically considered public goods have more recently going private, such as with the advent of satellite radio and cable television, but this model has seen a resurgence in popularity in more recent years as small startups and individuals create independent computer software which is then distributed for free, as the company earns money selling ad space within the software interface. As a result, the digital era has seen a huge increase in the availability and variety of public goods, as some of the world's largest companies like Alphabet offer a huge variety of products for free, including their most well-known service: Google. This model has also helped to stimulate innovation and competition, as new entrants and companies entering new markets are able to take market share from suppliers more established within a given market by offering a more competitive price – free.

Note that the difference between public and private goods has nothing to do with the ownership status of the supplier. Public goods are not necessarily publicly-owned or operated, such as when operated by a government agency, but rather are publicly available regardless of supplier. Again, the defining features are non-excludability and non-rivalrous. By contrast, **private goods** are those which are excludable and rivalrous, regardless of who offers it. The postal service is a public agency offering a private good, since it requires people to each pay for a service which increases in production volume with higher demand, and also prevents people from receiving this service if they fail to pay for the cost of postage. Nearly any product or service you buy is a private good.

The optimal provision of public goods comes not from demand of a good at a given price, like private goods. Private goods are measured "horizontally", which means that they're measured in terms of quantity at a given price. By contrast, public goods are considered to have a fixed quantity, since they are freely available, and the demand is measured vertically, in terms of price. This means that public goods are measured in terms of the **marginal rate of substitution**. In other words, how much private goods is a person willing to forego in order to make a public good available to themselves, as well as everyone else?

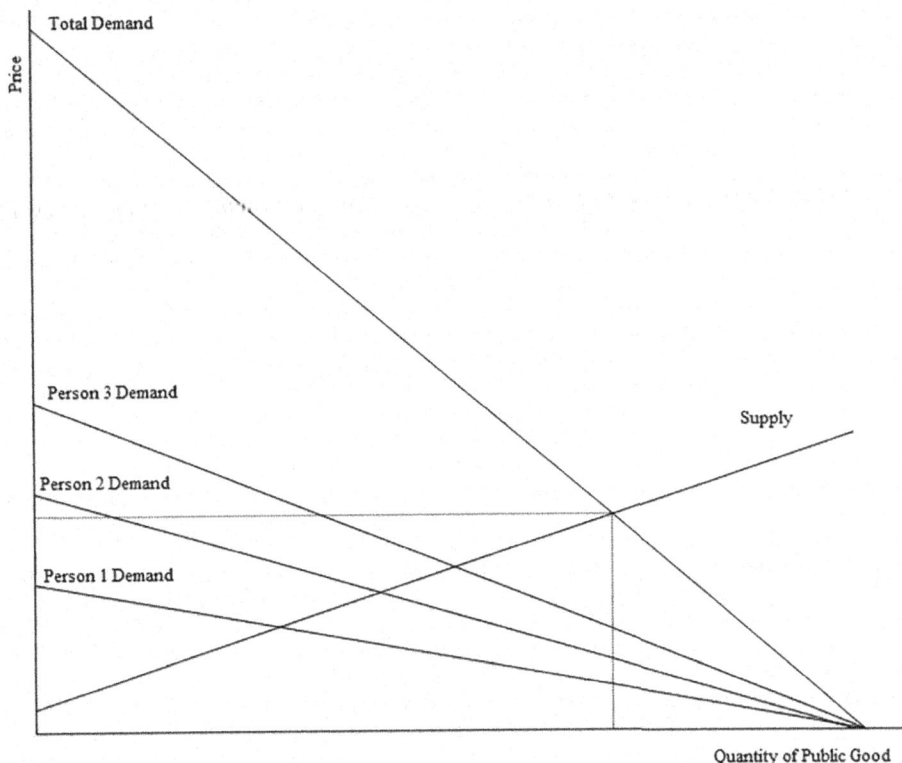

The point at which the **provision of public goods** has reached optimal efficiency is the point at which the utility received from the pubic goods is equal to the opportunity cost in private goods. In other words, when a person helps pay for a public good, they are then not able to use that money on private goods. As people pay more and more, they will receive less comparative value, as per the law of diminishing marginal returns. As a result, the optimum supply of public goods is the amount at which the total value of the public goods is equal to the total value received from foregone private goods – the opportunity cost.

The cost of a public good comes in two primary forms. Those public goods being provided by the government are funded using tax revenues. The public goods being provided by private companies are paid for in the prices of other goods. For example, a radio station earns revenues by charging for advertising, and the high cost of advertising causes firms to increase their selling prices in order to account for selling expenses. As a result, the radio services you receive are paid for when you pay the higher prices goods offered by those firms which advertise on the radio station. Either way, just as the consumption of public goods distributed publicly, so is the expense of funding those public goods.

The real problem with public goods arises when those who are consuming the good are failing to pay for their consumption. Air pollution is a common example, as companies and people create waste fumes into the air that people breathe. By doing this, the air around us is being consumed, making it unsuitable for other uses such as breathing, medical purposes, inflatables, and so forth. Since air is consumed as a way to distribute waste rather than adding economic value to the end product, it typically isn't included as a factors of production. As an overlooked public good, for a very long time it was consumed without anyone paying for that consumption. This means air was drastically underpriced, causing consumption levels to be well above equilibrium levels under market conditions, allowing firms to keep their costs lower than was truly representative in terms of resource consumption. The result is that the air in many places is toxic to breathe, systematically causing elevated levels of disease simply by living there. Since those who are consuming the resource are not paying for their consumption, the resource will continue to be depleted until the resource is no longer available for important purposes. At that point, the government gets involved to fix the problem, which means that the public pays the high price of fixing the problem through tax revenues, rather than accounting for its consumption at the time it is depleted.

The third market failure listed is the existence of monopolies, and the inherent inefficiencies which result from their operations. In particular, predatory practices used by monopolies who abuse their market influence have been targeted for government intervention. Natural monopolies, by contrast, have something of a complicated relationship with the markets. The reason is that natural monopolies truly do have the potential to operate more efficiently and lower market price by taking a greater percentage of the market, but the tendency for this to cause abuses of that market by the monopoly firm leaves many distrustful. As a result, natural monopolies such as utilities tend to be kept as a governmental or quasi-governmental operation, utilizing a publicly-elected board to manage operations.

Besides natural monopolies, there are laws which strictly prevent the existence and market abuses of monopolistic firms, known as antitrust laws. The very first antitrust law was the **Interstate Commerce Act** of 1887, passed under the administration of Grover Cleveland, which applied specifically to modes of transportation, and particularly railroads, in response to rampant price-fixing across the nation. The first major act outlawing certain practices in the nature of monopolies in all markets, and still the most famous of the antitrust laws, is the **Sherman Antitrust Act**, passed by Benjamin Harrison in 1890. Part 1 prohibits the formation of monopolies and cartels, Part 2 prohibits attempts to monopolize markets, and Part 3 defines the areas to which the law applies. In 1903 and 1906, Teddy Roosevelt passed the **Elkins Act** and **Hepburn Act**, respectively. Both these laws once again targeted the railroad industry, which had now made it common practice to participate in price discrimination. So, the Elkins Act banned price discrimination in transportation, while the Hepburn Act expanded the powers of the Interstate Commerce Commission, giving them new jurisdiction while also giving them power to dictate pricing. The first sweeping antitrust law passed since Sherman came under the administration of Woodrow Wilson in 1914: the **Clayton Antitrust Act**. This banned all forms of anticompetitive price discrimination, banned some forms of **exclusive dealings** (requiring buyers to note deal with competitors) and **tying** (requiring buyers to purchase some product other than the one being bought, banned certain types of significant mergers and acquisitions, and banned any person from taking a board position when they have a conflict of interest between multiple firms within the market. In the same year, **Federal Trade Commission Act** was passed, which both created the Federal Trade Commission, and also defined the types of practices it would prevent by using its authority to enforce a variety of commerce regulation laws, including antitrust laws. In 1936, the **Robinson-Patman Act** was passed by Franklin Roosevelt, in an effort to stop systematic price discriminator between wholesalers and retailers. In other words, suppliers to retailers would sell to large chain stores more cheaply than to small businesses, even if the sales quantity and terms remained the same. This practice ended in 1936. Things stayed quiet for a while, and then in 1976 the Ford Administration passed the **Hart-Scott-Rodino Antitrust Improvements Act**. The sole purpose of this act was to require companies to report to the Federal Trade Commission and Department of Justice before executing any kind of merger, acquisition, equity exchange, or other forms of major business integration. This allowed for a review of any potential violation in antitrust laws before they occur.

The final market failure addressed in the AP test is that which relates to the **income/wealth inequality**. It's a convoluted problem with several connected elements, so there isn't an exact name for the whole of the mechanisms which make this happen, but I personally refer to it as national income misallocation. The largest and most problematic symptom of this is the fact that the difference in income and wealth between the average person and the very wealthy continues to increase. In other words, the rich get richer and everyone else get poorer. In recent years there's been talk of the top 1% of the wealthiest people in the world, but that's a bit of a misconception. There's a few different ways to look at it. The top 0.01% of wealthy in the US own 11-12% of all wealth in the US, equal to 66% of lower and working-class households. This group is by far wealthier than even the .09% directly below them. The top 1% earn above $400,000 per year, but it is the top 2% whose incomes fluctuate most directly with national GDP. Earning $320,000 per year, and claiming 22-25% of the nation's total wealth, this small group of people own so much of the entire nation that their net value is directly tied to the nation's gross domestic product (a value measure of the entirety of a nation's production). The top 10% in income, those earning above $145,000 per year, are the start of the real disparity, though. Below this point, the rate of increase of income is relatively linear. In other words, for 90% of people, the income they earn increases evenly compared to others. Once you reach the top 10%, though, income levels start to increase exponentially.

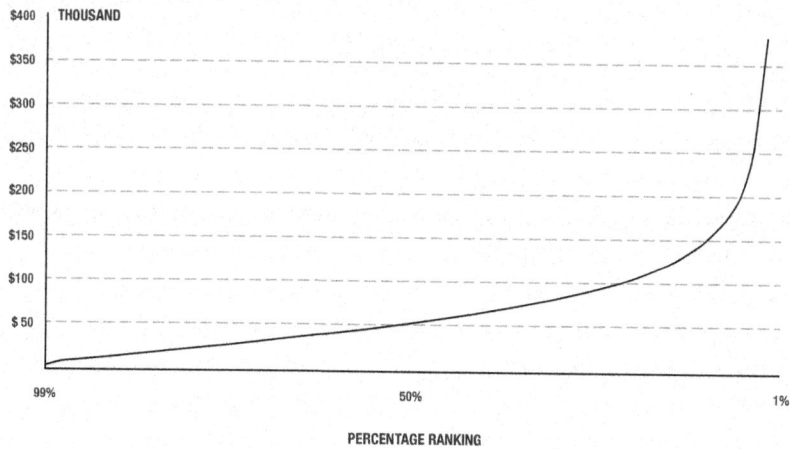

$400 THOUSAND
$350
$300
$250
$200
$150
$100
$ 50

99%   50%   1%

PERCENTAGE RANKING

By contrast, 98% of the nation, and especially the 90% who aren't ultra-wealthy, struggle to keep their real income from decreasing. This is known as the disappearance of the middle class, as incomes for 90% of the nation fail to keep-up with the ever-increasing price of things like food. **Real income** and real wealth account for changes in price over the years, so that you can compare the ability of people to buy things, rather than just increase the volume of money they collect. It is only by constantly fighting for constant updates to labor policy that real income has remained constant, and even then there has been a decrease in real income since 2008. The difference has become so large that it is difficult to visualize since it has gotten so large, so quickly. In 1965, the average CEO earned just 2,000% more than that of the average American, but by 2014 that number grew to 30,300% more than the average worker. Odds are good that the CEO of your company earned in a single day more than you will the entire year, but odds are also good that you don't believe that person work harder in a single day than you do all year.

The socioeconomic disparity is measured using something called the **Gini Coefficient**. This is a value between 0 and 1 which expresses the ratio of total national income earned by a given percentage of the population. A Gini coefficient of 0 indicates pure equality, wherein 1% of people earn 1% of the nation's income, 10% of the population accounts for 10% of income, and 99% of people earn 99% of all the money earned in the nation. A Gini coefficient of 1 indicates pure inequality, wherein 1 person owns 100% of all income in the nation. This can be illustrated using a particular type of graph called a **Lorenz Curve**.

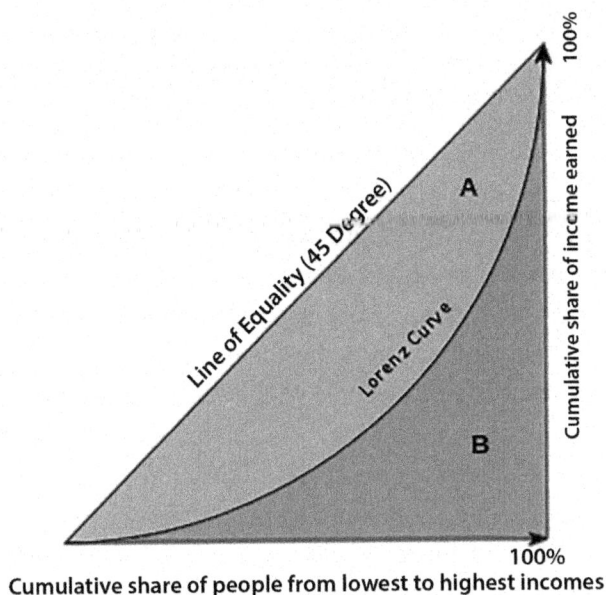

Cumulative share of people from lowest to highest incomes

Note that the line of equality is the same as a Gini coefficient of 0, that the vertical line on the right is equal to a Gini coefficient of 1, and that A+B compromise the entirety of the nation's income. The Lorenz Curve, then, is the curve which illustrates the actual distribution of income within a nation. Those nations which are most equal are mostly found in Northern and Central Europe, including Denmark, Sweden, Netherlands, Slovenia, Germany, Czech Republic, and others. The lowest Gini coefficient is roughly 23. Those which are most unequal tend to be in Africa and South America, including Botswana, Sierra Leone, Haiti, Honduras, and Guatamala. The highest Gini coefficient is roughly 63. The United States is the 43rd most unequal country (101st most equal), with a Gini coefficient of roughly 42. Nations with a similar Gini coefficient include Cameroon and Peru.

Differences in earning power is not inherently a bad thing, and in fact it is necessary in some ways, particularly when considering the role of investing in national growth (a matter discussed more thoroughly in the portion on macroeconomics). However, once the socioeconomic disparity gets too large, some very serious problems occur. It's a matter discussed in macroeconomics, but to be brief, the entire national economy starts to break-down for everyone, rich and poor, and the whole of society ceases to function as it should. Again, see the portion on macroeconomics for more on this.

The growing socioeconomic starts with differences in the **marginal propensity to consume** (MPC) between people. MPC refers to the proportion of a person's income which is spent. If a person spends 50% of their income, then their MPC would be 0.5. By contrast, the **marginal propensity to save** (MPS) is the proportion of a person's income which is stored-away or invested. You can look at MPS at 1-MPC, since 1 is equivalent to 100%, or you can think of MPC as 1-MPS. The vast majority of people have a MPC of 0.99 or more, spending all their money on subsistence requirements like housing, food, and transportation to work. As a result, they have no money to invest, which means they never get their money to earn gains and never accumulate any kind of wealth. They never learn how to manage money because they never have any to manage, so the decisions made are sometimes not the best, and financial management skills are not taught to their kids. They are in a position where they cannot afford quality food or healthcare, thereby decreasing their health, nor can they afford a top-tier education, which inherently puts them at a perpetual disadvantage. In order to acquire a home or a vehicle or an education, the average person must borrow money and repay it with interest, which means they pay more for the things they buy than someone who can afford to pay in cash. In fact, people with lower income have to pay higher interest rates since they are considered a higher-risk loan, despite the paradox that charging higher interest rates puts them at greater risk of defaulting. The average worker also cannot properly negotiate in the labor markets. Having little in their savings, people are generally desperate to maintain work at any price since they cannot afford their bills for long without it, preventing them from taking the opportunity to search the market for competitors, or otherwise negotiate price. It's been proven that when there is a perceived shortage of some kind, then those who perceive that shortage are more aggressive and even violent toward each other, so those who have moderate-to-low skilled jobs tend to have an ongoing struggle with mental and social health, and extremely low morale. They are the first to lose their jobs in an economic slump, and the first to lose their jobs to automation, and are keenly aware that there are other desperate people ready to take their place should their employer decide that they could hire new people for lower wages. Such an incident is likely to cause a person to lose their home, and financial struggle is by far the #1 cited reason for divorce. Poverty increases crime, terror, and even revolution.

By contrast, when you earn lots of money your MPC tends to be very low, affording you many possibilities to grow your wealth and influence. The very rich only make about 35% of their total annual earnings from their wages, while the remaining amount comes primarily from investments of various types. When you are able to save more of your money, it becomes possible to invest it, making even more money. This additional income stream also gives you a better negotiating position in the labor markets, since you can rely on your other income for a time while you search the market for the best wages possible. With very high wealth you can afford to pay for things in cash, rather than taking loans on which you must repay interest, so you're spending less for the same goods that someone else buys. With lots of money also comes the ability to guarantee economic policy which benefits you, personally. By giving money to politicians, political campaigns, political action committees, political parties, and so forth, you are placing a bid on national policy. Besides providing money to campaigns, it's also legal for federal politicians to participate in insider trading on the stock market, they are allowed to accept positions on the board of directors, or other high-paying positions, with the companies for whom they are writing policy. In the case Citizen's

United vs. FEC, the Supreme Court deemed that corporations are people. So, rather than giving all the people within the corporation political influence, the corporations themselves now influence politics with huge sums of money. This is all considered an investment because spending a $10 million on a particular politician might get $100 million worth of government contracts, tax cuts, or some other benefit. With great sums of money it also becomes possible to manage that money in ways which avoids taxation. For example, income from investments are taxed at a much lower rate than even middle-class income, so it's not uncommon for CEOs to accept $1 in wages per year, just to make them technically employed, and then receive the remainder of their income in stock options or other investments. The use of overseas tax shelters is a very popular choice, as well.

So, the national income/wealth disparity becomes a self-perpetuating thing. The differences permeate every aspect of life, from health, happiness, education, probably of being a victim in a crime, relationships, and so forth. This continues to happen until some point is reached where so many people have become so poor that the whole of the nation devolves into chaos, as seen through revolutions in France, several ex-Soviet nations, and more. There is no consistent point at which this occurs, and there has been debate as to whether the US is on that verge, especially in the wake of the Occupy movement. It is most definitely necessary to engineer a mechanism by which this problem can be fixed. Such attempts have included policies which support organized labor, giving people a better negotiating position in labor markets, and this was very successful but these have largely been eroded through the political influence of large corporations. The use of tax and stimulus policies which create programs which benefit the public was very successful at the end of the Great Depression and the period afterward, but these, too, have been largely eroded by opponents of upper-class taxation. The minimum wage and social security policies were implemented to guarantee that all Americans who are employed full-time, or retired, are guaranteed that they will be able to maintain at least a living wage, but the minimum wage has failed to increase with inflation since the 1970s. There is currently a great degree of research and debate on the merits of a guaranteed minimal annual income issued by the federal government, and a variety of other models have also been proposed, but so far it seems as those these models are also likely to fail in the long-run (in the unlikely event that they pass, at all) since they fail to address the matter of money influencing government policy. Once again, this matter clearly overlaps macroeconomics heavily, but you'll be encountering it in the microeconomics test, so be prepared.

There is about a handful more market failures which you'll be unlikely to encounter on the AP microeconomics exam, but which will help you better understand the mechanics of microeconomics, preparing you for the exam through a solid foundation of economic knowledge rather than rote memory. The first, and most basic, is that of market inefficiency. Though there has not yet been any developments to effectively improve upon this problem, the fact of the matter remains that markets are inherently inefficient. There's a little joke in the field which helps illustrate this point. I would cite the source but the truth is that I can't remember where I heard it, anymore, so I apologize for failing to provide proper credit. "Two economists are walking down the street when they see $100 laying on the ground. The first stops to pick it up when the second says, 'Don't bother. If it was real, someone would've grabbed it already.'" This illustrates the problem with the efficient market hypothesis, which states that markets will respond instantly and perfectly to changes in the market. Well, this is clearly nonsense. Even assuming everyone knows that the market has changed the instant it does, no one can change their activities so quickly.

Reversing that, even if people and companies were able to change their activities instantly, they wouldn't all receive the information at the same time and in-advance of their need to respond to that information. This is another market failure called information asymmetry, which may or may not be included as a part of the inefficient market, depending on how you define it. At any rate, for a time it was common for the exchanges in a market to be laissez faire, which means "let the buyer beware." So, if you bought something, it was completely up to you to ensure that you're not being swindled, despite the fact that the companies know something about the product which you do not. Then in the mid-20th century we began to see a wave of consumer protection laws, truth-in-advertising laws, and transparency laws for particular types of investments. These laws weren't passed to prevent consumer abuses from happening in the future, but rather to stop widespread problems which were occurring from the systematic abuse of the information asymmetry which occurred within markets.

Inefficiency and information asymmetry are thought to contribute to another failure of the free market: volatility. If there is anything good which can be said about attempts to fully-plan economies such as that found in North Korea, it's that they are very stable – they consistently suck. If we knew of some way to maintain that kind of stability within an economy that's successfully growing, then that would be great. Unfortunately that's not the case. So, we end up with periods of growth, recession, markets which are overvalued or undervalued, and all sorts of large variation in the quantity and price of different resources. In response to that we are able to use different types of economic policy to minimize the amount of variation which occurs by influencing them indirectly via the free market, itself. It works ok – not great, but a heck of a lot better than nothing, at all. That's all discussed in the portion on macroeconomics, though.

Those three market failures are all very closely related, so it's sometimes debated whether or not they are distinct things. They are very fundamental to every aspect of the economy, though, which is why they were included in this guide. There are several more market failures which are more common to specific markets, so we won't get into them here, but in the end there's roughly 10 of them in all, and it is the ideal role of government to create minimally-invasive mechanisms to resolve the problems associated with these failures while remaining uninvolved in everything else.

Macroeconomics

Macroeconomics is a field of economics which deals specifically with studying the manner in which groups of firms function collectively. Whereas individual firms maintain consistent, predictable traits and behaviors, there are regular, predictable patterns and trends which occur when you look at all of them together. This can best be illustrated by looking at a term unique to macroeconomics: aggregate. Aggregate, in other contexts, refers to a type of cement. When you look at aggregate very close, you'll see lots of individual and unique pebbles, bits of sand, sometimes some crystalline rock, and so forth. You could look at any one of these tiny elements and come to learn how it looks. When you step-back, though, what you'll see is a much larger, constant substance which makes streets, sidewalks, and so forth. You don't see the tiny rocks and sand anymore, but each one contributes its own unique traits to make something larger that looks like a single entity, in itself. In this same way we see the relationship between microeconomics and macroeconomics. In microeconomics we study the individual firms – people, households, companies, charities, etc. Each firm is unique from any other in some ways, but when you step-back and see how the economy as a whole looks, then each firm found within that economy contributes its traits to something much larger that looks like a unique entity, in itself.

The term aggregate, in economics, refers to the way in which each firm contributes its own traits to the whole. For example, each firm has its own supply and demand curves which can be measured, and then when you add-up all the supply curves, and add-up all the demand curves, you'll get what's known as aggregate demand and aggregate supply. This in the total amount of demand and supply for all things within a given geographic region, usually a nation. Even though we can look at everything we produce as a nation – its total volume and value – as a single aggregate supply curve, the traits it exhibits are determined by the individual supply curves of every firm in the nation. That is the nature of macroeconomics – it studies the traits of a collection of firms and generates unique principles of its own.

Measurement of economic performance.

Economics is the study of resource allocations, not the study of individual things. If things aren't in motion, then it's not really an economy at all, it's just a bunch of items. Looking at a pile of money, economics isn't really concerned with what the money is made of or the pretty designs on it (that would fall more under the field of anthropology, though there is an overlap), but rather economists are concerned with the manner in which that money is going to be used. So when you're looking at the nation's economy as a whole, it's not just a list of the stuff which exists, but the way in which those things were used. That's why the national economy is referred to in terms of the circular flow of national income. Refer to the image below:

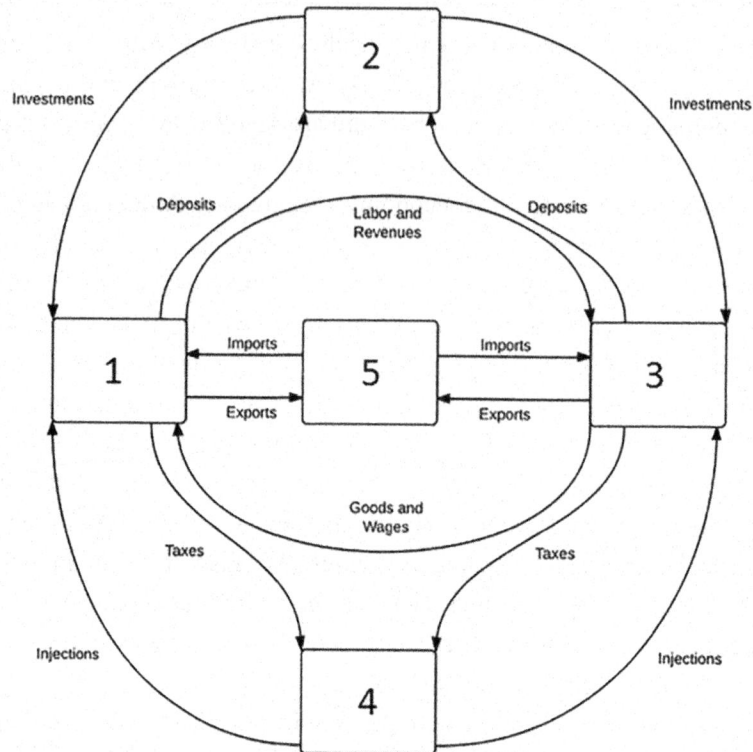

In the graph, there are 5 sectors, each of which interacts with the other sectors in their own, unique ways by both consuming value from, and adding value to the other sectors. The arrows in the graph show the flow of value from one sector to another, and are labeled as the type of transactions which are occurring when that value is moving. Based on these arrows you can probably guess what each of the sectors are, but let's go over it anyway:

Sector 1: **Households**. These includes every individual person. As workers they provide value to companies by offering their labor, and in return they receive value in the form of wages. Households also receive value from companies in the form of goods and services, and give value in return in the form of revenues. Households, along with companies, are a part of the core economy. Households are the foundation of all demand.

Sector 2: **Financial**. This includes banks, credit unions, investment brokers, and things of that nature. The defining feature of the financial sector is that it functions as an intermediary between those who have resources to invest, and those who are trying to attract investors. The financial sector receives value in the form of deposits, as people and companies put their money into bank accounts or brokerage accounts. They then send value back into the economy in the form of investments – they give loans to people and businesses, or purchase other types of financial products such as stocks. The financial sector grows by earning more money on the investments than it pays for deposits, though a portion of the money earned from investment does go to the depositors in order to give incentive to make deposits.

Sector 3: **Companies**. This includes businesses of all sorts, non-profit organizations, self-employed individuals, and so forth. The defining feature of this sector is that it produces goods and services by applying processes to some combination of inputs. Together with households, companies are a part of the core economy, forming the foundation of all supply. That's why the relationship between households and companies is so unique, and why there are so many more types of value moving between them than between any other sectors. Companies provide goods and wages, and receive revenues and labor.

Sector 4: **Government**. As you might have guessed, this is the government. More specifically, this refers to any administratively-defined collection and distribution of resources. It might be the federal government, or it might by your local community. The point is that the government sector receives value in the form of taxes, and then provides value back to the economy in the form of injections. The term "injection" is probably the only one in that graph which seemed strange to you, but it's just the term that's used to refer to anything of value the government puts back into the economy. That could be infrastructure development, it could be providing fire and law enforcement services, or it could be economic stimulus in the form of a tax credit.

Sector 5: **Foreign**. This includes any interaction with foreign nations and the economic sectors within those nations. Any value sent to other countries is called an export, and any value received is called an import. We will, of course, delve into the matter of imports and exports in greater detail in the chapter on international trade and finance. For now, there are a couple types of exports/imports which tend to trick people. When a person goes to another nation to work, that's an export, but when people go to another nation as tourists, that's an import. Despite the fact that tourists go to the foreign nation to receive that value, and must consume the value while there since the experience cannot be brought home, people from your domestic nation are still receiving value from a foreign nation, making it an import. Everything they consume while there is an import. On the flip side, foreigners who come to your nation on vacation are receiving exports, but if they come to your nation to work then you're receiving an import.

Between these 5 sectors, everything which happens within a nation's economy takes place. Value continues to move between these sectors in what's known as **circular flow**. As value flows from one sector to another, it generates economic value added – wherein

Like all macroeconomic measurements, GDP is not 100% precise, either are price indices, or sentiment indices, or anything else, really. Does that mean they're completely useless? Not at all, it just means that you need to be aware of these things if you are to use them correctly.

Let's say you want to know the total value of production in the nation. Using just one measurement will help you get a fuzzy picture of the truth, and with each measurement you use, the answer becomes a little clearer.

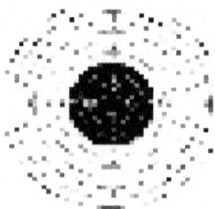

If the true value of the nation's production is the center of that target, then by using just GDP the target might look like this. You have a general idea of about how much the nation is producing, and the kinds of things it's producing, but it's not exactly precise. So, you go-on and try to add a few more measurements, like inflation, payroll, and some

the sector provides more value than they receive. As this value continues to grow, it is said that the economy is growing, which just means that there is more total value flowing throughout these sectors than there was in the past. Without people participating in transactions with each other, all this stuff would just lie stagnant, but as people we are uniquely able to take these resources and turn them into something more valuable than they once were by applying our efforts and processes to them. It is the amount of this added value – the total amount of value produced between all these sectors of a single nation within a given year – which we call **gross domestic product** (GDP).

Since GDP is the value of production within a nation, GDP growth refers to our ability to continue to increase the amount of economic value added each year. How much more (or less) are we producing this year than we produced last year?

$$Y = C+I+G+(X-M)$$

Where:

Y = GDP. Technically, Y is the variable used to denote income (even personal income, when we're talking microeconomics), so it means national income. Since GDP and national income are the same thing, though, it doesn't matter.

C = Consumption. Everything that is purchased.

I = Investments. All the value that's invested.

G = Government. All the money spent by the government.

X = Exports. All the value sent to other nations.

M = Import. All the value received from other nations

$(X-M)$ = Net exports. The total change in value in the nation based on its interactions with other nations.

You can explore US GDP, it's exactly content and breakdown of its value, at the Bureau of Economic Analysis website at http://www.bea.gov/iTable/index_nipa.cfm.

In contrast to GDP, another measure of national production is **gross national product** (GNP). Whereas GDP includes the value of all production within a nation, regardless of who makes it, GNP is the value of all production by a nation's citizens, regardless of where they are in the world. If you were to move to China for a year for work, you'd be contributing to Chinese GDP but US GNP.

Without getting into a lot of long-winded jargon, let's just say that prices change over time. Your grandparents paid a lot less for bread than you did, but at the same time the price of computer memory has gone down a lot over the past few decades. At the macro-scale we're not so worried about changes in the price of most individual products, but the manner in which the changes in all products contribute to the overall change in average price levels of all the stuff. Of course, there are some exceptions when you start talking about individual types of products that really influence overall production and price levels, such as changes in the price of energy (e.g.: oil, natural gas, etc.). As a general rule, though, when talking about price in macroeconomics we mean the average price of everything.

In order to get an estimate for the overall price of everything, you need to use a thing called a **price index**. Each price index is developed by picking the types of goods which are the most common and in roughly the same volumes that the average person buys them, which is known as a **basket** (i.e.: a basket is any selected collection of measurement, including baskets of goods, or baskets of currencies, etc.). The total price of everything in that basket changes over time, and it's measured as a percentage. So, if the total amount you'd need to spend in order to buy everything in that basket goes up 10%, then your price index would say that the nation's prices have gone up 10%. Whereas the year being used as your reference point would have a price index of 1, the next year would have a price index of 1.1. That's simply because 1 = 100%, while 1.1 = 110%, and that you can use any year you want as your reference point. If you want to start at 1960 then 1960 will have an index of 1, or if you want to start at 2020, then that will have an index of 1, and everything else is measure relative to that point.

There are two primary price indices used today: the Consumer Price Index (CPI) and the Producer Price Index (PPI). **Consumer price index** refers to the things that your average consumer buys on a regular basis, and includes a wide array of food, shelter, clothing, transportation, medical, education, communication, entertainment, and other such things. By contrast, producer price index includes the price of wholesale stuffs of a huge range, from food, to energy, to industrial machinery, and on and on and on.

Overall price changes almost invariably mean that things become more expensive, a state of change called **inflation**. If you have inflation of 10% in a single year (which is really high, by the way), then it means you have to spend 10% more money to buy the same volume of stuff. If prices go down, which really only happens during long periods of very high unemployment (e.g.: Great Depression, 2008 Financial Crisis, etc.), then that's called **deflation**.

First, let's get a common misconception out of the way: Inflation isn't always a bad thing. Trying to stimulate just a little bit of inflation can help to increase monetary velocity during a recession, helping to get the economy growing again. During the early-20th century, several Western nations engaged in a currency war, where they would each devalue their own currencies in order to increase demand for their own goods relative to the goods from foreign nations (a matter we'll discuss in the section on International Trade and Finance).

Inflation is really only dangerous when it gets too high, and there are some crazy examples of a state called **hyperinflation**. This is a state wherein a nation's currency essentially becomes useless. In 1946, Hungary experienced an annual inflation rate of 41.9 quadrillion percent – prices doubled roughly every 15 hours. By the time the Zimbabwe hyperinflation reached its peak at the end of 2008, it had reached a rate of 89.7 sextillion percent, requiring people to carry truckloads of the worthless currency to buy even small things. Germany between WWI and WWII experienced an inflation rate of 29,500%, and workers were asking to be paid for a half-day's wages at lunch so they could buy groceries before the prices went up at the end of the day. These types of

other things, and the target starts to look like this:

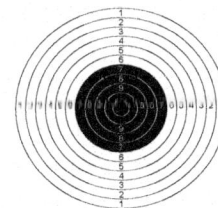

Still not 100% clear, is it? Well, there are some things that are really hard to measure. Most measurements, for example, don't include the grey market or black market. The grey market is completely legal, but it's all the transactions which occur outside typical distribution channels. Garage sales and lemonade stands are included in the grey market, as is the use of Craigslist to buy or sell stuff. When you barter, that's a grey market transaction, and all the food you grow is included, too. There's nothing wrong with any of these types of transactions, but they are just outside the scope of traditional distribution channels.

Black markets, on the other hand, include any type of illegal activity. Not surprisingly, people aren't exactly willing to admit to black market activity, so this is easily the hardest to measure. The market for drugs, or weapons, or counterfeit items, or rhino horn, function no differently than the markets for simple things like carpeting or dog shampoo. All the basic mechanisms are functionally identical, and they are still a form of production. They turn raw materials into products by hiring workers to create value, they still have target markets and work to make a profit, and so forth. That part of the economy didn't just disappear – it's still there and it contributes to the nation's total production, but it has been deemed illegal, which makes it really hard to properly measure.

circumstances are created exclusively through blatant and reckless mismanagement, or the elimination of the government which issued it such as the Soviet Ruble in the 1990s (defunct currencies later regain value as collectors' items rather than as functioning money). In Germany, for example, they simply started printing huge volumes of money in order to pay the war debts resulting from losing WWI. During times of hyperinflation it's common for people to simply resort to bartering, while companies and government agencies will often rely on foreign currencies. Hyperinflation is really quite rare.

That being said, there are some costs associated with inflation. If you have money in a bank account earning 0% interest, then inflation means that the money in your account loses value over time. Even though it might be the same volume of money, it can purchase less stuff, so that you're actually losing value. This also poses a risk for people on fixed income, or for investors who buy fixed-return assets like bonds. As a result, theoretically, expenditures are made to try and counteract the effects of inflation. It's said that people will spend their money instead of holding it, but let's be honest: when is the last time you heard someone say "Well, I better go spend all my money today because it will be worth slightly less tomorrow!" The reality is that most people don't do much of anything to manage the influence on inflation on their finances, and those who take the steps to be proactive put their money into investments. So, while you have to know this for the AP exam, it's total nonsense. Also B.S. is the idea that inflation creates costs in that if a business doesn't properly keep-up with inflation then they'll lose money. Sure, that's true to an extent, but its zero-sum: what the business loses in foregone revenues just benefits consumers, so there is no total increase in costs. What's not B.S. is the fact that the more often a business increases their prices, the more they'll spend on price tags, ads, and other mediums of communicating price to customers. As a result, businesses must weigh whether the cost of changing all this stuff will generate enough added income to make the change financially beneficial. Realistically, the only time inflation has a negative impact is when it gets too high. Managing small levels of inflation can actually be beneficial, just so long as gross mismanagement doesn't lead to hyperinflation.

As for the normal rates of inflation, there are three sources:

1) **Cost-Push Inflation**. This occurs when the cost of production increases. For example, let's say one year there is a severe drought and farmers are forced to increase the amount of money they spend on irrigation. Since farm profit margins are so small, they have to increase the selling price exactly the same amount that production costs increased. Since all other production relies on food, the price of everything else goes up, too.

2) **Demand-Pull Inflation**. This occurs when AD>AS. Yeah, we haven't talked a whole lot about aggregate demand (AD) or aggregate supply (AS) yet (that happens in the next chapter), but the point is that when that the people of a nation demand more than the nation can provide at its current production potential, then prices will go up. This is, in part, a result of producers needing to invest in greater production potential and consume higher volumes of

the factors of production (at lower marginal product, of course), resulting in lower production efficiency that raises prices. This is also, in part, because the producers can increase prices without dropping their current sales volume, thereby increasing profitability, so why not?

3) **Monetary Inflation**. Monetary inflation occurs when the government uses monetary policy to decrease the purchasing power of a currency. This is done by increasing the amount of currency in circulation relative to the total production of the nation. For example, let's say that a nation has total production of $100 per year, and total volume of 100 units of currency. Well, the next year that nation increases its production volume by 100% but does not increase the volume of its currency. In that case, each unit of currency represents twice the volume of goods. The result will be that each unit of currency can buy more stuff, but that the monetary velocity decreases. By contrast, if that nation kept its production volume constant but printed 100 more units of currency, then each unit of currency would represent half as much total production, so that each unit buys half as much stuff.

These distinctions between the different types of inflation is critically important to understanding the behavior of inflation, as well as to developing proper policy to manage inflation rates.

Inflation is also the source of many necessary adjustments in the measurements of any other calculation of money-type stuff. Consider the money you make at work – if you don't get a regular raise, then you're actually earning less money each year than you did before. As prices go up, you can't buy as much as you could the year before. That's the difference between the terms "nominal" and "real". **Nominal** refers to the quantity, while **real** refers to the value. If you make $100 dollars every year then your **nominal income** is $100, but if prices go up by 10%, then your **real income** is just $90.

A few of the things which must be adjusted for inflation:

1) **Real GDP** vs. **Nominal GDP**. As GDP changes, it must be considered, too, that the change in the value of money is also changing the measure of GDP. In other words, if total production remained completely the same, year after year, but prices went up, then GDP would also go up. Well, that doesn't make any sense, so we use Real GDP.

2) **Real Income** vs. **Nominal Income**. If your income doesn't increase at least with the rate of inflation each year, then you're actually making less money than you did last year in terms of purchasing power. Don't worry about the volume of money you're making, but rather focus on real income.

3) **Real Interest** vs **Nominal Interest**. The amount of interest you're earning on an investment, or paying on a loan, will not be exactly what you think it is, because inflation is playing a role in the purchasing power of that money

which is owed. If you're earning 1% on your bank account, but inflation is 2%, you're actually losing l% of the value of your account each year.

4) International Trade. When dealing with other nations, whether through investment or purchases, both nations have their own unique rate of inflation. If that just blew your mind, then don't panic – we'll deal with that in the chapter on international trade and finance. For now, suffice it to say that large international contracts quite frequently have clauses accounting for possible changes in relative value.

For reasons we'll discuss in the chapter on stabilization policies, inflation and unemployment are related. They're not opposites of each other, but one does influence the other, and managing inflation rates is one way to indirectly manage the rate of unemployment. That's why you always see these two concepts taught back-to-back, so if the jump from inflation to unemployment seems somewhat abrupt, then that's the reason why it happens. So, that being said, to understand unemployment you first need to know about the nature of the labor force.

The **labor force**, also known as the **workforce** (the two terms are interchangeable), includes all the people who are working or trying to work. Generally this includes people over the age of 18 (when you're legally an adult) and under the age of 62 (legal retirement age), who do not have disabilities which prevent them from working, and are not full-time students. It is those people who are actively seeking employment but not actively working which are considered to be **unemployed**, contributing to the **unemployment rate**. Those people who fit the requirements of being included in the labor force but are not working or actively seeking employment are said to have dropped from the labor force, contributing to a decrease in the nation's **labor force participation rate**. During very long and deep recessions (e.g.: Great Depression, 2008 Financial Crisis), it is common for people to temporarily give-up their search for employment until more jobs become available – especially after a home foreclosure, until they can once again maintain a stable address. This type of dropping from the labor force is considered a type of long-term unemployment, since it requires a change in economic state in order to once again increase the labor force participation rate.

There are a few unique states of employment that can sometimes be considered to be a flux between employed and unemployed. In particular, **underemployment** is a matter of great concern. Underemployment occurs when people are not able to work as much as they would like, or when they accept work below their skill level. This is particularly common when nation is recovering from a recession, as people with years of experience take entry-level positions, thereby crowding-out those with entry-level credentials. This often has the side-effect of causing those who have been crowded-out to have long-term, sometimes lifelong professional struggles. Underemployment after a recession also occurs as people accept part-time or temporary work. Since the period after a recession can be precarious, employers often don't want to commit to hiring full-time individuals, and so will resort to hiring people on a limited basis. Part-time work, almost by definition, will not earn sufficient wages to accommodate the cost of living, however.

Another state which can sometimes float between a state of employment and unemployment is **self-employment**. Self-employed people do not have traditional jobs, wherein they work for an employer, and they are not seeking an employer, but they are still working. Instead of employers, self-employed people seek customers, as they function as a business in their own right. Except through tax-filings, self-employed people tend to fall-through the gaps of employment measurements, so they often don't get included as employed or unemployed, since they don't engage many of the same bureaucratic systems. There are no qualifications or procedures necessary to be legally self-employed other than to say that you're self-employed. The only way to be included as a measurement of self-employed people is to file the tax forms for independent contractors (usually 1099-Misc). Right now, as I write this book that you're currently reading, I am functioning as a self-employed individual who has been contracted by XAMonline. At any given point whether I have active clients or not, I'm still self-employed, even though there is really no way for economists to include me in the labor pool other than by looking at my income tax statements. If I fail to secure any work for the entire year, I can still consider myself self-employed (though very poor at it) and there would be no way for anyone to include me as employed or unemployed, so I'd be considered to have dropped out of the labor force entirely.

As for those who are not working but are actively seeking employment, as noted before, they are considered unemployed. Like inflation, unemployment is not just some singular force – there are several different types of unemployment. The distinctions between them is very important to understand the state of the labor force, as well as how to manage the influences upon that labor force. Also like inflation, there are three types of unemployment:

1) **Frictional Unemployment**. This occurs when people are in transition between jobs, between employers, between cities, between career fields, etc. For one reason or another, the person's employment in one particular job has ended and they have not yet begun working in another job yet. This is considered to be a good type of unemployment because it means that the efforts are being made to better match available jobs with the skill sets each person has to offer.

2) **Structural Unemployment**. This occurs when there is some mismatch in the skill sets demanded in the market and the skill sets which people have to offer. This can occur for a variety of reasons, but it is most inherent as a result of improved technologies. As machinery and computers replace some people in the workforce, the people who were replaced no longer have that job available to them, but new work is created in making and operating machines and computers. For example, with the advent of electrical lighting we forever

lost such jobs as lamp lighters (the people who would go out each evening and light the lamps along the streets), and there was a severe reduction in the demand for people who know how to make candles or lamps. Instead, though, there was an increase in demand for people to maintain electrical lights, make lightbulbs, and so forth. It was rather unfortunate for the people who lost their job, but protecting the employment of people should not come at the cost of harming everyone. The nature of this is best expressed by Frederic Bastiat, a French economist who wrote what is colloquially known as *The Candlestick Makers' Petition*, in which the candlestick makers of the time write a letter to the government urging them to block-out the sun in order to increase demand for candles and sustain high rates of employment. This is, of course, a bit of ironic fiction intended to illustrate just how ridiculous it is to prevent progress in the name of protecting jobs. That is why structural unemployment is considered a good thing, as it represents a fundamental change in the economy that requires people to develop new skills (usually indicating improvements in the economy, as opposed to apocalypse).

3) **Cyclical Unemployment**. This is the bad type of unemployment – the kind we don't like to see. This type of unemployment is the polar opposite of demand-pull inflation. Cyclical unemployment occurs when AD<AS. Again, I know we aren't going to talk in detail about aggregate demand and aggregate supply until the chapter on national income and price determination, but suffice it to say for now that cyclical unemployment occurs when there is more supply than is being consumed. Companies are never going to hire even 1 more person than they need to meet production demands, so if there is too much production capacity then the company will reduce their volume of labor. The problem is that this becomes a self-perpetuating cycle (hence, the name). When companies fire people, people have less money, so they spend less money, so companies are selling less stuff and earning fewer revenues, so they have to fire more people, who then have less money, etc. Starting with the New Deal under President Franklin Roosevelt, we learned that to end a deep recession (and lessen the severity and length of smaller recessions), a degree of intervention used to stimulate demand can help to get the economy growing again. When people buy stuff, then it puts companies back into production, which forces them to hire people. There are many ways to accomplish this that will be discussed in the chapter on stabilization policies.

Both frictional and structural unemployment are considered to be good things. They both represent the ongoing reallocation of labor resources so that they can be more productive. Both of these types of unemployment will always exist, even when the economy is doing great and unemployment is at all-time lows. That is why it is not required that unemployment be 0% in order to reach **full employment**. Full employment is the state in which everyone in the labor force is actively employed, except for those currently in a state of frictional or structural unemployment. In the US, full employment tends to float around 2-3%. Full employment is also often referred to as the **natural rate of unemployment**, though the two concepts are technically unique. The natural rate of unemployment is the rate of unemployment that the economy tends to gravitate toward in the long-run. There's little or no evidence to think that this is anything different than full employment, but it's technically possible that the economy will gravitate toward a point that is somewhat more or less than full employment. It's a difficult thing to assess, so for functional purposes, full employment is used as the natural rate of unemployment.

National income and price determination. _____

You're probably thrilled to know that national income and price levels are determined, like just about everything else, by supply and demand. It looks a little different this time, though. See the graph below:

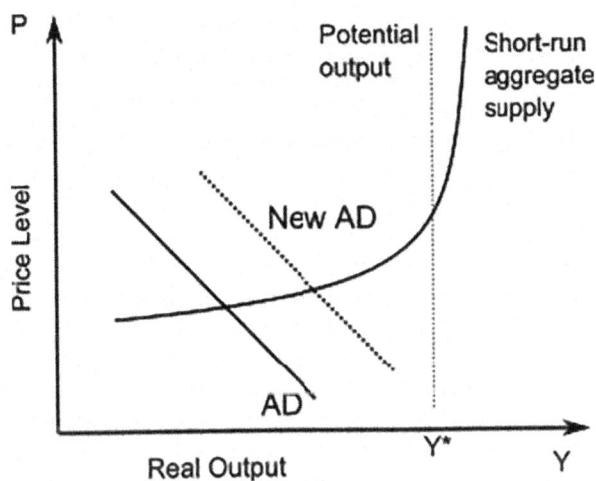

Since this is macroeconomics, we're still talking about aggregate demand and aggregate supply. Remember that P is price, and that Y is both national income and GDP. Well, let's go ahead and add another layer to that insanity and call it aggregate demand, too. You read that right – national income is the same thing as gross domestic product, and they're both the same as aggregate demand. If you haven't figured it out by now, economists seem to enjoy taking things which are either simple or obvious, and explaining them in ways that no one understands, because why not?

The things which determine the level of aggregate demand are known as the **determinants of aggregate demand**. The most obvious thing and most significant ting influencing aggregate demand is the size of the population. Each living person, in order to remain a living person, needs to consume resources – food, water, clothing, shelter, etc. Each person will also have a degree of demand for other things like energy, transportation, entertainment, etc. So, as the population gets bigger, more resources will be in demand.

Another major determinant of demand is income. No, not national income this time, but the amount of money that people make. This is called the income effect, and sometimes the Pigou Effect, which says that as wages increase relative to price levels that consumption will increase. Of course, the impact of this is not equal across all income levels – when you can already afford everything you could ever want, then increase your income won't influence your buying habits. It's all a matter of marginal propensity to consume, which is a matter we'll revisit just a little later in this chapter. Both demand, and the income effect, as influenced by consumer sentiment – when people are confident in the economy, their spending tends to increase. When people are worried about their job or other sources of income, then they'll tend to be more frugal in order to save money in preparation for a period of time in which their income will drop.

Interest rates also have an influence on demand. As interest rates decrease, investors borrow more money for the purpose of investing, and people are more prone to buying things like houses, which are big-ticket items that involve a lot of resource consumption. Relative interest rates between nations, in addition to relative differences in inflation and exchange rates determine the levels of demand between nations. Depending on how these things between nations compare, it might increase both domestic and foreign demand for the goods of one nation or the other. That's a topic that we'll explore more in the chapter on international trade and finance, though.

This one is going to get a little complicated, so pay attention. The last determinant of aggregate demand we're going to talk about is the national multiplier. The multiplier effect states that an injection of money will create more economic growth than the nominal value of the injection. The logic of this is simple: when people have more money, they'll spend more money, but not 100% of it – only a proportion. The amount of money spent then goes to businesses, who spend a proportion of it, and whoever those businesses give the money to will spend a proportion of what they receive, and so forth. So, the multiplier is the amount of increase in GDP that results from an injection of money. Another way to look at this is that the multiplier effect is an accelerator monetary velocity, but we won't talk about monetary velocity until the chapter on the financial sector, so don't worry about it just yet but when you get to that part of the book just think back on the multiplier effect and it'll all make sense.

Recall how we talked about the income effect, and how that lower-income households spend a greater percentage of their income. Well, this is called the **marginal propensity to consume** (MPC). We discussed this in microeconomics, but macroeconomics is another test, and now we're going to expand on it, so let's touch on it again. MPC is the total percentage of your income that you spend. If you have a MPC of 0.8, it means you spend 80% of your income. The opposite of this is the **marginal propensity to save** (MPS), which is the amount of money you don't spend. If your MPC is 0.8, then your MPS is 0.2; 1-0.8 = 0.2 (100%-80%=20%).

So, given any injection of money, if a higher percentage of that money is spent, there will be a greater impact on economic growth – a bigger multiplier effect. The multiplier effect is calculated as:

$$1/MPS$$

So, if you have MPS of .25 (meaning that people spend 75% of their total income), then your multiplier would be 4. Using this information, we can say that an injection of $25 million would create total economic growth of $100 million, since you're multiplying the amount of the injection by the multiplier.

$$25 \text{ million}/0.25 = 100 \text{ million}$$

Understanding relatively differences in MPS across specific demographics of household or business can mean quite a lot of difference in the effectiveness that an injection has in stimulating economic growth. When using this as a stimulus measure, ideally those with the highest MPC (lowest MPS) will be targeted.

That being said, it is projected by some that the multiplier is actually close to 1, meaning that the amount of economic growth in an economy is exactly equal to the amount being put into the economy. The reason for this is the **crowding-out effect**. That is to say that any money spent through the government sector is money not being utilized in the other sectors, so that private stimulus of economic growth goes down in order to accommodate public stimulus. This is both right and wrong. Under ideal conditions, stimulus measures through economic policy would be quite effective at creating GDP growth. Under real conditions, governments tend to not make ideal decisions, thereby preventing us from utilizing what would otherwise be a much higher multiplier.

This is all typically illustrated using a particular type of graph called the **Keynesian Cross**, as seen below:

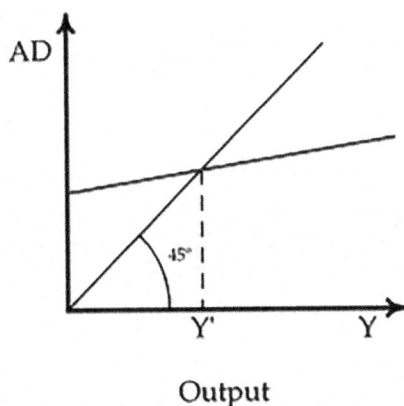

The black line is at a perfectly 45 degree angle, expressing that AD and Y are the exact same thing (which, if you're mathematically-inclined, is known as an **identity**).

The blue line is intended to express the "C" part of C+I+G+(X-M); the consumption element, with the other elements being held constant. Note that as national income increases, so does consumption. If you included the I+G+(X-M) part, to the blue line, then the blue line would also be at a 45 degree angle, laying right on top of the black line. The point at which the blue line intersects the black line is considered the ideal level of production. Producing at higher levels of output, higher GDP, means that there will be inventory surpluses which are not being bought, potentially indicating an impending recession. Producing at lower levels means that there are shortages, limiting potential economic growth. Let's say, for example, that there is surplus production – inventories are overloaded, people aren't buying it fast enough, so companies may have to start firing people until they need to go back into production, again. Well, the government has the option to take advantage of the multiplier effect by injecting money into the economy as a way to raise the blue line up higher until it meets the appropriate spot on the black line. This results in higher consumption rates of the current GDP production.

That brings us to the next point. If productive potential can exceed (or fall behind) consumption rates, then what, exactly is driving aggregate supply? The answer depends on whether you're talking about short-run or long-run aggregate supply. Let's refer to this image:

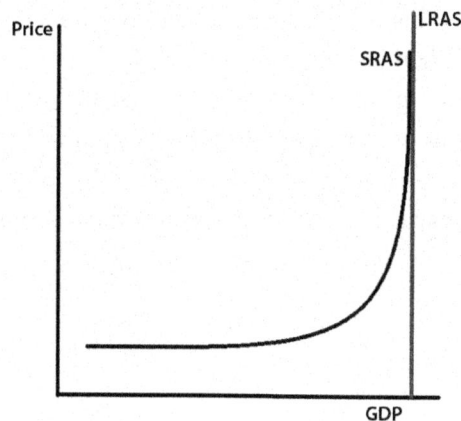

Recall that in economics, short- and long-run is defined by the ability of a business to adapt to the market by changing their factors of production. So, if demand increases and a company has no more production capacity, they'll need to buy a new machine. That means that in the long-run, when all companies are able to hire more people, buy the best equipment, and do everything they can to change their production capacity, it doesn't matter what the price level is because you've maxed-out your supply capabilities. You're already utilizing all the resources available in the economy, so there's nothing more you can do to produce more unless something increases that LRAS (long-run aggregate supply).

The determinants of LRAS include things like technological advances, size of the labor force, skill/education and health of the labor force, natural resources available, sociopolitical paradigm, and so forth. Anything which fundamentally increases either the volume or the quality of the factors of production available will just about do it.

In contrast to LRAS, short-run aggregate supply (SRAS) looks and acts a little more like a traditional supply curve. At low-enough rates of GDP, companies can change production levels without a corresponding change in price because of excess capacity available – in fact, the cost of maintain the surplus production capacity would cause deflationary pressure and contribute to a recession. At increasing rates of GDP, the increase in production as a function of price beings to decreases until it approaches LRAS. The determinants of SRAS include the same things which determine microeconomic supply curves.

Since no sector of the economy can respond instantly and/or perfectly to fluctuations in AS and AD, or in the flows of national income between the different sectors of the economy, many things are called **sticky**. All this means is that some things are slow to respond to changes in the market – though they'll eventually adapt, it doesn't happen right away. Some things which are sticky include prices, wages, and, in some more extreme cases, production levels. For example, if costs increase suddenly, perhaps as a result of an increase in minimum wage, companies will not be able to increase prices right away in response. Instead, they'll have to reduce their levels of profitability for a period of time. There are several reasons why this occurs:

1) Contracts. Any contract which were created prior to the change are still legally obligated to be fulfilled at the terms expressed prior to the change.

2) Market Supply and Demand.

3) Short-Run Limitations.

Just because stickiness results in a temporary decrease in market responsiveness doesn't necessarily mean that it's inherently a bad thing. First of all, stickiness tends to be zero-sum, which means that although some will experience a temporary loss of value, others will generate a temporary increase in value. For example, if a sales contract is signed and then prices increase, the seller will lose value because the exchange is happening at a price lower than current market price, but the buyer is benefitting by getting a price that's lower than current market price. Since these will equal 0 (cancel each other), there is no total loss or gain in value. These small and temporary deviations from market responsiveness can even be utilized as a form of economic policy intended to stimulate growth, but that is something which will be discussed in the chapter on stabilization policies.

The point where aggregate supply meets aggregate demand is known as macroeconomic equilibrium. In the long-run there will always be a return to this equilibrium point, but it is due to stickiness that, in the short-run, shortages and surpluses can occur. Even in the long-run, though, there are limitations. When at full employment, even in the long-run the production levels cannot increase without some change in the available capital, such as advances in technology. What tends to happen at full employment, though, is that short-run production capacity surpasses long-run consumption levels, causing cycles of expansion and contraction.

The image below illustrates these cycles by showing how GDP grows over time on average, but that this occurs in a wavelike manner instead of consistently.

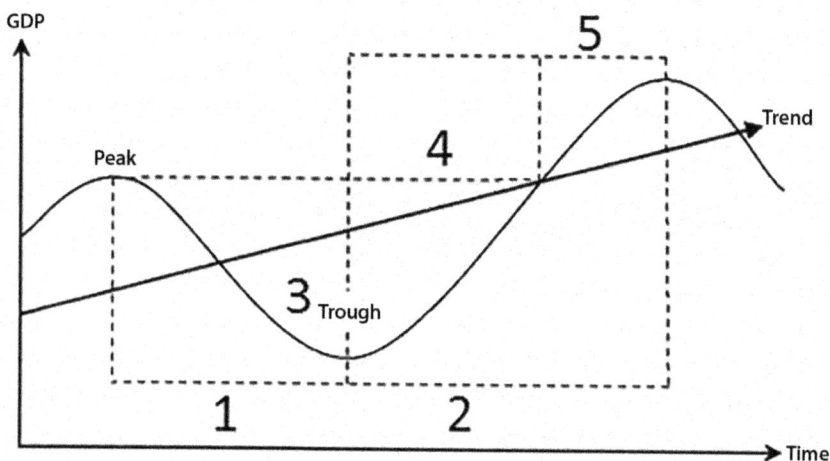

There's a lot going on here, so let's go through it step-by-step:

1) When GDP is decreasing, this is known as a **contractionary period**. It starts with a **slump**, which is a brief period of decreased production. If the negative growth lasts for at least 2 quarters (6 months), then it's called a **recession**. A slump usually begins with lower-than-expected company revenues, decreased payroll, and lower consumer and producer confidence indices. The term **depression** isn't really a formal thing – just a term used for the deep recession that was the **Great Depression**.

2) When GDP is increasing, this is known as an **expansionary period**. It starts with **recovery**, as the economy comes out of a recession, and goes on to be a **boom**.

3) **Recessions** are the only terms with a definition that includes clearly-defined criteria, but that criteria can only be measured in hindsight, after it's already happened, making it somewhat less than useful. Recessions always have high rates of unemployment, surplus inventories and low company revenues, low tax revenues, and so forth. Basically, all the transactions in the economy decrease in volume and value.

4) As GDP once again beings to increase after a recession, it's known as **recovery**. Unemployment rates stabilize, surplus inventories are slowly depleted, which eventually forces companies to begin hiring again as they need to once-again meet production demands. Profitability increases, often exceeding previously-pessimistic outlooks, and the stock markets very quickly exceed their previous highs.

5) Once GDP growth exceeds the trend, the economy is said to be in a **boom**. It operates at full-employment, has high rates of investment and excess risk-taking which leads to investment bubbles, companies expand production potential, the rate of new entrants is high, and so forth. Basically, all the transactions within the economy increases in volume and value, often growing at unsustainable rates.

When you combine both sections 1 and 2, which includes a single contractionary period and a single expansionary period, this is considered 1 full cycle in economic growth.

Financial sector.

People not familiar with economics tend to think it's the study of money, but money is to economics what the kilometer is to physics. Money is a very useful type of measurement used to quantify things otherwise impossible to evaluate. Specifically, **money** is a way to measure how much value or importance that humanity places on particular types of resources. It isn't the money itself that people want – it's just little bits of metal cheap metal and ornately-decorated cotton. Even gold has far less functional value than it has as a store of measuring value. Adam Smith called this **the paradox of value**: water is among the most valuable things on earth, yet it is extremely cheap, while gold is mostly useless (at least it was in the days of Adam Smith, before electronics) but given great value. The reason these kinds of currencies have value is that they can be exchanged for things of functional usefulness. This type of currency is called a **fiat currency** – its anything which derives its value from its ability to be exchanged for things of functional value. By contrast, other things which have historically been used as currency are those things which are widely in demand for their functional value: salt, spices, silks, etc. Under some circumstances, objects such as cigarettes or medicine are very valuable as currency.

As you go to work, chances are you don't want to exchange your efforts for whatever it is your employer makes, so they give you money in an amount equivalent to the value they place on your efforts. You then take that money and exchange it for things of value to you, and this happens again and again. Some of it may even end-up back at your employer, if it finds itself in the hands of someone so inclined to purchase from your employer. In this way, money functions as a kind-of debt. As a measure of value, the amount of money you have is a quantity of the resources which are owed to you, but you can transfer that money to someone else so that the resources are owed to them, instead. This is the fundamental trait required of all currencies – **transferability**. This simply means that you can easily transfer the given measure of value easily between individuals without forming new contracts of debt. Currencies are also easy to transport (i.e.: small and conveniently-shaped), and is not generally not made of something which is consumed. For example, although salt is extremely valuable, it's heavy, bulky, and prone to being depleted by whomever holds it. So, despite such common saying about money being the root of all evil, it really is something more mundane: a measure of the amount of value in resources that is owed to the holder of the money.

This is where things get interesting. Having established that money is a measurement of value owed to the holder in the form of resources, the concept of price becomes a representation of our cultural values and ideas. Every time a transaction takes place, both the buyer and seller must consider how much value they place on the thing being exchanged which, in turn, is a representation of the amount of value they place on themselves. For example, how many hours must you work in order to afford a particular item? The answer will define not only how much value you place on that item, but on the value of your own work. These exchanges occur, then, on an ongoing basis via an auction mechanism whereby the sellers and buyers must agree both on the value of the goods, and the value of the money. If sellers value their product more than they value the amount of money willing to be given in exchange for the product, then they will not sell anything unless they drop the price. That very rarely occurs, though, as prices almost invariably increase. As buyers and sellers agree to higher prices, people are getting fewer resources for a given quantity of currency – a thing called **inflation**.

Money does not have a fixed value. Each unit of money is defined by the willingness of buyers to spend it, and sellers to accept it, in exchange for some quantity of resources. The volume of resources offered almost exclusively decreases. This means that the currency has lower **purchasing power** – that is to say, a single unit of some currency has less ability to be exchanged for goods. It is possible for deflation to occur, wherein a currency increases its purchasing power, but this is rare and only occurs during deep recessions, but that's a matter which will be discussed in great detail later.

The tendency of currency to decrease in value over time is called the **time value of money**, and it is a matter of great importance. The reason is simple: Your future, and that of anyone else, is dependent on their ability to manage money relative to its loss of value over time. If you were to just hide all the money you make in a hole in the ground, then over the years you'd find you have less than you think. It's not that the volume of money would change, but rather the same volume would not sustain you for nearly as long, since its purchasing power has decreased. This is something called **inflation risk** – the possibility of losing money resulting from a failure to ensure its growth is at least as fast as the inflation rate. This is the conundrum associated with investing: the failure to invest comes with inflation risk, but the act of investing also comes with some risks of losing the money you invest. So, it becomes a matter of risking the loss of money by investing, or guaranteeing the loss of money by refusing to invest. Bummer.

There are two primary types of investments: debt or equity. This comes from the accounting equation:

$$Assets = Debt + Equity$$

Any firm which needs to acquire assets must do so either by borrowing the resources to do so, or by using the resources of someone who owns the firm, at least in-part. Since there is a wealth of firms who want to acquire both debt and equity, this provides opportunity invest. Since time will cause money to lose value over time, it's not enough to simply give your money to some firm with the expectation that they will pay it back over time. Instead, they must repay you the full amount, plus an amount that is at least equal to the rate of inflation during that time, if not more. The amount which a firm must be able to provide to investors depends on how risky the investment is. If the firm is large, has a history of repaying investors on time, has stable income, and so forth, then it's considered a safe investment, so the amount of money which needs to be paid in order to attract investors will be lower, on average. If the firm is new or small, has a poor history of repaying investors, or their success depends on succeeding in a bit of research or invention, then the firm will be considered higher risk. There's an old saying "No risk, no reward", implying that if you want to earn more money you must be willing to make risky investments. The truth is actually that for riskier firms to attract investors they must be willing to offer more money to investors. Simply assuming you'll earn higher income because a firm is risky or offering a higher rate of return isn't enough – the returns must be proportional to the risk, and there must be at least some reasonable expectation you'll get your money back, otherwise you're just being swindled.

So, firms want your asset, and there are two primary ways they can request them. The first is **bonds**. Bonds are a type of debt. A firm could go to a bank or other type of traditional lender to get a loan, or they can appeal to the public by issuing bonds that people can buy. Just as one must repay a bank loan, in the same manner a firm must repay their bond debt. The terms of the debt are all created prior to the issue, so that investors know exactly how and when the debt will be repaid, and what happens if a firm fails to repay it. Generally it's pretty similar to a bank loan, wherein the full amount of the loan is repaid with a specified percentage extra. Sometimes partial repayments are made at regular intervals, which occurs with coupon bonds, and sometimes the entire amount of repaid upon **maturity** (i.e.: the end of the contracted repayment period).

Bank loans a little different in the manner of their function, however. The basic idea is the same, but investors don't purchase the loans so directly. It is the purpose of a bank to function as an intermediary between potential investors (people who have money they aren't spending, even for a short time), and potential borrowers (people who are in need of money which they don't have). When you have a bit of extra money then you put it in a bank account, along with lots of other people. The bank then pools that money together, and lends it to people. Borrowers must repay that money in-full plus a percentage extra, and then the bank gives you a little bit of the money they earn by adding it to the value of your bank account. The difference in the amount the bank earns and the amount they pay depositors is called the **spread**, and this is the primary manner in which banks earn their money. The amount of money which must be paid to lenders is called **interest**. When a bank lends you money, for the bank this is a type of investment – they are investing in you and your ability to pay them back with interest.

If you're thinking about making an investment that earns interest, you'll want to know how much money you'll have in the future. In a moment of inspired creativity, this has been dubbed **future value** (FV).

The most basic calculation of this is:

$$P(1+r)^t$$

Where:

P = Principle balance (the amount deposited in a bank, the value of a loan, etc.)
r = Rate. This is the interest rate expressed as a decimal. If you're earning 5% interest, then this would be 0.05
t = Time (the number of years you'll be earning interest)

For example:

P = $100
r = 5%
t = 3 years

$$100(1+0.05)^3$$

By starting with the part in the parentheses, we get 1.05, which means 105% of the principle balance will be used, so that the interest is added to the initial investment in the final calculation. We then take 1.05^3, which is 1.158. Then multiplying that amount by the principle gives us $111.58. Conclusion: In the matter of an investment of $100 which earns 5% interest over 3 years, we can conclude that:

$$FV = \$111.58$$

This calculation is also called **simple interest**, but frequently you'll find that interest **compounds**, which means that the amount of money you make at the end of each period is based on the current balance at that time, rather than the amount of the principle investment:

$$P(1+[r/n])^{nt}$$

The only new variable here is n, which refers to the number of times in a year the interest compounds. For example, if you invest $100 with a rate of 12% compounding monthly, that means dividing the annual 12% rate into 12 compounding periods, which is 1% per month.

Month 1 = $1
Month 2 = $1.01
Month 3 = $1.0201

Notice how the amount earned in each month increase. That's because the only month in which interest is based on principle balance is Month 1, which would total $101. The interest earned in Month 2 is based on the balance during Month 1, giving a balance of $102.01, and so forth.

There is a special type of compounding interest called **continuously compounding interest**. In these types of investments, the number of compounding periods in a year approaches infinity, dividing-up the year into periods of time which are nearly infinitely small. The math behind this is really simple, but math behind the explanation is really hard. Suffice it to say that for our purposes, interest compounds constantly rather than in periods. This is accomplished using the following:

$$Pe^{rt}$$

The value e is an irrational constant. You're probably familiar with another famous irrational constant, π (pi), which is 3.14159, and critical to calculating things related to circles. Well, e is 2.71828. The constant e is used in calculating exponential and logarithmic change – curves which have a constant rate of change in their slope. Consider the graph below, comparing rates of compounding – the smooth curve at the top is continuously compounding:

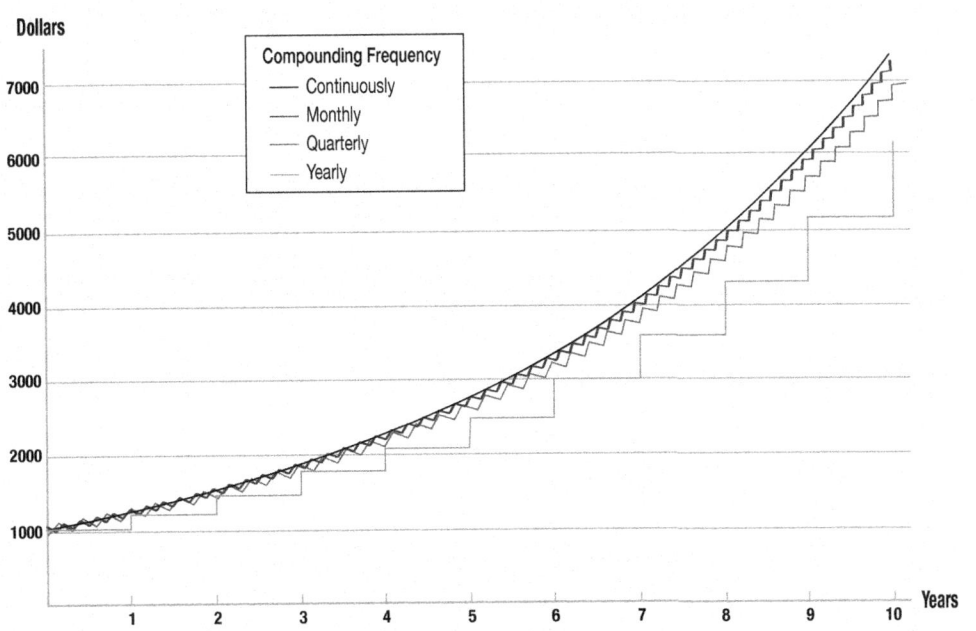

While future value is all about how much an investment will be worth in the future, **present value** (PV) tells you about some money you'll receive in the future and the value that it has right now. For example, if you bought a bond earning 5% interest and will earn $1,000 in 5 years, you may want to know what the bond is worth right now so you can decide whether to resell it to someone else. In order to accomplish this, use the following formula:

$$C/[(1+r)^t]$$

This formula should look familiar, because it almost identical to the calculation for simple interest. The only difference is that instead of multiplying by the principle, you are dividing by the future cash flow, denominated as C. A cash flow includes any movement of cash into our out of a firm. In this case we are looking at an investment which generates a one-time positive cash flow in 5 years. Another way to look at this is that you have bought a bond with FV = $1,000. So, the equation would be:

$$\$1,000/[(1+.05)^5]$$

So, the interest calculation at the bottom comes down to 1.05, and over 5 years it is 1.276. Dividing the FV of the bond by the interest calculation shows that the bond is currently worth $783.53. In FV calculations you'd be wondering how much interest is adding to the value of an investment in the present. In PV calculations you're using the interest rate you're earning to subtract value from an investment in the future, and so it's called the **discount rate**. Yes, it's the exact same rate – the percentage you are earning on an investment – but now you want to calculate how much the investment is worth if you take away the interest you haven't yet earned.

Present value calculations are particularly important in dealing with investments that have multiple cash flows. This occurs coupon bonds, large pieces of equipment, and some other types of investments you won't learn about here. It's getting dull writing about bonds, so let's talk machines. You own a manufacturing company that produces hair gel for guinea pigs, and are have a choice of 3 different machines, each of which produces one huge batch per year. You need to figure-out which one is the best deal, so to do that you're going to use a calculation called **net present value** (NPV). Once you know how to calculate PV, it's amazing easy to learn NPV, because NPV is nothing more than the sum of all PVs. In our example, you decide to buy the biggest machine, which has a FV of $10,000 each year for 3 years (i.e.: Each batch produced earns $10,000, and it makes 1 batch each year). In this case we'd have 3 PV calculations, one for each year.

$$PV_1 + PV_2 + PV_3$$

In our example this means that:

$$\$10,000/[(1+.05)^1] + \$10,000/[(1+.05)^2] + \$10,000/[(1+.05)^3]$$

When calculated this comes to:

$$\$9,523.81 + \$9,070.29 + \$8,638.38$$

Notice that each year's cash flow is $10,000, but that each year the PV goes down. The reason is that you're discounting it at the same rate but over more years. When you add-up all the PVs of the machine, you get:

$$NPV = \$27,232.48$$

So, when you consider the present value of all future cash flows the machine will generate, the NPV is the present value on the machine over the course of its entire life. As a final note on NPV, you're probably wondering how I got a discount rate of 5% on it. Quite frankly, I've been using 5% for all the calculations, but generally speaking it's best to use the rate of profitability per year on the investment. Just like the present value of a bond is discounted at the interest rate, which is the percentage of profit you earn on the bond, so too you can use the profitability rate on any investment.

When talking about government debt, there's three primary types: **Treasury Bills**, **Treasury Notes**, and **Treasury Bonds**. The only real difference between these is the amount of time it takes them to **mature** (end the period of repayment so that you can collect the money you are owed plus interest). T-bills mature in less than 1 year and pay the lowest rate of interest, T-Notes mature between 2-10 years, and T-Bonds mature in 30 years and have the highest rate of return. The government issues debt through the Treasury when they run a budget **deficit** – they are spending more money than they're making in a given year. In order to account for the difference in spending, they sell these forms of debt in order to raise more money.

So far we've only talked about debt investments, but returning back to the accounting equation we see that assets can also be purchased using equity. While you can invest directly into a firm by purchasing a portion of a private company, the more common method of investing in equity is by purchasing stocks. When a firm needs to raise money, it has the option to do so through an **initial public offering** (IPO). A corporation is a company whose ownership is split into several pieces, called a **stock**, so whoever buys even a single stock owns a piece of that company. Typically speaking, the company only raises money at the initial public offering, which is the point at which the stocks are first sold by the company. The volume of stock they sell, and the price at which the shares sell, determines how much money the company raises. A company's first initial public offering, also called the primary market, happens when they first become incorporated, but any time the company wants to raise more money by issuing more shares of stock it can have another initial public offering of the new set of stocks. After stocks are sold on the primary market, they can be bought and sold between investors, called the secondary market. Corporations generally do not make money on the secondary market – their capital has already been raised at the initial public offering, and every time a stock is sold after that point is merely a gain or loss for some other investors.

Equity investments are generally considered to be riskier than debt investments. Debt investments are typically **fixed-rate** (meaning that the annual rate of earnings you make doesn't change), leaving them subject to **inflation risk** (wherein inflation rates exceed your rate of return) and **credit risk** (the chance that a firm will **default** on its debts, which means they exit the market or otherwise have their debts legally excused). By contrast, equity investments are variable – their value is derived from the success of the firm. This is no different than being an owner of a **sole proprietorship** (where you are the only owner of a firm); how much money you make depends on how successful the firm is, and your lenders will always make sure you pay the proper payments to them before you earn anything.

Since equity investments are variable, measuring their present and future value is much more difficult. An immense amount of time and money is spent figuring-out ways to improve these measurements, make better predictions, develop strategies to mitigate risk, and so forth. Some people try to find companies that will experience strong, stable growth in the future, while others try to buy and sell stocks frequently to earn money on temporary changes in market price. **Stock exchanges** function a bit like banks, in that they function as an intermediary to connect potential investors with potential investments. Companies list their stocks on a particular exchange, brokers buy and sell those stocks on behalf of investors, and the investors are the ones who actually maintain ownership of the stocks. You really won't have to know much about stock investing for the AP economics exam, though, so if you're interested in knowing more you should check-out some other book like *Introducing Personal Finance: A Practical Guide* from Icon Books.

When talking about the financial sector it is, of course, necessary to understand the flow of money, itself. The amount of money in existence really doesn't matter that much, the question is more one of the amount of money that's being productive and the amount of production that money is creating. In economics 101 you learn that people can either save or spend money, and that any money you save will be invested by the bank in which you deposit it unless you invest it, yourself. This isn't exactly true, but let's go with it for a moment to make a few points, and then we'll come back to this point.

There are several different measures of money supply, the three primary are M0, M1 and M2. M0 refers to just the amount of actual money in circulation – bills and coins. **M1** includes actual money and things which function like money (e.g.: traveler's checks, etc.). **M2**, the most commonly used measure of the money supply for applied research, and will be the measure of money supply we use throughout this book, includes things that take a little longer to turn into money, like timed accounts (i.e.: bank accounts that pay a higher interest rate but from which you can't withdraw funds for a specified period of time). The total amount of money supply is managed by the **Federal Reserve Bank** – money is produced by the US Treasury and distributed to the Federal Reserve and other banks. The Federal Reserve Bank, a quasi-governmental entity which manages the money of the nation, then decides how much of that money will be made available. It also controls the price of money, which refers to interest rates for investing or lending. Together, the management of money supply and price is known as **monetary policy**.

There are several ways to manage the supply and price of money, sometimes both at the same time. The most commonly utilized is known as **Open Market Operations** (OMO), which is a way to manage both the price and supply of money. OMO works by utilizing the free market, allowing the Federal Reserve to either sell or buy more government debt on the open market. If they want to increase the amount of money in circulation or decrease interest rates, they'll buy-up debt from other investors so that those investors have cash that's ready to be used for something instead of a bond which won't become cash for many more years. By buying-up these debts, it increases the total demand and lowers the total supply, so that the price investors must pay increases (i.e.: lower interest rate offered). If the Federal Reserve wants to decrease the amount of money in supply, or increase the price of money on the open market, they can sell some of their own holdings. In recent years there's been a lot of talk about **quantitative easing**. This is more of an advertising term than anything, and only refers to efforts by the Federal Reserve to increase the money supply by buying-up privately-issued debts, rather than just government debts. The basic mechanism is the same, though.

Other ways to control the money supply includes changing the **reserve ratio**. The reserve ratio is the percentage of a bank's total holdings which must be kept in-house, rather than loaned. Banks maintain a reserve ratio in order to guarantee they have enough cash on-hand in order to manage their own costs while also fulfilling the withdrawals of their customers. Looking at the 2008 Finance Crisis, we see that the banks had loaned a lot of money to people considered high risk, in the subprime mortgage market (issuing mortgages to people who had an elevated probability of failing to repay their loans). During that same time, the banks failed to increase the amount of money they kept in reserve, so when people stopped repaying their loans, the banks didn't have as much money as they needed in order to pay their own bills and handle the increase of withdrawals that came as people pulled from their savings to pay for mortgages they couldn't afford. Thankfully we had learned about **bank runs** (people get scared that the bank will run out of money and pull all their money out) during the Great Depression and had measures in place to avoid it, but it still brought the entire financial sector to a total halt.

The price of money, again, is the interest rate. Besides changes to the market rate through open market operations, the Federal Reserve directly controls one key interest rate: the **federal discount rate**. Yes, we've already used the term "discount rate" when talking about present value, and unfortunately this same term is used to describe something totally different also related to interest rates. This time "discount rate" refers to the rate of interest that the Federal Reserve charges when lending money to other banks. By raising or lowering this rate, it causes other banks to increase or decrease their own interest rates in order to maintain the same spread.

So, all that is well and good, but we're still just talking about the amount of money in existence. An economy is an engine, though – no matter how big it is, it's useless unless it's in motion. Money has to change hands to be worth anything. A single dollar is spent by a consumer, and then spent again by the business to hire employees, and then spent again, and again, and again. Every time that single dollar changes hands, it's facilitating production, consumption, and investing. It's only once that dollar stops moving from one person to another that it stops stimulating economic growth.

The rate at which money changes hands is called **monetary velocity**. This is a very important measure of economic health, because it's a bit like measuring the oil pressure of the nation's growth – it tells us how freely money is flowing through all the moving parts of the economy, keeping those moving parts functioning properly. If the flow of money stops at any point, then the entire economy seizes, and growth comes to an abrupt stop. For example, in both the Great Depression and the 2008 Financial Collapse, mismanagement of the financial sector began to thin the flow of money through that part of the economy until it eventually stopped functioning entirely, bringing to a halt the flow of money to households, businesses, investors, and everyone else; even the government, as lower household incomes and business revenues caused a drop in tax revenues.

In fact, monetary velocity is intrinsically connected to economic growth. GDP can be expressed as a function of the money supply, M2, and the nation's monetary velocity:

$$GDP = M2*V$$

As noted, if money is stagnant, it's not doing anything to stimulate production. Since GDP is a measurement of the value of a nation's production, it can be described as a measure of how much money is moving throughout the economy. Contrarily, by using a little bit of basic algebra, monetary velocity can be measured as:

$$V = GDP/M2$$

US monetary velocity usually floats around 1.8, but took a hit after 2008 and is now floating around 1.5. Even though the US economy is growing again, this has had implications for the rate at which it's growing, on wages/unemployment, and so forth, to the degree that some people are predicting another recession in the near future (of course, there are always people predicting recession, though some tend to be more accurate in their predictions than others). So if the US had a GDP of $16.77 trillion in 2013 (which it did), and monetary velocity of roughly 1.55 during the same time, then we can safely say that there was a money supply of $10.82 trillion. In fact, according to the Federal Reserve, the money supply in 2013 was $10.8187 trillion.

Another way to look at this is through the **quantity theory of money**, which describes the relationship between prices and the total volume of money, written as:

$$MV = PQ$$

Where:
Money = Money supply
V = Velocity
P = Price
Q = Quantity of exchanges

In other words, M2*V is equal to GDP, and since GDP is measured as the total volume of exchanges and the price of those exchanges, the money supply can be expressed as a function of the exchanges. Using simple algebra, we can rearrange this into:

$$P = (MV)/Q$$

As a result, this states that price levels are a function of money supply, monetary velocity, and quantity of exchanges. This is actually a very formal way to describe something that is very intuitive. If people are spending the same amount of money, but over fewer quantity of exchanges, then clearly the price of those exchanges must be higher. If monetary velocity increases while price levels and quantity of exchanges remains equal, then people must be spending more money in each of those transactions.

The problem is that it's really not that simple. It was popular for a time to think that price levels were purely a function of money supply, velocity, and quantity of transactions, as described in the model. It's nice and neat, and there are handful of well-meaning fringe economists (known as monetarists) who still believe this to be true, but they are very much on the fringe of the science, because the quantity theory of money is ultimately wrong. This model says nothing about the nature of demand for money. We've already talked about several types of inflation, but monetarists tend to place the emphasis for all inflation on, as you might guess, monetary inflation. It's ridiculous on its face.

Make sure you're paying attention, because this is where things can get a little tricky. The demand for money is quantitatively written as:

$$M^d = P*L(r, Y)$$

Where the demand for money is a function of price, and the amount of preference to hold money rather than investing it. P is price, and L(R, Y) describes the relationship between the desire to hold money, interest rates, and GDP. It's expressed

The Gold Standard is a type of policy which pegs the currency of a nation to the value of gold. This is not a thing unique to the US, and it's not always gold, either. There have been identical policies utilizing silver, as well. The ultimate goal, though, is to stabilize the value of a nation's currency by establishing policy that keeps the value of your currency equivalent to some ratio of an ounce of gold or silver. For example, the value of each dollar might be kept at a value exactly equivalent to 0.01 ounces of gold. As the value of gold goes up and down, so too will the value of the money. Taking it even further, it is argued that the treasury should only be allowed to print more money if a greater volume of gold is acquired. In the US, money was also considered to be directly exchangeable for the currency's value in gold – anyone holding US money could literally turn-in their money for gold. There are many very good reasons why no one actually uses this system anymore, despite many attempts throughout history. Ask yourself: what intrinsic value does gold have?

most effectively through a specific type of supply/demand model known as the **IS-LM Model**. **IS** stands for **Investment/Savings**, and **LM** stands for **Liquidity/Money**. Since the term "liquidity" is new here, let's define it. **Liquidity** is the ease with which something can be turned into cash. Money is as liquid as it gets, and short-term investments are very liquid, as are inventories. Less liquid are things like real estate, bonds, any basically anything else that will take some time to turn into cash. Refer to the image below:

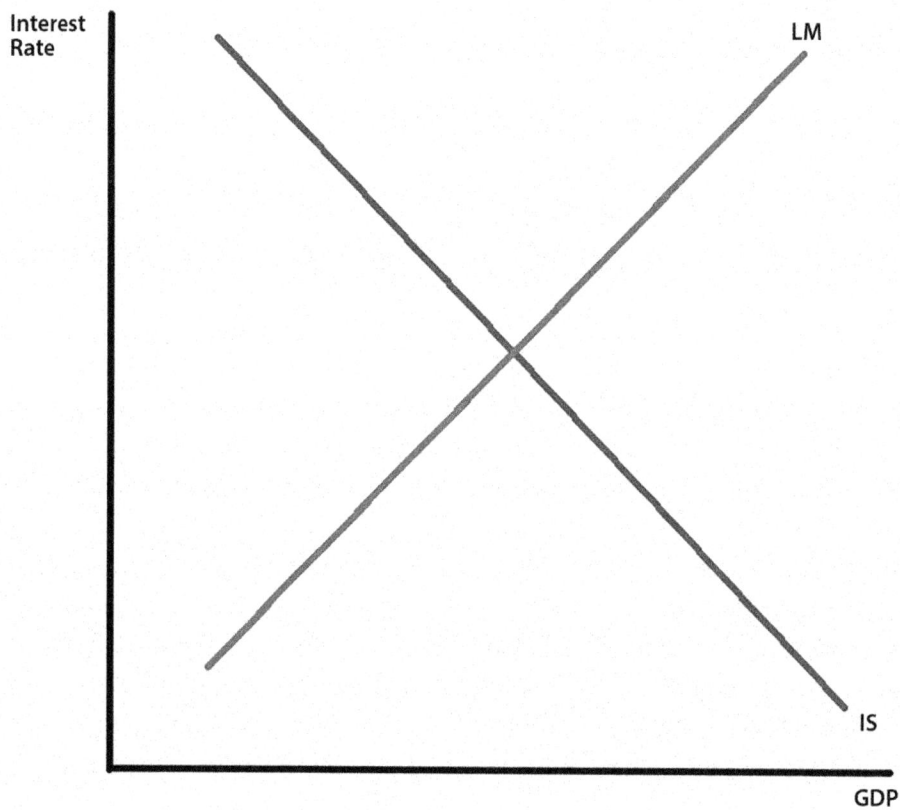

Simply put, when interest rates go down it is cheaper to borrow money, which means that businesses and entrepreneurs will borrow money in order to invest in new productive activities, and people will borrow money for things like houses. That's why the IS curve in the graph shows that GDP increases as interest rates fall, and why lowering interest rates is a typical first response to impending recessions. The preference for liquid money (holding cash, rather than investing it) does the total opposite, though. As GDP increases, there will be a greater volume of transactions, resulting in greater demand to have money available, and pressuring interest rates back up again. This interplay between the supply and demand for debt as a determinant of interest rates is known as the **loanable funds market**.

If that seems a little counterintuitive to you, then you're not alone. As GDP increases, investments tend to increase, as well, as investors are increasingly attracted to the future growth potential of firms in a strong economy, and since interest rates vary much less than investment growth, future earnings potential has a much greater influence on the demand for investments. When GDP growth is down, people also tend to shift their investments to things like gold or foreign investments, rather than holding money. Saving will increase to a degree, but there's little incentive to hold money since that doesn't generate earnings, so they'll find some other way to generate returns on their investment. If investment markets are in damage-control mode, and investors aren't investing in anything because the outlook is poor, then no matter how much money is poured into supply it just won't increase investing – there really needs to be something worth investing in. This state is known as a liquidity trap – a state in which OMO or other expansionary monetary policy fails to increase prices, interest, or growth. Under other conditions, increasing the supply of loanable funds would decrease interest rates and stimulate investing, but that completely fails to take into consideration the fact that investors are an animated group of people – very bold under stable conditions, but with seeming ninja-like ability to disappear the very instant things start to go poorly.

An expansion on the IS-LM model, called the Mundell-Fleming model, takes into consideration the role of the movement of capital between nations, as the GDP growth and interest rates of trade partners also alter domestic IS and LM curves.

Let's not forget about the role of the government sector in this, either. As previously noted, the government sells debt to investors when they are running a budget **deficit**. By increasing the supply of debt, interest rates will naturally increase, making them cheaper for investors to buy, as debt issuers must compete even more to attract investors. This is a situation known as **crowding-out**, but it's really nothing more than the role of the government sector in contributing to the supply and demand of money, altering the IS and LM curves which determine **equilibrium interest rates**. Oh yeah, and by the way, the point at which IS and LM meet is called the equilibrium interest rate.

Stabilization policies.

The tools available to the central bank – the management of the supply and price of money known as monetary policy – is only 1/3 of economic policies. The other 2 are **regulatory policies**, and **fiscal policies**, both of which are managed directly by the government rather than the central bank. There's been some talk in recent years about shutting-down the Federal Reserve, but remember that the only other alternative is to put monetary policy in the hands of Congress, and when you consider how ineffective they've been at managing other forms of economic policy, it's clear that some separation of the types of economic policy is warranted.

At this point in the book, we're not really worried about regulatory policy. That was touched-on just briefly in the Microeconomics chapter on market failure and the

What is it about gold that gives it more or less value than money? The answer is nothing. Gold have no real intrinsic value other than what we place on it. This is the same thing which gives money its value too – just the ability to buy things with it. If no one believed that a currency or gold had any value, then you couldn't use it as a medium of exchange. They are both fiat currencies. Whether gold is more stable as a currency than the money issued by a treasury depends largely on the individual nation - nations with smaller economies tend to fluctuate more than nations with large economies. Even nations with highly variable economies, though, now fix their money to a basket of several currencies, usually weighted as a proportion of some global reserve currency (e.g.: US dollar, Euro, British pound, Japanese Yen, etc.).
The only thing that gold and silver standards accomplish is to limit the range of economic tools available. You're nearly completely eliminating your nation's ability to use monetary policy – to manage the quantity and price of money. This leaves you completely helpful to adjust

these variables in response to changes in the market, making it only a matter of time before your economy deviates so far from free market equilibrium that it starts to have a serious impact on growth and development.

By implementing a gold standard, what you're essentially doing is taking your nation back to a mercantilist system, in which one nation can only benefit if another nation loses – the total amount of wealth available is determined by the amount of gold. It's an idea which violates even the most basic, and well-proven principles of economics.

So, next time someone tells you that we should switch to a gold standard, remember that they don't know a single thing about economics.

role of government, and it will be discussed again just briefly in the Macroeconomics chapter on international trade and finance. Monetary policy was discussed most thoroughly in the chapter on financial markets, so if you need a refresher, that's the best place to start. In this chapter, we're going to talk about two different things: the nature of fiscal policy, and how monetary and fiscal policies can be used to manage volatility.

Fiscal policy refers to **taxation** and **spending**. Congress establishes fiscal policy as a way to raise money in order to afford the cost of their spending. These are extremely nuanced topics, because there are many types of both taxation and spending. Taxes refers to the money raised by the government, and common types include:

1) **Sales Tax** – A tax you pay anytime you buy or sell something. This generally does not include medicine or food, except in restaurants where the cooking and serving of food is considered a service rather than actually buying the food, itself. Sales taxes vary by state.

2) **Excise Tax** – A tax based on the volume of commerce, and when placed on those things which have negative externalities, which is frequently, it is sometimes known as a **vice tax**. Fuel is an industry which attracts a lot of attention for excise taxes, as is gambling, alcohol, tobacco, tanning, and so forth.

3) Income Tax – A tax on the amount of money made by individuals and corporations. These vary a lot (and I mean a *lot*), depending on how much is being made, the sources of the earnings (e.g.: **capital** gains tax is a tax that's applied only to income generated from investments, **royalties tax** is a tax that's applied only to income from things like book sales, etc.), and even what the money is being used for. Payroll taxes are paid by workers but taken from paychecks by employers before it's received in order to pay for Social Security, Medicare, and FICA.

4) Tariffs – A tax on imports, which vary depending on the type of thing being imported, the nation from which it's being imported, and the value or volume being imported.

When people talk about raising or lowering taxes, generally they have no idea what they're talking about. There are far too many different types of taxes, levels of taxation, and degrees of economic impact in order to simply lump them together for most purposes.

That being said, we're now going to lump together all the taxes. I'm only half-kidding – even though all taxes are unique, they do have some things in common. In particular, they all have their **Laffer Curve**, as shown in the image below.

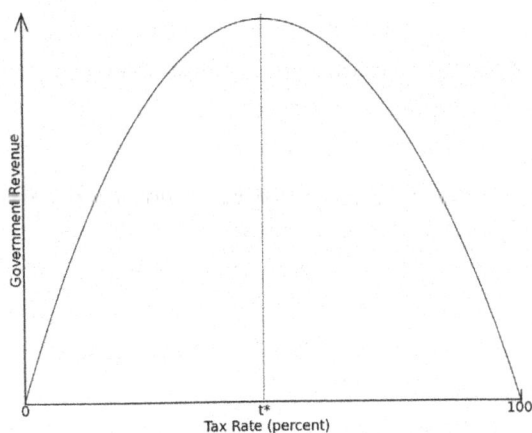

The Laffer Curve illustrates, broadly, the relationship between the rate of any particular type of tax and the amount of government revenues received. Clearly, very small tax rates will not collect as much revenues as moderate tax rates, but what people tend to forget is that very high tax rates also tends to decrease revenues because people are unable to pay it. Each unique tax has an equally unique Laffer Curve, which change in height, flatness/pointiness (technically called kurtosis), and the direction that the central hump points (technically called skew).

The ideal approach to taxes is very different to the real approach to taxes. Ideally, a government will look at all their options and choose the one with the lowest opportunity cost. In other words, money stimulates the economy depending on how it's being used (or not used), so a government will look at the different want in which money is being used and choose those things which have the smallest impact on the economy for their source of tax revenues. For example, think back to the multiplier effect and monetary velocity and how they differ depending on the amount of money people earn – due to the law of diminishing marginal returns, as people earn more and more money, the amount of money they earn will contribute less and less to economic growth as they spend and invest a smaller percentage of their total income (only spending or investing stimulates income). As a result, taxing the income of higher income individuals tends to have little or no negative impact on economic growth, while taxing low-income individuals has a much larger negative impact since those people spend and invest 98-100% of their income. The reality of taxation, though, is somewhat less effective than ideal. I won't say exactly what makes this happen, but I'm sure you have some ideas of your own on what makes this happen.

Besides asking what sources of taxation have the lowest opportunity cost, the manner in which the money is spent must also be considered. Ideally, the goal is to choose those expenditures which have the highest return on investment. Even debt can be a good thing, so long as the manner in which that money is used generates greater value than the amount of money being spent on interest payments. For governments, this is measured in the amount of tax revenues raised after accounting for any change in tax rates. In other words, if the government is stimulating more economic activity through its spending than it is eliminating through taxation, then the amount of tax revenues raised will increase without raising tax rates – everyone is earning more, spending more, investing more, working more, producing more, etc. As such, theoretically speaking, fiscal policy is successful when it generates a positive return on investment. Of course, once again the reality is somewhat less ideal for reasons which are better left discussed in this book, but you probably have a pretty good guess. A record of the US national debt can be attained from the website of the US Treasury: https://www.treasurydirect.gov/govt/reports/pd/histdebt/histdebt.htm

So what kinds of things to government buy? There's really a very huge diversity of things, and no real good way to categorize it. First, and foremost, a government must pay for its own operations, or else it will cease to exist and the nation will fall into anarchy. They also pay for military, they pay for infrastructure (e.g.: road, communication, energy, education, etc.), they pay subsidies (which theoretically keep the price low on things such as energy, food, and so forth), and much, much more. In the US, the single largest expenditure is Social Security, and despite common complaints about the amount of money spent on military operations, the US spends about an average amount on its military as a percentage of its GDP (even though that money is managed very poorly).

One of the big questions about economic policy is whether to influence aggregate demand or aggregate supply, and by how much. Economic growth and production is driven by demand – solid growth must be supported by consumption, otherwise you're producing things which no one will buy, which triggers recessions. A hundred years ago it was believed that there were "job makers" – by providing more resources to wealthy people, they would inherently invest more in the search for profits. Now we know this to be preposterous since investments tend to dry-up at the first signs of a slump, and even in the best of conditions investors tend to allocate resources toward what's already known rather than stimulating innovation. By contrast, so long as people have money to spend, there will always be someone there to sell something to them, and companies are forced to continue innovating in order to continue attracting consumers. In the end, it all comes down to the core of human existence – we pursue food, clothes, shelter, and so forth, and it is the drive to meet our needs which requires us to manage our resources; if we had ample resources then there'd be no reason to improve, regardless of potential investment opportunities. As one of my old undergrad professors used to say, demand creates its own supply, but supply does not create its own demand.

That being said, you cannot ignore either supply or demand in establishing policy. Just because growth is based in demand does not mean we should give supply any less attention. If AD is less than AS, it is prudent to expedite the process of increasing AD just as we absorb all the surplus inventories and production capacity. If AD is greater than AS, it's prudent to stimulate increases in aggregate supply by focusing on technological innovations, while tempering any volume of demand which exceeds sustainable rates (i.e.: spending more money than can continue indefinitely, such as through overproduction, inflated levels of debt consumption, etc.).

Both AD and AS are managed using methods we've already talked about – using OMO and managing interest rates influence the ratios of money being used for consumption or investing, changing reserve ratios and debt management to manage supply of currency in circulation, spending money in different ways to stimulate consumption or investing, using the multiplier and velocity to increase production requirements, and so forth. Generally monetary and fiscal policy are used in combination to manage the economy, but in recent years fiscal policy has been largely lost to political gridlock, leaving monetary policy to function independently in order to end one of the deepest recessions in US history.

Regarding economic policy, there's a couple matters which are at the forefront of almost every conversation and every news headline: unemployment and inflation. Of course these matters are important to everyone, and economic contraction almost by-definition necessitates a loss of jobs, so the manner in which policy can be used to manage these two things is given a lot of attention.

For a long time it was thought that unemployment and inflation were opposites – that as inflation went up, unemployment went down, and vice versa. Then, in the 1970s, there was a period of **stagflation**, which is a state of high unemployment and high inflation. According to previous models, this wasn't supposed to happen, so a new explanation was needed. Of course, as we've already discussed in this book, only demand-pull inflation and cyclical unemployment are opposites, but there are three types each of unemployment and inflation. There is no reason to think that other permutations of these 6 things couldn't exist together. They were looking for a relationship between unemployment and inflation, though, and the new model they developed was known as **NAIRU**. NAIRU is the non-accelerating inflationary rate of unemployment, as shown below:

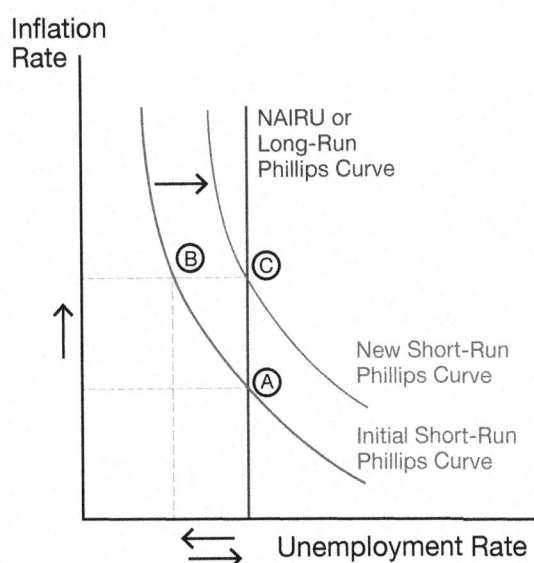

At this point we need to differentiate, once again, between short-run and long-run. In the short-run we have a curve called the **Phillips Curve**, which is the one that expressed a direct, inverse relationship between unemployment and inflation. In the short-run, this is still a reasonable assumption, because as we already know, stimulating a little inflation during a recession can help to reduce the unemployment rate (pushing us from Point A to Point B on the graph) by increasing monetary velocity via the multiplier effect. For example, let's say the minimum wage increases during a recession, allowing the income effect to increase consumption and forcing companies into higher rates of operation. This contributes to inflation, but it also reduces unemployment rates.

In the long-run, though, this simply doesn't hold true. NAIRU states that there is an equilibrium, or natural rate of unemployment, and that when unemployment is maintained at that point inflation will stabilize. If unemployment drops, then inflation rates will increase; if unemployment increases, then inflation rates will slow.

I personally find it helpful to think about it in terms of pressure. When unemployment drops, it increases the amount of inflationary pressure by shifting the AD=AS matter closer to demand-pull inflation (AD>AS). When unemployment increases, it relieves some of the inflationary pressure by moving closer toward cyclical unemployment (AD<AS). This doesn't state that the change in unemployment will naturally change the direction of inflation, or even the rate of inflation necessarily. If inflation is already going up and unemployment drops, then inflation is likely to increase faster, but if unemployment increases then inflation might still increase but perhaps at a slower rate.

The thing that makes NAIRU difficult to use is that it isn't a constant – the NAIRU varies relative to economic conditions and is difficult to predict. This creates something of a problem for **rational expectations theory**, as related to NAIRU, which states that people will anticipate changes and respond normally back to the natural rate. Well, since the NAIRU fluctuates in ways that are difficult to predict, there is no constant reference point which people can use as a basis for any expectations.

Economic growth.

The entire point of understanding the fine details of macroeconomics, and giving all this attention to macroeconomic policy, is to maintain stable, consistent growth. Well… Kind-of; that's the answer you'll typically get, anyway. Really, the entire point is to maximize peoples' quality of life, but a big part of that is ensuring that there is enough volume of resources available with which to make that happen. As the population grows, as it always does, we have greater resource requirements, and we are in constant pursuit of improving the quality of our lives, and ensuring that such quality can be sustained for the indefinite future. It's a pursuit we're really, really bad at. Before we get into that, though, let's look at some of the basics.

Economic growth is defined as an increase in GDP. Simply put, that means the nation has produced more stuff this year than the year before, and that it will produce more stuff next year than it did this year. We already talked about nominal and real GDP in the chapter on the measurement of economic performance, but then when talking about growth we also become much more concerned with **GDP per capita**. To calculate this you start with GDP and then divide it by the population – the total number of people in the nation. In fact, anything per capita means you divide some measurement by the population. In terms of growth, this helps us understand changes in the per-person levels of productivity. If GDP is growing at the same rate as the population, then this represents a kind-of stagnancy, wherein our total production is determined by the amount of people. This was true for most of human history and even before that – from the dawn of time until of the **Industrial Revolution** in the late-1700s. Before that time, even through the use of domesticated animals to assist with farming, our total per-person output remained the same. After that point, through the assistance of automation, our output per-person just skyrocketed, as shown below in the image from the Federal Reserve.

Figure 2
World Population and Production

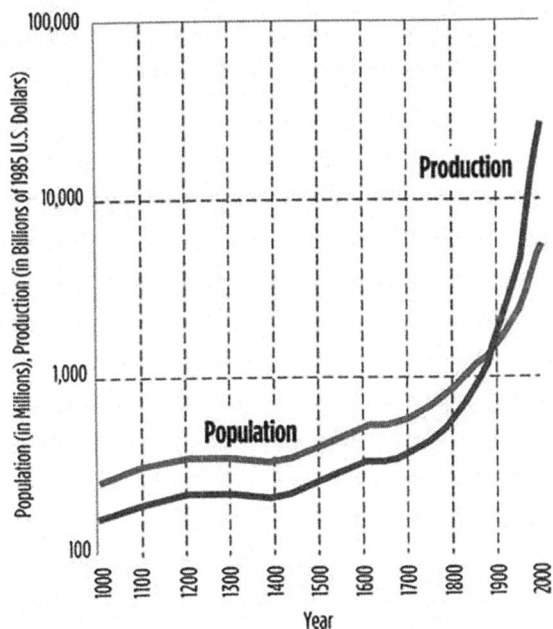

A point that's really interesting is that population and production were linked for a long time, but that once production levels per person increased so much, then the rate of population growth also increased, but much less dramatically. Rather than the population driving production growth, not production was driving population growth. People had more stuff, so they could afford to support more kids, and there were more medical and educational resources available to help improve the survival rate of children and age expectations.

Clearly there's something to be said about growth, then, since it can have such a dramatic impact on our lives. The issue then becomes understanding what causes growth, and finding ways to use economic policy in order to help create more growth. There are several different models of growth, each with pros and cons, but they all basically come-down to just a few different variables, as you'll see.

1) **Harrod-Domar Model**. This is the first model of economic growth that was truly popularized. Very simply, it states that output is the result of capital availability. It treats all money that isn't spent inherently as investments, and states that these investments will generate greater volumes of capital, and that this capital is used to create more income, which increases the volume of investing, and so forth. Of course, we can extend this to include the implications of changes in the savings rate in response to interest rates or anything else, or include the loss of value that any given piece of capital experiences over time (called **depreciation**), but that's not necessary to understand the core of the model.

2) **Solow-Swan Model**. This was an extension of the Harrod-Domar model, and replaced its predecessor as the prevailing model of growth in its time. This model separates labor and capital, paying special attention to the relative amount of investment dedicated to each, and then includes the nature of improvements in technology which make both labor and capital more productive. Otherwise, it functions pretty much the same as Harrod-Domar.

3) **AK Model**. This is typically the first endogenous growth model you'll learn. Whereas the other two models assume that all advances in technology/capital are driven by investments (they are exogenous), endogenous growth models attempt to explain such improvements in the productivity of labor and capital as a result of endogenous factors, such as learning and creativity by people and the impact this has on capital even with stagnant investment rates (sometimes stimulated in spite of a lack of resources, as people are forced to adapt and innovate in order to meet output requirements). The AK model is essentially the simplest way to illustrate this relationship, and the manner in which endogenous factors can sustain long-run growth, which is something exogenous models tend to fail to explain. Unfortunately, the AK model is also extremely simplified and poorly defined, so it is best used to illustrate the points rather than make useful calculations.

In recent years it seems that endogenous Schumpeterian growth have been seeing something of a resurgence in popularity, as some matters of growth and geography can best be explained by Schumpeter's models. Schumpeter states that the primary driver of long-run growth is creative destruction. That is to say, growth is determined less by capital and more by labor – specifically, the ability of people to be creative and develop innovations. The more we advance our understanding of the world and use that information in innovative new ways, investors will make investments necessary to fund these innovations and turn them into physical capital. Investors, themselves, are driven by the desire to attain monopolistic profits which result from having access to innovations not yet available to others. It is now relatively widely accepted that knowledge is the primary driver of economic growth, and that Schumpeter's explanations of growth account for knowledge externalities and knowledge spillover within competitive markets (matters we'll discuss in the chapter on international trade and finance).

Note that regardless of whether growth models are endogenous or exogenous, the core determinants of growth always includes 3 basic things: labor, capital, and knowledge (i.e.: technological progress). Though the models differ in the way they treat these things, they are always included in some fashion. As a result, these are typically the target of economic growth policies. Whether using policy to adjust the rate of investments or consumption, and the things in which people are investing/consuming, there is always consideration given to the impact on labor, capital, and knowledge.

1) Labor. Decreasing unemployment rates helps to increase the amount of active labor, helping people and companies to match jobs with people that have the right skill sets helps to improve the efficient utilization of available labor, helping people stay healthy and functional increases the rate of labor participation, and helping people become educated helps to increase the value of labor (see the end of this chapter for a note on the nature of education). Note how major topics of economic policy all come-down to emphasizing labor productivity.

2) Capital. Policies focusing on increasing capital production include those intended to increase business investments and entrepreneurship, such as lowering interest rates, increasing trade, encouraging manufacturing industry growth, and so forth.

3) Knowledge. Again, referring to technological advancements, policy can target this by facilitating education (particularly in STEM fields), encouraging speculative investing, helping entrepreneurship in tech and research firms, facilitating the free and open communication and sharing of information within industries, and things of that nature.

Since 2008 there has been a lot of question regarding the nature of long-run growth, and whether we've reached a global plateau. Well, globally, we have plateaued, but the question is whether this slowing of growth is a permanent state. This is a matter of debate, but there is a lot of research and discussion regarding new types of economic paradigms intended to facilitate minimum levels of consumption in order to support base demand, vastly increase the amount of innovation explored by a broader population, and so forth. Growth economics is about to become very bold, and very interesting, so keep your eyes open.

What's the point of all this growth? While giving so much attention to more and more stuff, what happens to all that stuff? Many people, even economists sometimes, tend to forget that growth is not the final goal. Once we have achieved growth, the final step is determining how to use all that stuff in a manner which improves the quality of life, known as **development**. Economic development is measured using any of several different indices, the most popular of which is the **human development index** (HDI). HDI, like most development indices, include measurements of health, wealth, and education. Specifically, health is typically measured using things like life-expectancy at birth (how long you're expected to live) and infant mortality rates; wealth is usually measured using GDP per capita or some measure of average income; and education is measured using combinations of average number of years of schooling completed, expected number of years completed, and so forth. Some indices also include measures of egalitarianism (people being treated equally), conflict, income disparity, and sometimes even metrics such as divorce rates. In the end, none of them are perfect, but just broad assessments of the quality of life people have in a given nation.

Policies intended to improve development include increasing the size of those earning middle class income, decreasing the number of people in poverty, making education available, making healthcare available, making basic utilities like water and internet available (yes, internet is now considered a basic utility, necessary for applying to jobs), ensuring that basic infrastructure is maintained, and guaranteeing the fair and equal treatment of all people. Over the past few decades there has been a huge increase in focus on sustainability as a matter of economic development. The global population is huge, and its consuming resources faster than those resources can be replenished, resulting in difficulty maintaining access to clean water, clean air, and all the basics of subsistence. Policies to address this matter emphasize increasing efficiency through improved capital and processes. For example, there's been increased attention given to the input ratio of food, wherein the production of some foods actually require more inputs than outputs (beef requires more resources be consumed than are produced), while some crops require significantly more water than others to grow.

The point of sustainability in economics is to optimize dynamic efficiency. In other words, it is to ensure that if any short-run gains produce any long-run deficiencies, that the gains are great enough to then fulfill those deficiencies. It's a thing which humanity fails at, terribly, but that's the goal, in theory. There is an ideal point of consumption we strive to achieve, where our consumption of any resource is exactly equivalent to the rate at which that resource is replenished. Consuming at a faster rate results in degradation and is not sustainable. Consuming at a slower rate will result in regeneration, but indicates that we have unutilized resources which can be safely consumed to increase growth and development. The goal is to get it just right.

International trade and finance.

It's actually something of a misnomer to think of international economics or international trade as something unique. People tend to think that it deals with the way in which the economies of entire nations interact with each other, and with good reason given that we use the term "international". The truth, though, is that the same behaviors which nations exhibit while engaging other nations in economic activities are no different from those which are exhibited by individual people. Not only is the behavior of a nation's economy composed directly of the behaviors of the people within that economy, but even on an aggregate scale, a nation will act just like a big person working with other big people.

The **balance of payments** (BoP) is a record of all the transactions which occur between a nation and all other nations in the world. This isn't some abstract idea, I mean it's a literal record, one which you can get from the US Bureau of Economic Analysis at http://www.bea.gov/iTable/index_ita.cfm. In it is found all the goods and services that come into the country or go out of it, and the money which is transferred, all the investments which are made, and so forth. The BoP is divided into 2 primary parts: the current account and the capital account.

The **current account** is the one that everyone thinks of when talking about trade. It includes the transfer of all goods and services between nations. When a nation exports more than it imports, it's called a **trade surplus**; when a nation imports more than it exports, it's called a **trade deficit**.

The **capital account**, also known as the **financial account** based on IMF rules, wherein the capital account is then a narrow type of capital transfers in which the US almost always has a 0 balance. The capital account includes all the movement of investment and reserve assets between nations, such as money, stocks, debt, gold, and so forth. When a nation has a current account deficit, it will have a capital account surplus; and when a nation has a current account surplus, they will have a capital account deficit. Theoretically speaking, the final values of the current and capital accounts will equal 0. They are said to balance, which is why it's called the balance of payments. Due to insufficiencies in data collection, though, they rarely ever do. So, in order to account for the remaining balance, a statistical discrepancy adjustment is used.

The relationship between the current and capital accounts does more than just balance – it demonstrates an important element of trade, and gives insight into the nature of trade between nations. When a nation imports or exports goods to another nation, there is an equivalent value of capital exchanged. So, when the US imports stuff from China, financial capital is exported. It's popular to demonize this exchange, but the reality is that it is literally no different than going to the store to buy your stuff. There's not some monolithic imposition of Chinese imports flooding the United States, it's just people going to the store and buying things which are frequently made in China because the Chinese markets currently have a competitive advantage in many types of simple manufacturing. You chose to go to the store to buy something rather than make that thing yourself as a result of the specialization of labor – you make the things you're good at, and buy the rest. Well, it just so happened that the person you bought from was Chinese, and they were very good at producing whatever it is you bought.

3. Semi-skilled labor is anything that falls between skilled and unskilled. Note that these aren't clear definitions, and that some jobs likely fall into a grey area that could be categorized in more than one category (e.g.: could be skilled or semi-skilled). One could make the argument that non-fiction authors should be categorized as semi-skilled labor. Even skilled labor doesn't necessarily include a lot of schooling, but it definitely requires a lot of education. Education comes in many forms, though. Besides schooling, you can get an education through trade schools, tech schools, internships, apprenticeships, mentoring, and so forth. Self-teaching one's self by using guides is also very common, especially for jobs like computer programmers, whose employers tend to be more concerned with whether a person is proficient in some type of programming language rather than whether they have a degree.

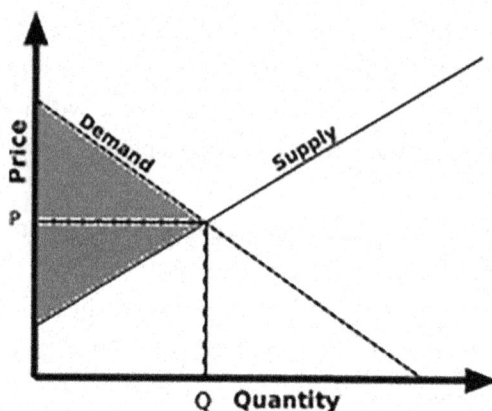

In this exchange, you are both earning value – the seller got more value from the money than they did from holding inventory, and you got more value from the thing you purchased than you would from holding money. It all still follows the basics of consumer and producer surpluses, but now the exchanges are just happening between people who are farther away from each other.

Would the Chinese sell stuff to the US if they thought the US dollar was going to be worthless? No! They wouldn't bother to send the US valuable resources for scraps of cloth that have no value. From their perspective it's an investment – a majority of China's foreign currency reserves is US dollars. If the US economy collapsed, it would be a big hit to the Chinese economy, too; and it wouldn't do the US any favors if the Chinese economy collapsed and suddenly the resource cost of meeting demand skyrocketed, causing our own exports to become less competitive. As shown in the basics of economics at the beginning of this book, nations accomplish more together than they can alone.

So what does China, or any other nation, do with all those US dollars? A percentage of them are held in reserve for those "just in case" moments when some government needs them for international transactions (sort-of like banks hold money in reserve), but for the most part all that money will be spent. Eventually, each dollar finds its way back to the US, whereupon US companies will export valuable outputs in exchange for that dollar. As the US imports stuff, it is able to produce its own things more efficiently, and then when they are finally obliged to export their own things, since the economy has grown, each dollar received will obligate the US to export less than they had imported using the same volume of money as a result of inflation. That doesn't mean that foreign nations lose in these transactions, because quickly-growing businesses require capital in order to expand, so the increased availability of capital resulting from all those export sales help to fund the growth in other nations, too. In the end, the proof is simple: the BoP balances, even if the current account doesn't.

Now, let's complicate things. Let's say you have US dollars (USD) and you want to buy Chinese Renminbi (RMB). How can you decide what each currency is worth in terms of the other? There are two measures which compare the relative values of currency. The one most people think of is the **exchange rate**. As of the moment I am writing this, the market exchange rate between the USD and RMB is 1/6.5. That means each 1USD you have for exchange will get you 6.5RMB (minus the price charged for the exchange at the exchange desk, of course). How is this determined, though? The answer depends on whether you're talking about a fixed or floating currency.

Fixed currencies, also called **pegged currencies**, are those whose value is established by government policy as a static exchange rate with some other thing. For example (a purely fictional example), if the RMB is pegged to the USD at a rate of 2/1, then no matter how the value of the USD changes, the RMB will always trade at a rate of 2RMB for each 1USD. Even in dealing with the Euro, the exchange rate of the Euro and RMB would be measured using USD. Generally nations don't peg their currencies wholly to one other currency – that never really ends well because the exchange value of the pegged currency won't respond at all to market forces. Instead, what nations tend to do is peg their own currency to a basket of currencies. For example, Nation A might peg the value of its currency to the USD, Euro, GBP (British Pound), gold, and oil; and all in different ratios. Maybe 50% of the currency's value is pegged to the USD, so if the USD increases in value 1%, then Nation A's currency would increase in value by 0.5%. Generally, nations choose currencies from their trade partners, and roughly in the ratios in which they trade with each nation (or at least in a modified variation on it).

Exchange rate policy, then, is based on changing the policy of the peg, rather than market forces. To increase the value of the currency is called **revaluation**. Revaluating a currency means that you are increasing the amount of foreign currency you can purchase with your own currency by manner of a change in the policy that set the pegged rate. In the opposite direction, there is **devaluation**, which means decreasing the value of the currency by decreasing the amount of currency you can buy with each unit of your own currency.

Even if pegged currencies are pegged to other pegged currencies, they are all eventually pegged to a floating currency, which is one whose value fluctuates with market forces. That means that pegged currencies also respond to market forces, but it's someone else's market forces rather than your own. This can be beneficial for nations who have volatile economies, or whose currency value tends to fluctuate wildly. The increased stability improves production and trade, and the impact of a failure to respond to one's own market forces is minimized so long as the peg is carefully managed.

Floating currencies fluctuate in value through **appreciation** and **deprecation**, which mean that they increase or decrease in value through market forces. If demand for a currency suddenly increases, that currency will appreciate in value, whereas a sudden increase in supply will depreciate the currency. The policies used to manage exchange rate, then, take advantage of these market forces, and are nearly identical to the same monetary policy used to manage the currency domestically. Exchange rates of floating currencies can be influenced by relative changes in inflation, supply, demand, and so forth, which means it can be managed through relative changes in interest rates, reserve ratios, OMO, and generally any type of monetary policy.

The most important long-run determinant of exchange rates, particularly floating exchange rates, is the relative rates of inflation. Remember that inflation is a decrease in the purchasing power of a currency, so if one currency decreases in its purchasing power more quickly then will also be a tendency to be a decrease in the exchange rate of that currency. Let's say that the USD and RMB have the same purchasing power and an exchange rate of 1/1. With either currency, you'd be able to buy the same amount of stuff for the same price, and you could exchange equal amounts of one currency for the other. Then in one year the US has 10% more inflation than China, which means that now you have to spend 10% more USD in order to buy the same amount of stuff. This relative comparison in the purchasing power between two currencies is known as the **purchasing power parity** (PPP). PPP is a valuation of the values of currency by comparing their ability to buy things, similar to the manner in which inflation is measured (i.e.: using changes in how much of each currency it takes to purchase the same basket of goods). In our example, even though the exchange rate is still 1USD/1RMB, the PPP is actually 1.1USD/1RMB. Since inflation increased 10% in the US, it takes 1.1USD to buy the same amount of stuff that you can buy with 1RMB. Needless to say, it's less beneficial to have USD, so demand for the currency drops thereby causing depreciation.

When an exchange rate is higher than PPP, then the currency is said to be **overvalued** and it is expected to decrease in value in the long-run. When an exchange rate is higher than PPP, then the currency is **undervalued** and it is expected to increase in the value in the long-run. This is most famously illustrated in a measurement developed by *The Economist* (a news magazine and research center), called **The Big Mac Index**. The Big Mac Index collects the price of a Big Mac (a McDonald's hamburger) in every nation, and uses that as its measure of PPP. If it costs 2GBP to buy a Big Mac in Britain, and 1USD to by a Big Mac in the US, then according to the Big Mac Index it is said that the PPP is 2GBP/1USD. This is then compared to the exchange rates between each nation to determine whether the exchange rate is overvalued or undervalued. Clearly this isn't the most accurate method of measurement, but it does have the benefits of being very easy to understand, very easy to measure, and just a bit amusing.

Have a weak currency is not necessarily a bad thing. In fact, the US has been accusing China of keeping their currency undervalued by keeping the RMB peg well below market equilibrium. The reason for this is that decreasing the value of your exchange rate causes your exports to increase, and decreases demand for imports from other nations. In our example from earlier, since it takes 10% less RMB to buy things in the US, and 10% more USD to buy things in China, demand for US-produced goods will increase (but probably not by 10% or 20%, as you may guess). So, whether you want to increase the value of your currency so goods from other nations are cheaper, or decrease the value of your currency to stimulate production, depends entirely on the state of your nation's economy and its goals for the future.

It is therefore common for nations to use economic policy in order to ensure that their currency continues to deviate from PPP. This is one reason why exchange rates tend to not return to PPP, despite the pressure from market forces to do so. Since relative inflation rates are one of the biggest influences on changes in PPP and exchange rates, monetary policy is the most effective manner in which to manage exchange rates. Illustrating this most effectively is something called the **International Fisher Effect** (IFE).

Strictly speaking, the IFE says that a 1% increase in interest rates relative to another than will result in a 1% decrease in exchange rates with that nation. Strictly speaking, the IFE is wrong, but only because it's so very specific. The principle of the IFE is sound – an increase in interest rates relative to another nation will decrease the exchange rate with that nation – but the elasticity of that cause-and-effect will vary (i.e.: the amount of response in exchange rates relative to a 1% change in relative inflation will not necessarily be 1%, nor necessarily even the same each time). It's also been shown that the decrease in exchange rates is temporary, since the higher demand for a nation's goods which results from the change in exchange rates tends to strengthen that nation's economy and currency in the long-run (which is usually a good thing).

The amount by which a nation's trade actually changes in response to a change in exchange rate can be best illustrated by understanding the **Marshall-Lerner Condition**. If the goal of devaluation is to increase exports and decrease imports, then the total increase in the current account will depend on the amount of devaluation and the amount of change in trade. Since a devaluation in the currency means that the monetary value (i.e.: price) of your exports decreases and increases the monetary value of imports, this will look like a decrease in the value of your current account. The value of your current account will only increase if the volume of trade is great enough to negate the loss in monetary value. This is a kind-of trade elasticity – the degree of change in trade in response to a change in exchange rate; $\Delta T/\Delta X$. If the absolute value of this elasticity is greater than 1, then you've met the requirements of the Marshall-Lerner Condition.

Helping to estimate the impact of trade policy is by closely tracking the **terms of trade** (ToT). A nation's ToT is a measure of the total value of a nation's imports relative to the nation's exports. This can be used when considering the whole of a nation's trade, or just trade with any given nation, but it always includes the aggregate of all trade. ToT is calculated as:

$$p_x q_x / p_m q_m$$

Where:

p = price
q = quantity
x = exports
m = imports

The ToT can be thought of as the value of exports you must sell in order to afford your imports. In the end, this tells you the total value of your exports as a ratio of the total value of your imports. If you have a trade deficit, then your ToT will be between 0 and 1; if you have a trade deficit, your ToT will be greater than 1.

The last topic we'll discuss is trade policy. There are two broad categories of trade policy: protectionism and integration. **Protectionism** is policy intended to limit the amount of trade with other nations in a typically-failed effort to protect domestic industry. There are several types of protectionist policies, some of the more common including:

Tariffs – A tax on imports levied by the federal government, making imports more expensive relative to market price.

Subsidies – A payment by the federal government made to producers who export certain types of goods, making exports cheaper relative to market price.

Quotas – A restriction on the volume of particular types of goods which will be allowed to be imported, or the amount that is allowed to be imported tariff-free.

Any attempt to restrict free trade only succeeds in limiting gains from trade. Any failure for a nation to benefit from free trade is a failure of that nation to effectively utilize its gains, rather than a problem inherent with trade.

At the opposite end of the spectrum we have **integration**, which refers to policies intended to increase free trade between nations. Economic integration is a more complicated than protectionism – it's not hard to understand, there's just a lot more to know. I find it's easiest to express it in spreadsheet form, as shown in the image below:

	Reduced Restrictions	No Restrictions	Common Non-Member	Free Factor Movement	Common Monetary Policy	Common Fiscal Policy	Example	
Free Trade Zone	A single city in an otherwise restricted nation that allows for value-added import/export, but not the market sale of foreign goods.						Pre-WTO China	
Preferential Trade	X						SPARTECA	
Free Trade Area	X	X					NAFTA	
Customs Union	X	X	X				MERCOSUR	
Common Market	X	X	X	X			SAFTA	
Monetary Union	X	X	X	X	X		EU	
Economic Union	X	X	X	X	X	X	US	
Involuntary Integration	Global integration which cannot be consented to, such as through the internet, global crime and terrorism, and the movement of pollution via air and water currents.							

Organizations of International Economics

	Gives Advice	Loans Money	Does Research	Promotes Trade	Mostly Just for Show	Part of World	Talking Forum		Private Sector
WTO	X		X	X			X	X	
IMF	X	X	X	X					X
OECD			X	X	X		X		X
IBRD	X	X	X			X			X
IDA	X	X	X			X			X
IFC	X		X			X			X
MIGA	X		X		X	X			X
ICSID	X			X	X	X	X		X
OPEC			X						X
G8				X	X		X	X	
NGOs	Organizations which pursue non-profit goals in global industrial standardization (W3C), charity (Red Cross), and political issues (Human Rights International)								X

Private Sector Integration

	Domestic Operations	Import/	Foreign Presence	No Domestic	Example				
Domestic Company	X				White Castle				
International Company	X	X			Glico				
Multinational Company	X	X	X		McDonalds				
Transnational Company	X	X	X	X	Nestle				

Economic integration not only increases the amount of buying/selling between nations, but it also increases the amount of investment between nations, the amount of capital moving between nations, the amount of people moving between nations, and so forth. It gives nations access to greater pools of capital, investors, investments, customers, sellers, labor, employers, and even knowledge. Since people of different skill sets and backgrounds are able to more freely interact with each other, particularly within a given industry, there is an increase in the amount of **knowledge spillover**. Knowledge spillover is the sharing of ideas and information in a non-competitive manner which improves the factors of an endogenous growth model, such as those found in Schumpeterian growth.

Conclusion

People tend to say that economics is tough. It includes a lot of very specialized info unique to the field, uses a lot of math, and tends to use words and phrases that are great to know if you want to sound smart (unless you're actually an economist, in which case it just comes across as confusing and elitist, so using simple explanations tends to get the best response). There's also a lot of misinformation about economics pushed on the nation, primarily from politicians and politically-interested sources trying to convince you to support nonsense. Everyone learns different, of course, but in my experience teaching I have found that there are two ways to study this stuff that tend to be very helpful.

1) Know your history. Learn what economic models, policies, and theories were prevalent in the past, understand why they were eventually replaced, and know what replaced them. Economics is a really new science, relatively speaking, less than 200 years old (as compared to physics which is ancient), so people have made lots of mistakes from which you can learn.

2) Know how things interact. All the visual and mathematical models, and even all the crazy-long names we give stuff actually tend to be pretty intuitive, if not obvious, when you consider what they're explaining. All of economics deals with the manner in which people and organizations interact together in the utilization of resources, so by remembering the way things act and how they respond to their environment will help you better remember the more abstract elements.

That's it for now. Good luck!

AP
MACROECONOMICS
Sample Test 1

Multiple Choice Questions

1. A decrease in _____ is likely to shrink a nation's production possibilities curve:
   (Basic Economic Concepts)

   [A] inflation

   [B] labor forces

   [C] taxes

   [D] GDP

   [E] interest rates

2. _____ causes a rightward shift in the short-run aggregate supply curve:
   (National Income and Price Determination)

   [A] Increased prices

   [B] Decreased fiscal spending

   [C] Improved technology

   [D] Decreased investing

   [E] Decreased savings

3. Ceteris paribus, a $100 million increase in GDP can be accomplished through an _____ injection, with MPC of 75%:
   (Inflation, Unemployment, and Stabilization Policies)

   [A] $75 million

   [B] $100 million

   [C] $25 million

   [D] Government can't increase GDP

   [E] $200 million

4. _____ causes real interest rates to increase:
   (Financial Sector)

   [A] Decreased investing

   [B] Decreased savings

   [C] Decreased consumption

   [D] Decreased production

   [E] Decreased inflation

5. _____ will ease deflationary pressure during a period of economic recession:
(Inflation, Unemployment, and Stabilization Policies)

[A] Increasing taxation

[B] Increasing interest rates

[C] Increasing money supply

[D] Decreasing money supply

[E] Stopping new currency production

6. _____ decreases long-run economic growth:
(Economic Growth and Productivity)

[A] Decreasing expenditures on corporate subsidies

[B] Increasing privatization

[C] Decreasing expenditures in education/training

[D] Increasing taxation

[E] Increasing government spending

7. _____ results from appreciating a nation's currency in the forex market:
(Open Economy: International Trade and Finance)

[A] No change in imports or exports

[B] Decreased imports, increased exports

[C] Decreased imports, decreased exports

[D] Increased imports, decreased exports

[E] Increased imports, increased exports

8. Tariffs are not used to _____:
(Economic Growth and Productivity)

[A] Increase tax revenues

[B] Decrease import prices

[C] Increase import prices

[D] Mitigate the impact of dumping

[E] Impose sanctions

9. **Federal Reserve Open Market Operations means:**

(Inflation, Unemployment, and Stabilization Policies)

[A] Changing federal reserve ratio

[B] Buying and selling of federal debt to manage money supply and interest rates

[C] Printing money to cause inflation

[D] Changing tax rates

[E] Increasing government spending

10. **____ will not cause an increase to a nation's current account :**

(Open Economy: International Trade and Finance)

[A] Federal debt purchased by a foreign nation

[B] Exporting consumer goods

[C] Foreign tourists visiting

[D] Food aid from foreign nations

[E] Exporting agricultural goods

11. **According to the International Fisher Effect, a 1% appreciation in nation A's currency relative to Nation B will result from:**

(Open Economy: International Trade and Finance)

[A] A 1% increase in real interest rates relative to Nation B

[B] A 1% higher nominal interest to nation B

[C] A 1% lower nominal interest rate relative to Nation B

[D] A 1% increase in inflation relative to Nation B

[E] A 1% increase in exports to Nation B

12. **A currency with PPP of 1 and exchange rate of 1/2 is considered:**

(Open Economy: International Trade and Finance)

[A] Undervalued

[B] Overvalued

[C] Appreciated

[D] Depreciated

[E] In equilibrium

13. A fiat currency is:

(Open Economy: International Trade and Finance)

[A] Any item whose value is derived from its ability to be used as a measurement of value

[B] Any pegged currency

[C] Any currency subject to inflation

[D] Any floating currency

[E] Any currency currently in print

14. "Output is a function of capital" is indicative of:

(Economic Growth and Productivity)

[A] Solow-Swan model

[B] Harrod-Domar model

[C] Endogenous growth model

[D] Exogenous growth model

[E] Unified growth model

15. "Growth is a function of capital and technology" is indicative of:

(Economic Growth and Productivity)

[A] AK model

[B] Exogenous growth model

[C] Solow-Swan model

[D] Harrod-Domar model

[E] Unified growth model

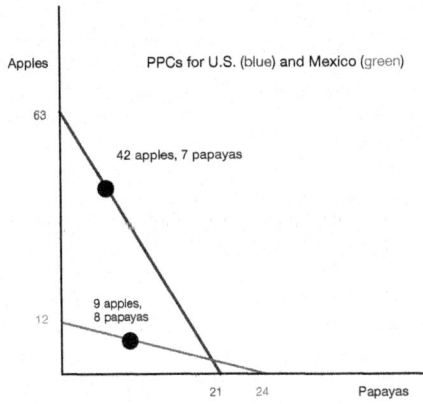

Apples

PPCs for U.S. (blue) and Mexico (green)

63

42 apples, 7 papayas

12

9 apples,
8 papayas

21   24   Papayas

16. Which nation has an absolute advantage:

(Basic Economic Concepts)

[A] US

[B] Mexico

[C] US in apples

[D] Mexico in papayas

[E] Mexico in apples

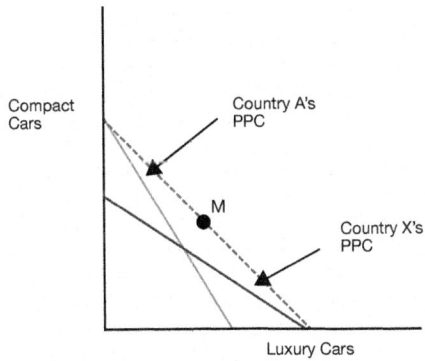

Compact
Cars

Country A's
PPC

M

Country X's
PPC

Luxury Cars

17. What is US's opportunity cost per papaya:

(Basic Economic Concepts)

[A] 0.33

[B] 3

[C] 63

[D] 21

[E] 2

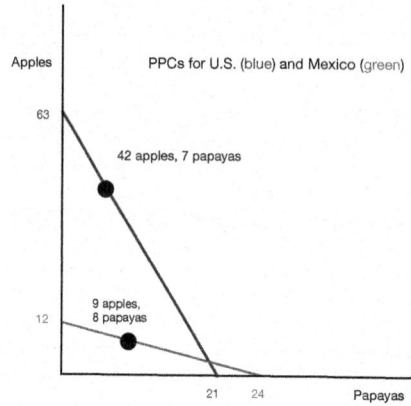

Apples

PPCs for U.S. (blue) and Mexico (green)

63

42 apples, 7 papayas

9 apples,
8 papayas

12

21   24   Papayas

18. **What is the maximum combined production with trade:**

(Basic Economic Concepts)

[A] 24

[B] 90

[C] 63

[D] 66

[E] 49

19. **_____ would cause a supply curve to shift right:**

(Basic Economic Concepts)

[A] Increased producer price index

[B] Shortages of raw materials

[C] Technological advancement

[D] Consumer demand

[E] Nothing

20. **A linear aggregate supply curve which starts at 0 and with point [$40 for 80 units] has a marginal price of:**

(Basic Economic Concepts)

[A] $0.5

[B] $2

[C] $40

[D] $80

[E] $0

21. It is true that:

(Economic Growth and Productivity)

[A] Investment creates its own supply

[B] Supply creates its own demand

[C] Demand creates its own supply

[D] Supply creates its own investment

[E] Supply creates its own savings

22. Lower consumption levels will:

(Inflation, Unemployment, and Stabilization Policies)

[A] Decrease company revenues, discouraging investment

[B] Increase savings, making more loanable funds available

[C] Create surplus supply, causing an immediate reduction in price

[D] Force investing in new innovations that people will want

[E] Be common during times of economic success

23. Increased inflation will:

(Inflation, Unemployment, and Stabilization Policies)

[A] Decrease exports

[B] Increase exports

[C] Increase imports

[D] Slow trade

[E] Slow economic growth

24. _____ can cause monetary inflation:

(Measurement of Economic Performance)

[A] Increased demand

[B] Birth of a natural monopoly

[C] Decreased money supply

[D] Reduction in federal reserve ratio

[E] Decreased taxation

25. _____ causes frictional unemployment:

(Measurement of Economic Performance)

[A] People changing jobs

[B] AS>AD

[C] Mismatch of labor demand and skills

[D] Wages below equilibrium

[E] Low inflation

26. _____ causes structural unemployment:

(Measurement of Economic Performance)

[A] Low levels of inflation

[B] Wages below equilibrium

[C] AS>AD

[D] Mismatch of labor demand and skills

[E] People changing jobs

27. Stagflation is:

(Measurement of Economic Performance)

[A] A state of high unemployment and high inflation

[B] A state of high unemployment and low inflation

[C] A state of low unemployment and high inflation

[D] A state of low unemployment and low inflation

[E] Inflation in the market for stag pelts

28. Full employment is:

(Measurement of Economic Performance)

[A] 2% unemployment

[B] A state wherein the entire labor for is actively employed

[C] A state wherein the entire population is actively employed

[D] A state wherein the entire labor force is actively employed or engaged in changing employment

[E] 0% unemployment

29. Monetary velocity is:

(Inflation, Unemployment, and Stabilization Policy)

[A] The speed with which money is created

[B] The amount of final income created from a stimulus package

[C] The number of times the same money changes hands, contributing to economic growth, within a time period

[D] Volume of foreign exchange transactions

[E] The rate of inflation created by monetary policy

30. **Which tariff gives domestic companies an unfair advantage:**

   (Open Economy: International Trade and Finance)

   [A] Domestic Price: $150

       Foreign Price: $125

       Tariff: 21%

   [B] Domestic Price: $75

       Foreign Price: $45

       Tariff: 60%

   [C] Domestic Price: $125

       Foreign Price: $100

       Tariff: 24%

   [D] Domestic Price: $100

       Foreign Price: $90

       Tariff: 10%

   [E] Domestic Price: $100

       Foreign Price: $80

       Tariff: 20%

31. **What is the relationship between federal deficit and federal debt:**

   (National Income and Price Determination)

   [A] Federal deficit reduces the federal debt

   [B] Federal debt causes an increase in the federal deficit

   [C] Federal debt is used to fund deficit spending

   [D] Federal deficit causes an increase in the federal debt

   [E] There is no relationship

32. **Who is included as a part of the national labor force:**

   (National Income and Price Determination)

   [A] People who were seriously injured on the job

   [B] People who have given-up seeking employment

   [C] People unemployed but seeking employment

   [D] Children

   [E] All of the above

33. A $10 tax return to an employee has a quarterly monetary velocity of 1.8, calculate how much economic growth it creates in 1 year:

(National Income and Price Determination)

[A] $18

[B] $10

[C] $72

[D] $40

[E] $22

34. Market shocks result from:

(Measurement of Economic Performance)

[A] Monetary mismanagement

[B] Volatility which lowers investor expectations

[C] Small, frequent change making production volume predictions difficult

[D] Fiscal mismanagement

[E] Sudden, large changes which impacts the economy more quickly than it can respond to those changes

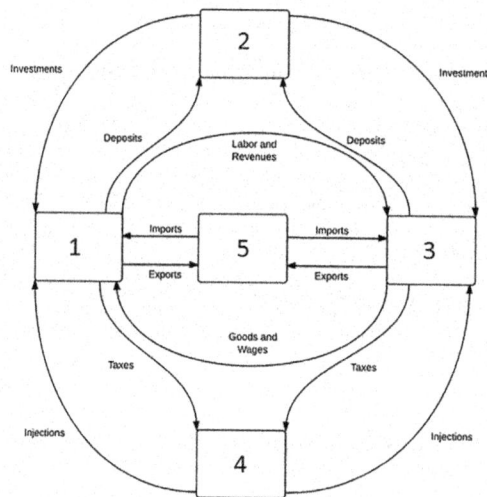

35. Sector 1 is:

(Measurement of Economic Performance)

[A] Financial

[B] Government

[C] Foreign

[D] Households

[E] Companies

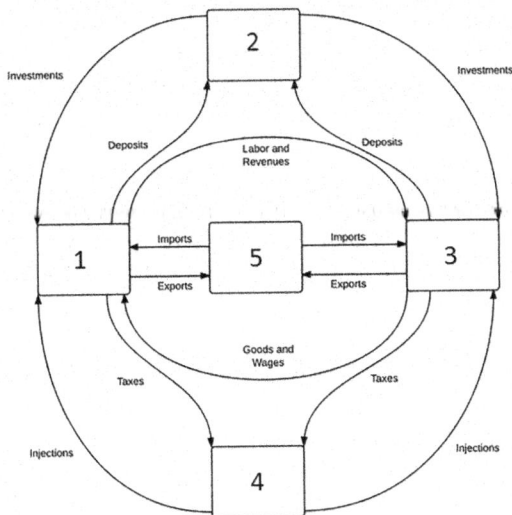

36. Sector 3 is:

(Measurement of Economic Performance)

[A] Households

[B] Companies

[C] Financial

[D] Foreign

[E] Government

37. Sector 5 is:

(Measurement of Economic Performance)

[A] Foreign

[B] Financial

[C] Government

[D] Households

[E] Companies

38. A recession is formally defined as:

(National Income and Price Determination)

[A] Any period in which unemployment exceeds 5%

[B] Any period in which unemployment exceeds 7%

[C] Two consecutive quarters of negative GDP growth

[D] Any period greater than one quarter in which AS>AD

[E] Any period in which gross wages drop more than 5% for greater than one quarter

39. **Aggregate demand, national income, and gross domestic product all share the same:**

(National Income and Price Determination)

[A] Income-based approach

[B] Consumption-based approach

[C] Mathematical formula

[D] Production-based approach

[E] Graphical model

40. **Nominal rate = 5%, Inflation = 2%**

Calculate real interest rate:

(Financial Sector)

[A] 2%

[B] 2.5%

[C] 10%

[D] 3%

[E] 7%

41. **Principle = $100,000**

Rate = 0.005

Time = 10 years

Calculate the balance using continuously compounding interest:

(Financial Sector)

[A] $150,000

[B] $105,000

[C] $105,127

[D] $150,127

[E] $105,126

42. **NPV is calculated by:**

(Financial Sector)

[A] Subtracting the sum of present values from the initial outlay

[B] Subtracting total returns from initial outlay

[C] Adding together all the cash flows on an investment

[D] Adding together all the present values on an investment

[E] Subtracting the sum of cash flows from the initial outlay

43. Fiscal policy is managed by _____ and monetary policy by _____:

(Financial Sector)

[A] Federal Reserve, Congress

[B] Congress, Federal Reserve

[C] President, Federal Reserve

[D] Federal Reserve, President

[E] Congress, President

44. Government debt that matures in 1 year or less is:

(Financial Sector)

[A] Treasury Bond

[B] Treasury Note

[C] Treasury Bill

[D] Corporate Bond

[E] Stock

45. _____ is a common method for slowing unsustainable rates of economic growth:

(Inflation, Unemployment, and Stabilization Policies)

[A] Increasing fiscal spending

[B] Decreasing interest rates

[C] Increasing bank reserve ratios

[D] Issuing a tax refund

[E] Depreciating foreign exchange rate

46. Banks earn the majority of their revenues by:

(Financial Sector)

[A] Charging fees and fines

[B] Borrowing money from deposits and then lending it to borrowers at a higher interest rate

[C] Buying investments and then reselling them through brokerage accounts

[D] Government benefits

[E] Laundering illegal funds earned through front-businesses

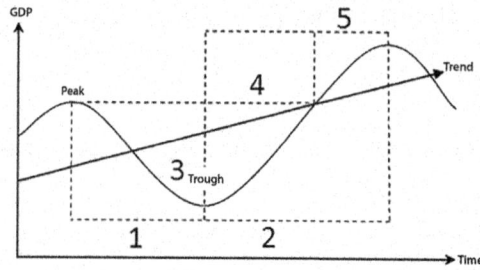

47. A period of _____ is shown at 2:
(National Income and Price Determination)

[A] contraction

[B] recession

[C] expansion

[D] boom

[E] recovery

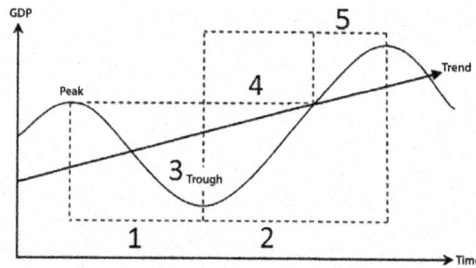

48. At 4, the economy is in _____:
(National Income and Price Determination)

[A] boom

[B] expansion

[C] recovery

[D] contraction

[E] recession

49. Economic terms include _____ and _____:

(Basic Economic Concepts)

[A] socialism, capitalism

[B] communism, capitalism

[C] socialism, communism

[D] capitalism, individualism

[E] free market economy, planned economy

50. A grouping of large numbers of unlike things for the sake of measuring trends between them:

(Basic Economic Concepts)

[A] Macro

[B] Aggregate

[C] Statistic

[D] Bundle

[E] Economy

51. Purchasing bonds through OPO is most effective for growth when:

(Economic Growth)

[A] Reserve ratio is high and investments are high

[B] Reserve ratio is low and savings are high

[C] Reserve ratio is low and investments are high

[D] Reserve ratio is high and savings are low

[E] Reserve ratio is high and investments are low

52. ___ and ___ can increase labor productivity:

(Economic Growth)

[A] Education, technology

[B] Education, population

[C] Employment, population

[D] Employment, technology

[E] Population, technology

53. ___ decreases the exchange rate of the USD:

(Open Economy: International Trade and Finance)

[A] Lower domestic inflation rates

[B] Higher foreign inflation rates

[C] Lower foreign interest rates

[D] Higher foreign interest rates

[E] The Federal Reserve

54. **Which will cause a $2.5 million decrease in the money supply:**

(Financial Sector)

[A] $500,000 purchase of government securities at a 20% reserve ratio

[B] $500,000 sale of government securities at a 20% reserve ratio

[C] $200,000 sale of government securities at a 50% reserve ratio

[D] $250,000 sale of government securities at a 25% reserve ratio

[E] $200,000 purchase of government securities at a 50% reserve ratio

55. **An increase in labor productivity will:**

(National Income and Price Determination)

[A] Increase AS

[B] Increase AD

[C] Decrease AS

[D] Decrease AD

[E] No change

56. **GDP = $___ trillion**

Money supply = $___ trillion

Monetary velocity = ___:

(Economic Growth)

[A] 6, 2, 3

[B] 4, 1, 2

[C] 8, 4, 3

[D] 6, 2, 4

[E] 4, 8, 3

57. Interest rates will most likely fall with _____ monetary policy and _____ fiscal policy:

(Inflation, Unemployment, and Stabilization Policies)

[A] contractionary, contractionary

[B] expansionary, expansionary

[C] expansionary, contractionary

[D] contractionary, expansionary

[E] nothing

58. Assume that US consumers increase their demand for Chinese Renminbi. This will cause:

(Open Economy: International Trade and Finance)

USD Supply, RMB Value, Chinese Imports

[A] Increase, Increase, Decrease

[B] Increase, Increase, Increase

[C] Decrease, Increase, Increase

[D] Decrease, Decrease, Decrease

[E] No change, Increase, Increase

59. Nominal GDP growth is -2%

Real GDP growth is 4%

The nation is experiencing ___ with an inflation rate of ____

(Measurement of Economic Performance)

[A] recession, 4%

[B] stagflation, -6%

[C] stagflation, 4%

[D] recession, 6%

[E] boom, -6%

60. The depreciation of USD on the forex market?

(Open Economy: International Trade and Finance)

[A] Decreases the balance of payments surplus if export elasticity is high

[B] Increases the balance of payments surplus if import elasticity is low

[C] Decreases the balance of payments deficit if export elasticity is low

[D] Increases the balance of payments deficit if export elasticity is low

[E] Increases the balance of payments surplus if export elasticity is high

Free-Response Questions

1. Nation A is in a recession

[A] Describe the interactions between growth factors

   (i)   Draw a graph demonstrating the shift in AS relative to AD

   (ii)   Explain how unemployment and underemployment perpetuate economic contraction

   (iii)   How will investors respond to worsening business performance? What will they do with capital instead of stimulating growth?

[B] Explain what monetary policies the central bank is likely to take

   (i)   Identify the open-market operations

   (ii)   Explain the impact of expansionary monetary policy on inflation rates

   (iii)   Given your answer from part [B](ii), explain how this will extend to influence exchange rates relative to nations which have remained constant, and how this will alter both the current and capital accounts of the balance of payments for Nation A.

[C] Assume Nation A has an MPC of 0.75 and a monetary velocity of 9.

   (i)   How much economic growth will result from a $1 million stimulus package?

   (ii)   If current GDP is $15 trillion, what is the money supply?

   (iii)   With average real GDP growth of -2% over the past 4 quarters, what value should the stimulus package be? Should this be supplemented with other policy measures? Why?

2. Nation A is in an economic boom

[A] Describe inflation

   (i)   What is the most likely state of inflation, and what causes it?

   (ii)   What conditions can cause deviations from the likely state? How?

   (iii) What is the likely impact on exchange rates and trade flows?

[B] What is the state of unemployment, if any?

   (i)   What types of unemployment are present? Why?

   (ii)   What factors contribute to the rate of unemployment at full employment?

[C] You are hired to provide advice on fiscal and monetary policy.

   (i)   What will likely result from expansionary policy during this time? Why?

   (ii)   What will likely result from contractionary policy during this time? Why?

   (iii) What specific steps would you recommend, if any? Why?

3. Consider the impact of The New Deal on the US economy

[A] List 3 specific programs created under The New Deal and explain the function of each

[B] List 3 specific regulatory reforms implemented and explain the function of each

[C] The banking industry during The Great Depression was dysfunctional

   (i)   Describe the nature of the dysfunction

   (ii)   How did these banking problems contribute to The Great Depression?

   (iii) How did New Deal policies help to alleviate the problem?

AP Macroeconomics: Sample Test 1- Answer Key

Question Number	Correct Answer	Your Answer		Question Number	Correct Answer	Your Answer
1	B			31	C	
2	C			32	C	
3	C			33	C	
4	B			34	E	
5	C			35	D	
6	C			36	B	
7	D			37	A	
8	B			38	C	
9	B			39	C	
10	A			40	D	
11	C			41	C	
12	B			42	D	
13	A			43	B	
14	B			44	C	
15	A			45	C	
16	A			46	B	
17	B			47	C	
18	B			48	C	
19	C			49	E	
20	A			50	B	
21	C			51	C	
22	A			52	A	
23	B			53	C	
24	D			54	B	
25	A			55	A	
26	D			56	A	
27	A			57	C	
28	D			58	A	
29	C			59	B	
30	A			60	D	

Sample Test One

AP Macroeconomics: Sample Test 1- Explanations

1. A decrease in _____ is likely to shrink a nation's production possibilities curve:

   (Basic Economic Concepts)

   [A] inflation

   [B] labor forces

   [C] taxes

   [D] GDP

   [E] interest rates

The answer is B

If fewer people are working, then the nation will have lower maximum production potential

2. _____ causes a rightward shift in the short-run aggregate supply curve:

   (National Income and Price Determination)

   [A] Increased prices

   [B] Decreased fiscal spending

   [C] Improved technology

   [D] Decreased investing

   [E] Decreased savings

The answer is C

Technological advances facilitate higher volumes of production at lower costs

3. Ceteris paribus, a $100 million increase in GDP can be accomplished through an _____ injection, with MPC of 75%:

   (Inflation, Unemployment, and Stabilization Policies)

   [A] $75 million

   [B] $100 million

   [C] $25 million

   [D] Government can't increase GDP

   [E] $200 million

The answer is C

A high marginal propensity to consume creates a larger fiscal multiplier

4. _____ causes real interest rates to increase:

(Financial Sector)

[A] Decreased investing

[B] Decreased savings

[C] Decreased consumption

[D] Decreased production

[E] Decreased inflation

The answer is B

With lower loanable funds relative to demand for loans, the price of loans will increase

5. _____ will ease deflationary pressure during a period of economic recession:

(Inflation, Unemployment, and Stabilization Policies)

[A] Increasing taxation

[B] Increasing interest rates

[C] Increasing money supply

[D] Decreasing money supply

[E] Stopping new currency production

The answer is C

Deflation means the currency is increasing in purchasing power, which only happens during times of deep recession, so increasing the money supply will lower its value and increase monetary velocity

6. _____ decreases long-run economic growth:

(Economic Growth and Productivity)

[A] Decreasing expenditures on corporate subsidies

[B] Increasing privatization

[C] Decreasing expenditures in education/training

[D] Increasing taxation

[E] Increasing government spending

The answer is C

Human capital is a major component of all growth models, so less investing in the quality of human capital will result in lower long-term production potential

7. _____ **results from appreciating a nation's currency in the forex market:**

(Open Economy: International Trade and Finance)

[A] No change in imports or exports

[B] Decreased imports, increased exports

[C] Decreased imports, decreased exports

[D] Increased imports, decreased exports

[E] Increased imports, increased exports

The answer is D

A stronger currency will make your goods more expensive abroad, and imports cost less

8. **Tariffs are not used to _____:**

(Economic Growth and Productivity)

[A] increase tax revenues

[B] decrease import prices

[C] increase import prices

[D] mitigate the impact of dumping

[E] impose sanctions

The answer is B

Imposing a tariff will never decrease the price of imports

9. **Federal Reserve Open Market Operations means:**

(Inflation, Unemployment, and Stabilization Policies)

[A] Changing federal reserve ratio

[B] Buying and selling of federal debt to manage money supply and interest rates

[C] Printing money to cause inflation

[D] Changing tax rates

[E] Increasing government spending

The answer is B

OPO is the typical day-to-day activity of the Fed, and is used to maintain market stability

10. ____ will not cause an increase to a nation's current account :

(Open Economy: International Trade and Finance)

[A] Federal debt purchased by a foreign nation

[B] Exporting consumer goods

[C] Foreign tourists visiting

[D] Food aid from foreign nations

[E] Exporting agricultural goods

The answer is A

The current account is what people refer to when discussing trade deficits and trade surpluses; it deals with the exchange of goods

11. According to the International Fisher Effect, a 1% appreciation in nation A's currency relative to Nation B will result from:

(Open Economy: International Trade and Finance)

[A] A 1% increase in real interest rates relative to Nation B

[B] A 1% higher nominal interest to nation B

[C] A 1% lower nominal interest rate relative to Nation B

[D] A 1% increase in inflation relative to Nation B

[E] A 1% increase in exports to Nation B

The answer is C

IFE assumes a state of ceteris paribus, which is why it is used as a way to teach the basic mechanisms behind more complex calculations

12. A currency with PPP of 1 and exchange rate of 1/2 is considered:

(Open Economy: International Trade and Finance)

[A] Undervalued

[B] Overvalued

[C] Appreciated

[D] Depreciated

[E] In equilibrium

The answer is B

The intrinsic value of a currency is based in how much you can buy, so when an exchange rate goes much higher than the relative purchasing power, then it is considered overvalued

13. A fiat currency is:

(Open Economy: International Trade and Finance)

[A] Any item whose value is derived from its ability to be used as a measurement of value

[B] Any pegged currency

[C] Any currency subject to inflation

[D] Any floating currency

[E] Any currency currently in print

The answer is A

Fiat currencies have no functional value and can be easily transferred, which is what makes them useful as a measurement device

14. "Output is a function of capital" is indicative of:

(Economic Growth and Productivity)

[A] Solow-Swan model

[B] Harrod-Domar model

[C] Endogenous growth model

[D] Exogenous growth model

[E] Unified growth model

The answer is B

Harrod-Domar was the first growth model to gain popularity, but was too simplistic to be functional

15. "Growth is a function of capital and technology" is indicative of:

(Economic Growth and Productivity)

[A] AK model

[B] Exogenous growth model

[C] Solow-Swan model

[D] Harrod-Domar model

[E] Unified growth model

The answer is A

The AK model accounts for overall technological level using a constant

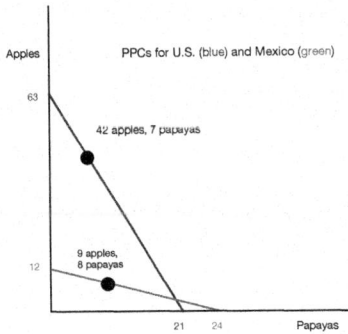

Apples

PPCs for U.S. (blue) and Mexico (green)

63

42 apples, 7 papayas

12

9 apples,
8 papayas

21 24   Papayas

16. Which nation has an absolute advantage:

(Basic Economic Concepts)

[A] US

[B] Mexico

[C] US in apples

[D] Mexico in papayas

[E] Mexico in apples

The answer is A

Absolute advantage just refers to which nation can produce the most total stuff and does not account for opportunity cost, proven by Ricardo to be the source of trade

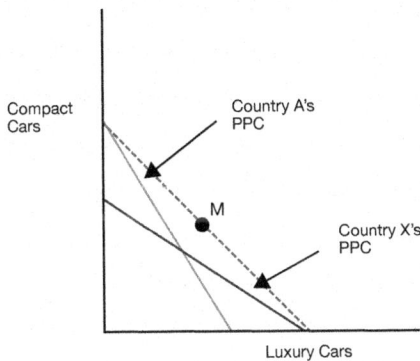

Compact
Cars

Country A's
PPC

M

Country X's
PPC

Luxury Cars

17. What is US's opportunity cost per papaya:

(Basic Economic Concepts)

[A] 0.33

[B] 3

[C] 63

[D] 21

[E] 2

The answer is B

The opportunity cost is the volume of good which must be given up to produce a unit of papaya

Apples

PPCs for U.S. (blue) and Mexico (green)

63

42 apples, 7 papayas

12

9 apples,
8 papayas

21   24

Papayas

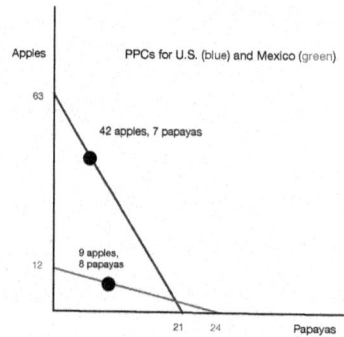

18. What is the maximum combined production with trade:

(Basic Economic Concepts)

[A] 24

[B] 90

[C] 63

[D] 66

[E] 49

The answer is B

With trade, each nation can produce more by reducing their opportunity costs

19. _____ would cause a supply curve to shift right:

(Basic Economic Concepts)

[A] Increased producer price index

[B] Shortages of raw materials

[C] Technological advancement

[D] Consumer demand

[E] Nothing

The answer is C

A right-shift in supply means producing more without raising prices, or producing the same at lower prices

20. A linear aggregate supply curve which starts at 0 and with point [$40 for 80 units] has a marginal price of:

(Basic Economic Concepts)

[A] $0.5

[B] $2

[C] $40

[D] $80

[E] $0

The answer is A

A linear curve will maintain the same margin

126   AP Macroeconomics/Microeconomics

Sample Test One

21. It is true that:

(Economic Growth and Productivity)

[A] Investment creates its own supply

[B] Supply creates its own demand

[C] Demand creates its own supply

[D] Supply creates its own investment

[E] Supply creates its own savings

The answer is C

There will always be someone ready to take your money

22. Lower consumption levels will:

(Inflation, Unemployment, and Stabilization Policies)

[A] Decrease company revenues, discouraging investment

[B] Increase savings, making more loanable funds available

[C] Create surplus supply, causing an immediate reduction in price

[D] Force investing in new innovations that people will want

[E] Be common during times of economic success

The answer is A

Investors are attracted to success and scared-off by failure

23. Increased inflation will:

(Inflation, Unemployment, and Stabilization Policies)

[A] Decrease exports

[B] Increase exports

[C] Increase imports

[D] Slow trade

[E] Slow economic growth

The answer is B

A decrease in foreign exchange rate makes your exports cheaper abroad

24. _____ **can cause monetary inflation:**

(Measurement of Economic Performance)

[A] Increased demand

[B] Birth of a natural monopoly

[C] Decreased money supply

[D] Reduction in federal reserve ratio

[E] Decreased taxation

The answer is D

Reducing the bank reserve ratio during an economic boom is a bad idea

25. _____ **causes frictional unemployment:**

(Measurement of Economic Performance)

[A] People changing jobs

[B] AS>AD

[C] Mismatch of labor demand and skills

[D] Wages below equilibrium

[E] Low inflation

The answer is A

"Friction" refers to reallocations of labor and resources in response to basic market changes

26. _____ **causes structural unemployment:**

(Measurement of Economic Performance)

[A] Low levels of inflation

[B] Wages below equilibrium

[C] AS>AD

[D] Mismatch of labor demand and skills

[E] People changing jobs

The answer is D

This is typical of technological advances and consumer preference changes

27. Stagflation is:

(Measurement of Economic Performance)

[A] A state of high unemployment and high inflation

[B] A state of high unemployment and low inflation

[C] A state of low unemployment and high inflation

[D] A state of low unemployment and low inflation

[E] Inflation in the market for stag pelts

The answer is A

"Stag" = Stagnation, "flation" = inflation

28. Full employment is:

(Measurement of Economic Performance)

[A] 2% unemployment

[B] A state wherein the entire labor for is actively employed

[C] A state wherein the entire population is actively employed

[D] A state wherein the entire labor force is actively employed or engaged in changing employment

[E] 0% unemployment

The answer is D

Even at full employment, a small percentage will still be unemployed just as a result of being a dynamic environment, rather than a static one

29. Monetary velocity is:

(Inflation, Unemployment, and Stabilization Policy)

[A] The speed with which money is created

[B] The amount of final income created from a stimulus package

[C] The number of times the same money changes hands, contributing to economic growth, within a time period

[D] Volume of foreign exchange transactions

[E] The rate of inflation created by monetary policy

The answer is C

Velocity is the speed of movement, and like a car, an economy is only useful when it's moving

30. Which tariff gives domestic companies an unfair advantage:

(Open Economy: International Trade and Finance)

[A] Domestic Price: $150

　　Foreign Price: $125

　　Tariff: 21%

[B] Domestic Price: $75

　　Foreign Price: $45

　　Tariff: 60%

[C] Domestic Price: $125

　　Foreign Price: $100

　　Tariff: 24%

[D] Domestic Price: $100

　　Foreign Price: $90

　　Tariff: 10%

[E] Domestic Price: $100

　　Foreign Price: $80

　　Tariff: 20%

The answer is A

Forcing foreign goods to be more expensive than domestic goods helps no one in the long-run

31. What is the relationship between federal deficit and federal debt:

(National Income and Price Determination)

[A] Federal deficit reduces the federal debt

[B] Federal debt causes an increase in the federal deficit

[C] Federal debt is used to fund deficit spending

[D] Federal deficit causes an increase in the federal debt

[E] There is no relationship

The answer is C

Only debt that generates more economic activity than the value of the interest costs is considered good debt.

32. Who is included as a part of the national labor force:

(National Income and Price Determination)

[A] People who were seriously injured on the job

[B] People who have given-up seeking employment

[C] People unemployed but seeking employment

[D] Children

[E] All of the above

The answer is C

Only people who are able and willing to work are part of the labor force, long-term employment causes people to give-up, and so post-recession unemployment numbers tend to be overly optimistic

33. A $10 tax return to an employee has a quarterly monetary velocity of 1.8, calculate how much economic growth it creates in 1 year:

(National Income and Price Determination)

[A] $18

[B] $10

[C] $72

[D] $40

[E] $22

The answer is C

Every time a single dollar changes hands, it creates economic growth – movement matters more than volume

34. Market shocks result from:

(Measurement of Economic Performance)

[A] Monetary mismanagement

[B] Volatility which lowers investor expectations

[C] Small, frequent change making production volume predictions difficult

[D] Fiscal mismanagement

[E] Sudden, large changes which impacts the economy more quickly than it can respond to those changes

The answer is E

A shock happens when the economy cannot respond to a large change

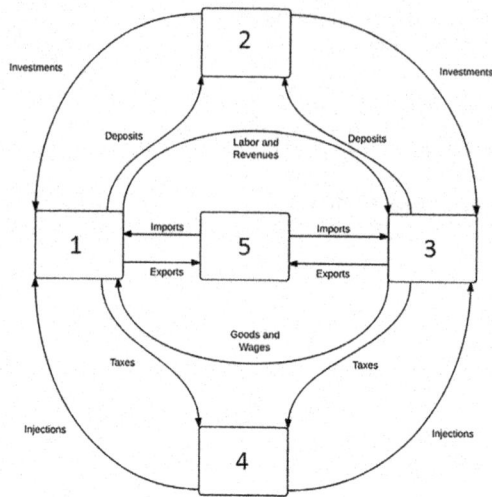

35. Sector 1 is:

(Measurement of Economic Performance)

[A] Financial

[B] Government

[C] Foreign

[D] Households

[E] Companies

The answer is D

Households are the driver of demand and growth

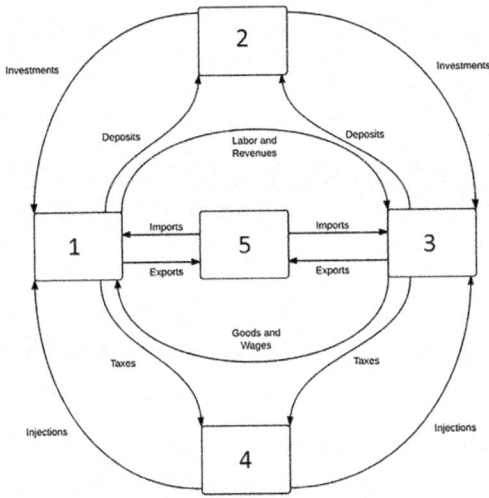

36. Sector 3 is:

(Measurement of Economic Performance)

[A] Households

[B] Companies

[C] Financial

[D] Foreign

[E] Government

The answer is B

Only companies pay wages, while also making deposits and paying taxes

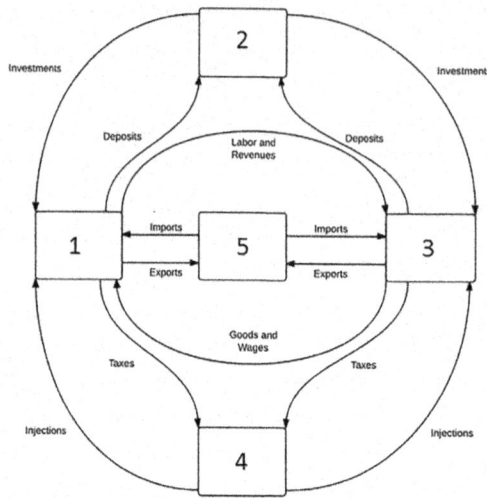

37. Sector 5 is:

(Measurement of Economic Performance)

[A] Foreign

[B] Financial

[C] Government

[D] Households

[E] Companies

The answer is A

Imports and exports are the domain of the foreign sector

38. A recession is formally defined as:

(National Income and Price Determination)

[A] Any period in which unemployment exceeds 5%

[B] Any period in which unemployment exceeds 7%

[C] Two consecutive quarters of negative GDP growth

[D] Any period greater than one quarter in which AS>AD

[E] Any period in which gross wages drop more than 5% for greater than one quarter

The answer is C

1 quarter of negative growth is usually considered a slump

39. **Aggregate demand, national income, and gross domestic product all share the same:**

    (National Income and Price Determination)

    [A] Income-based approach

    [B] Consumption-based approach

    [C] Mathematical formula

    [D] Production-based approach

    [E] Graphical model

The answer is C

They all measure the same thing but are used in different contexts

40. **Nominal rate = 5%, Inflation = 2%**

    Calculate real interest rate:

    (Financial Sector)

    [A] 2%

    [B] 2.5%

    [C] 10%

    [D] 3%

    [E] 7%

The answer is D

"Real" anything is the change in value after accounting for inflation

41. **Principle = $100,000**

    Rate = 0.005

    Time = 10 years

    Calculate the balance using continuously compounding interest:

    (Financial Sector)

    [A] $150,000

    [B] $105,000

    [C] $105,127

    [D] $150,127

    [E] $105,126

The answer is C

Pe^{rt}

42. NPV is calculated by:

(Financial Sector)

[A] Subtracting the sum of present values from the initial outlay

[B] Subtracting total returns from initial outlay

[C] Adding together all the cash flows on an investment

[D] Adding together all the present values on an investment

[E] Subtracting the sum of cash flows from the initial outlay

The answer is D

NPV stand for Net Present Value, which just means adding all the present values together

43. Fiscal policy is managed by _____ and monetary policy by _____:

(Financial Sector)

[A] federal reserve, Congress

[B] congress, federal reserve

[C] president, federal reserve

[D] federal reserve, president

[E] congress, president

The answer is B

Congress sets the budget for fiscal policy (or at least they're supposed to), and the Fed manages the volume and price of money

44. Government debt that matures in 1 year or less is:

(Financial Sector)

[A] Treasury Bond

[B] Treasury Note

[C] Treasury Bill

[D] Corporate Bond

[E] Stock

The answer is C

Bills mature in less than 1 year, making these investments very liquid, which is why they are considered the risk-free rate of return

45. ____ is a common method for slowing unsustainable rates of economic growth:

(Inflation, Unemployment, and Stabilization Policies)

[A] Increasing fiscal spending

[B] Decreasing interest rates

[C] Increasing bank reserve ratios

[D] Issuing a tax refund

[E] Depreciating foreign exchange rate

The answer is C

Increasing reserve ratios limit the supply of loanable funds, increasing interest rates

46. Banks earn the majority of their revenues by:

(Financial Sector)

[A] Charging fees and fines

[B] Borrowing money from deposits and then lending it to borrowers at a higher interest rate

[C] Buying investments and then reselling them through brokerage accounts

[D] Government benefits

[E] Laundering illegal funds earned through front-businesses

The answer is B

The difference between interest paid to depositors and interest earned on loans is called the spread

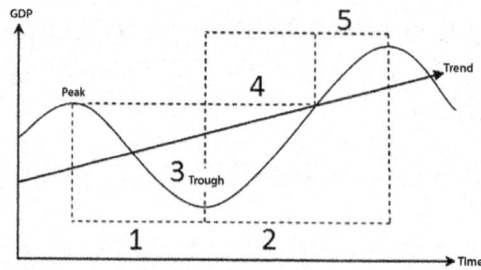

47. A period of _____ is shown at 2:

(National Income and Price Determination)

[A] Contraction

[B] Recession

[C] Expansion

[D] Boom

The answer is C

An expanding economy is one that is growing

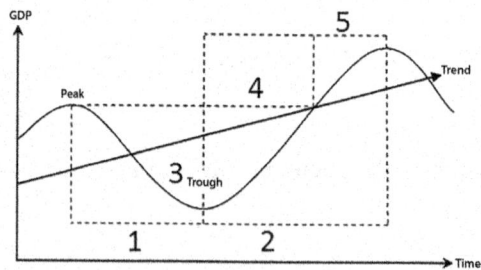

48. At 4, the economy is in _____:

(National Income and Price Determination)

[A] Boom

[B] Expansion

[C] Recovery

[D] Contraction

[E] Recession

The answer is C

Recovery occurs when the economy is growing but has not yet reached pre-recession levels

49. Economic terms include _____ and _____:

(Basic Economic Concepts)

[A] Socialism, capitalism

[B] Communism, capitalism

[C] Socialism, communism

[D] Capitalism, individualism

[E] Free market economy, planned economy

The answer is E

In economics, the degree of government influence on the economy is known as economic planning, and everything else is dictated by the free market

50. A grouping of large numbers of unlike things for the sake of measuring trends between them:

(Basic Economic Concepts)

[A] Macro

[B] Aggregate

[C] Statistic

[D] Bundle

[E] Economy

The answer is B

Aggregate is also a construction term referring to concrete, which includes unlike things such as cement, gravel, pebbles, and so forth to make something homogeneous

51. Purchasing bonds through OPO is most effective for growth when:

(Economic Growth)

[A] Reserve ratio is high and investments are high

[B] Reserve ratio is low and savings are high

[C] Reserve ratio is low and investments are high

[D] Reserve ratio is high and savings are low

[E] Reserve ratio is high and investments are low

The answer is C

When the reserve ratio is low, a greater amount of the available money supply can be borrowed by investors.

52. ___ and ___ can increase labor productivity:

(Economic Growth)

[A] Education, technology

[B] Education, population

[C] Employment, population

[D] Employment, technology

[E] Population, technology

The answer is A

Increased labor productivity depends on improvements in the production potential for the individual person, rather than changes in the size of the labor force

53. ___ decreases the exchange rate of the USD:

(Open Economy: International Trade and Finance)

[A] Lower domestic inflation rates

[B] Higher foreign inflation rates

[C] Lower foreign interest rates

[D] Higher foreign interest rates

[E] The Federal Reserve

The answer is C

When foreign interest rates are moved lower relative to the US it will cause their inflation rate to decrease, increasing the value of their currency relative to the USD on the forex market

54. Which will cause a $2.5 million decrease in the money supply:

(Financial Sector)

[A] $500,000 purchase of government securities at a 20% reserve ratio

[B] $500,000 sale of government securities at a 20% reserve ratio

[C] $200,000 sale of government securities at a 50% reserve ratio

[D] $250,000 sale of government securities at a 25% reserve ratio

[E] $200,000 purchase of government securities at a 50% reserve ratio

The answer is B

$500,000 is 20% of $2.5 million

55. An increase in labor productivity will:

(National Income and Price Determination)

[A] Increase AS

[B] Increase AD

[C] Decrease AS

[D] Decrease AD

[E] No change

The answer is A

Increased labor productivity comes from improvements in technology, including better capital and/or better methods

56. GDP = $___ trillion

Money supply = $___ trillion

Monetary velocity = ___:

(Economic Growth)

[A] 6, 2, 3

[B] 4, 1, 2

[C] 8, 4, 3

[D] 6, 2, 4

[E] 4, 8, 3

The answer is A

GDP = M1*V

57. Interest rates will most likely fall with _____ monetary policy and _____ fiscal policy:

(Inflation, Unemployment, and Stabilization Policies)

[A] contractionary, contractionary

[B] expansionary, expansionary

[C] expansionary, contractionary

[D] contractionary, expansionary

[E] nothing

The answer is C

Expansionary monetary policy includes reserve selling on OPO, increasing supply of money market assets; and contractionary fiscal policy involves lower investing, decreasing demand for those assets.

58. **Assume that US consumers increase their demand for Chinese Renminbi. This will cause:**

(Open Economy: International Trade and Finance)

USD Supply, RMB Value, Chinese Imports

[A] Increase, Increase, Decrease

[B] Increase, Increase, Increase

[C] Decrease, Increase, Increase

[D] Decrease, Decrease, Decrease

[E] No change, Increase, Increase

The answer is A

It would cause an increased demand for RMB, increasing its value while simultaneously flooding the market with cheap USD, resulting in a relative increase in the price of Chinese goods.

59. **Nominal GDP growth is -2%**

Real GDP growth is 4%

The nation is experiencing ___ with an inflation rate of ____

(Measurement of Economic Performance)

[A] Recession, 4%

[B] Stagflation, -6%

[C] Stagflation, 4%

[D] Recession, 6%

[E] Boom, -6%

The answer is B

If real GDP grows while nominal GDP shrinks, then there must be deflation

60. The depreciation of USD on the forex market?

(Open Economy: International Trade and Finance)

[A] Decreases the balance of payments surplus if export elasticity is high

[B] Increases the balance of payments surplus if import elasticity is low

[C] Decreases the balance of payments deficit if export elasticity is low

[D] Increases the balance of payments deficit if export elasticity is low

[E] Increases the balance of payments surplus if export elasticity is high

The answer is D

A depreciating US dollar makes foreign goods more expensive, but also makes US goods cheaper overseas; the impact on the balance of payments depends on the elasticity of imports and exports

AP
MACROECONOMICS
Sample Test 2

Multiple Choice Questions

1. ___ will not cause an increase to the capital account:

   (Open Economy: International Trade and Finance)

   [A] Foreign investment in corporate bonds

   [B] Direct investment into foreign nations

   [C] Foreign investment in government bonds

   [D] Importing consumer goods

   [E] Importing agricultural goods

2. The light-hearted measurement of purchasing power parity is called:

   (Open Economy: International Trade and Finance)

   [A] Fast Food Index

   [B] White Castle Index

   [C] Burger Index

   [D] Whopper Index

   [E] Big Mac Index

3. A tax on imported cars that begins after the first 5,000 is an example of:

   (Open Economy: International Trade and Finance)

   [A] Tariff-rate quota

   [B] Quota by unit

   [C] Quota by weight

   [D] Tariff

   [E] Embargo

4. A currency with PPP of 1 and exchange rate of 3/1 is considered:

   (Open Economy: International Trade and Finance)

   [A] Overvalued

   [B] Undervalued

   [C] In equilibrium

   [D] Appreciated

   [E] Depreciated

5. Nation B's currency is pegged to Nation A; if Nation A's currency strengthens 10% more than Nation B, then to maintain stability Nation B must:

(Open Economy: International Trade and Finance)

[A] End the peg

[B] Appreciate

[C] Depreciate

[D] Revalue

[E] Devalue

6. The AK model is a simple example of:

(Economic Growth and Productivity)

[A] Endogenous growth model

[B] Solow-Swan model

[C] Harrod-Domar model

[D] Exogenous growth model

[E] Unified growth model

7. "Growth is a function of capital and labor" is indicative of:

(Economic Growth and Productivity)

[A] Solow-Swan model

[B] Harrod-Domar model

[C] Endogeous growth model

[D] Exogenous growth model

[E] Unified growth model

8. An increase in supply without an increase in demand will:

(Inflation, Unemployment, and Stabilization Policy)

[A] Increase unemployment until surplus inventories and capacity are absorbed

[B] Increase unemployment in the short-run

[C] Decrease unemployment in the long-run

[D] Decrease unemployment in the short-run

[E] Increase unemployment until inflation slows

9. **Technological progress:**

(Economic Growth and Productivity)

[A] Replaces human capital

[B] Shifts the production possibilities curve left

[C] Decreases employment

[D] Increases employment

[E] Increases per capita production potential

10. **Knowledge Spillover is:**

(Economic Growth and Productivity)

[A] Increased production potential resulting from shared information between non-competitors

[B] Leaked industry secrets

[C] Unemployment from surplus human capital

[D] The result of investing in technology too quickly

[E] Gains from increased competition resulting from expired patents

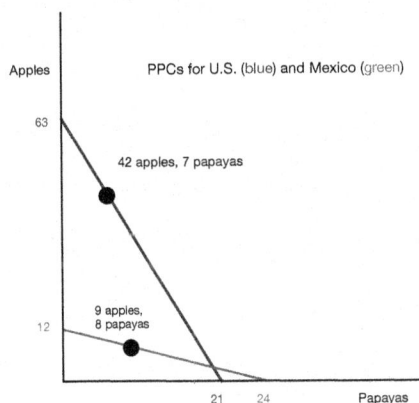

PPCs for U.S. (blue) and Mexico (green)

Apples

63

42 apples, 7 papayas

9 apples, 8 papayas

12

21   24   Papayas

11. **What is Mexico's opportunity cost per papaya:**

(Basic Economic Concepts)

[A] 0.5

[B] 2

[C] 12

[D] 24

[E] 0.33

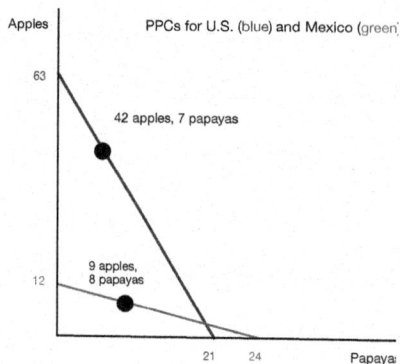

Apples

PPCs for U.S. (blue) and Mexico (green)

63

42 apples, 7 papayas

12

9 apples,
8 papayas

21   24   Papayas

12. What is the maximum combined production without trade:

(Basic Economic Concepts)

[A] 90

[B] 24

[C] 63

[D] 49

[E] 66

13. _____ would cause a demand curve to shift right:

(Basic Economic Concepts)

[A] Drought

[B] Increased median income

[C] Increased unemployment

[D] Inflation

[E] Overproduction

14. Long-run aggregate supply is:

(Basic Economic Concepts)

[A] Increasing with price

[B] The same at all price levels

[C] Decreasing with price

[D] Drops to 0 at any price other than equilibrium

[E] The same as short-run aggregate supply

15. Economics only matters because of:

(Basic Economic Concepts)

[A] Banks

[B] Government

[C] Trade

[D] Money

[E] Scarcity

16. **The New Deal was created to:**

(Inflation, Unemployment, and Stabilization Policies)

[A] End the Great Depression through conscripted labor

[B] End the Great Depression by increasing aggregate supply

[C] End the Great Depression by stimulating consumption through social investment

[D] Stimulate competition by providing companies with funds to invest

[E] Stimulate competition by breaking-up large companies called trusts

17. **The Square Deal was created to:**

(Inflation, Unemployment, and Stabilization Policies)

[A] End the Great Depression

[B] Stimulate competition by breaking-up large companies called trusts

[C] Reduce taxation

[D] Reduce the federal deficit

[E] Fund infrastructure development

18. **Decreased unemployment will:**

(Inflation, Unemployment, and Stabilization Policies)

[A] Have no influence on inflation

[B] Decrease inflation

[C] Increase inflation

[D] Decrease the amount of inflationary pressure

[E] Increase the amount of inflationary pressure

19. **_____ is an example of cost-push inflation:**

(Measurement of Economic Performance)

[A] Drought making agricultural production more expensive

[B] Production of new consumer products at higher prices

[C] Increased income driving demand higher

[D] Increased money supply driving money value down

[E] High interest rates reducing demand for money

20. ____ **can cause demand-pull inflation:**

(Measurement of Economic Performance)

[A] High interest rates

[B] Birth of a natural monopoly

[C] Population boom

[D] Increased taxation

[E] Increased money supply

21. ____ **causes cyclical unemployment:**

(Measurement of Economic Performance)

[A] Wages below equilibrium

[B] AD<AS

[C] Mismatch of labor demand and skills

[D] Low inflation

[E] People changing jobs

22. Phillips Curve states that:

(Measurement of Economic Performance)

[A] Unemployment and inflation are direct opposites

[B] High unemployment increases inflation

[C] High inflation increases unemployment

[D] Unemployment and inflation put inverse pressure on each other but are not direct opposites

[E] There is no relationship between inflation and unemployment

23. NAIRU states that:

(Measurement of Economic Performance)

[A] In the long-run, the labor markets will adjust to any rate of inflation to return to the natural rate of unemployment

[B] Inflation will accelerate at unemployment levels above natural

[C] Full employment will be reached at 0% inflation

[D] Unemployment and inflation are inversely related

[E] Unemployment and inflation are directly related

24. _____ and _____ unemployment are still seen during full employment:

(Measurement of Economic Performance)

[A] Structural, frictional

[B] Structural, cyclical

[C] Frictional, cyclical

[D] Cyclical, full

[E] No unemployment exists at full unemployment

25. **The multiplier effect:**

(Inflation, Unemployment, and Stabilization Policy)

[A] The amount of final income created from a stimulus package

[B] The number of times the same money changes hands, contributing to economic growth, within a time period

[C] The amount by which GDP multiplies in response to policy

[D] The amount that employment increases in response to increased spending resulting from initial employment stimulus

[E] The increase in monetary velocity created by monetary inflation

26. **Long-term NAIRU stabilization is possible due to:**

(Measurement of Economic Performance)

[A] Policies developed to reduce unemployment

[B] Policies developed to reduce inflation

[C] Expectations of inflation allowing a return to the natural rate of unemployment

[D] AS = AD

[E] Price stickiness

27. **A $100,000 economic stimulus package with a multiplier of 5 shows a MPC of _____:**

(Inflation, Unemployment, and Stabilization Policy)

[A] 8

[B] 2

[C] 0.5

[D] 0.2

[E] 0.8

28. A deficit of $100,000 funded with 20-year bonds at 1% will have a total nominal cost of _____ for taxpayers:

(National Income and Price Determination)

[A] $100,000

[B] $120,000

[C] $1,000

[D] $20,000

[E] $250,000

29. Which is not a measurement of inflation:

(Measures of Economic Growth and Productivity)

[A] Purchasing power parity

[B] Foreign exchange rates

[C] Producer Price Index

[D] Consumer Price Index

[E] GDP growth

30. The components of GDP by expenditure are:

(Measures of Economic Growth and Productivity)

[A] Y+P+R

[B] C+I+G+(X-M)

[C] GNP+NNI

[D] C+I+G+(M-X)

[E] C+I+G+(X+M)

31. The process of the state taking over industries and businesses is called:

(Basic Economic Concepts)

[A] Industrialization

[B] Nationalization

[C] Redistribution

[D] Amalgamation

[E] Reclamation

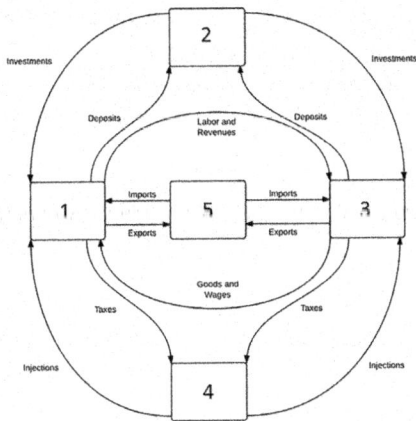

32. Sector 2 is:

(Measurement of Economic Performance)

[A] Households

[B] Foreign

[C] Financial

[D] Government

[E] Companies

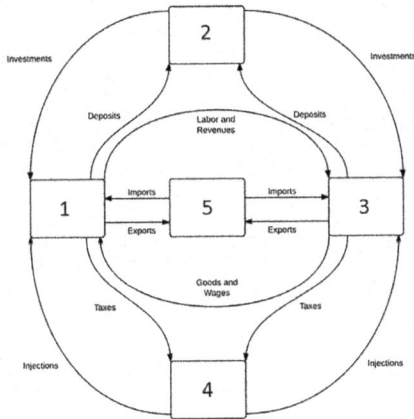

33. Sector 4 is:

(Measurement of Economic Performance)

[A] Government

[B] Financial

[C] Foreign

[D] Companies

[E] Households

34. Any period of time in which the economy cannot fully respond to a change, typically determined by the replacement of large capital, is:

(National Income and Price Determination)

[A] Long-term

[B] Short-term

[C] Medium-term

[D] Time value

[E] Business cycle

35. When government spending or investment impose-upon or hinder private spending or investment, it is:

(Inflation, Unemployment, and Stabilization Policies)

[A] Multiplier

[B] Privatization

[C] Nationalization

[D] Crowding out

[E] Municipalization

36. Principle = $100,000

Rate = 0.005

Time = 10 years

Calculate the balance using simple interest:

(Financial Sector)

[A] $5,000,000

[B] $5,000

[C] $105,000

[D] $150,000

[E] $50,000

37. Future value = $100,000

Rate = 0.005

Time = 10 years

Calculate present value:

(Financial Sector)

[A] $95,140

[B] $95,135

[C] $95,130

[D] $105,000

[E] $100,000

38. Monetary policy includes managing the _____ and _____ of money:

(Financial Sector)

[A] supply and price

[B] supply and velocity

[C] price and multiplier

[D] velocity and multiplier

[E] price and velocity

39. The Gold Standard:

(Financial Sector)

[A] Was highly successful

[B] Relied on the intrinsic value of gold to define the US economy

[C] Used gold as a fiat currency to which the dollar was pegged

[D] Did not create limitations on monetary policy

[E] Resolved the currency war between European and North American countries

40. The value of money is derived from:

(Financial Sector)

[A] The amount of hard assets owned by a country

[B] The ability to purchase things, backed by the production which is measured using that currency

[C] Supply and demand of currency markets

[D] Government promises of debt repayment

[E] Nowhere – it is valueless

41. With money supply of $100,000 at equilibrium with production, a $10,000 nominal increase in production with no change in money supply will result in:

(Inflation, Unemployment, and Stabilization Policies)

[A] Deflation of 10%

[B] Inflation of 10%

[C] No inflation

[D] Inflation of 90%

[E] Deflation of 5%

42. Aggregate supply, production possibilities curve, and economic growth all share the same:

(National Income and Price Determination)

[A] Factors

[B] Equation

[C] Usage

[D] Graphs

[E] Model

43. The market efficiency hypothesis fails as a result of:

(National Income and Price Determination)

[A] Sticky prices and wages

[B] Imperfect information

[C] Fixed nature of large capital

[D] A, B, and C

[E] Nothing, the market is efficient

44. Delayed response to sudden price changes by companies using LIFO inventory management is an example of:

(National Income and Price Determination)

[A] Price stickiness

[B] Price Rigidity

[C] Price flexibility

[D] Imperfect information

[E] Cost stickiness

45. A corporation with 10 million shares outstanding with share price of $2 has a total market capitalization of:

(Financial Sector)

[A] $20 million

[B] $10 million

[C] $5 million

[D] $200,000

[E] $15 million

46. The Federal Reserve lends money to _____ at the _____ rate:

(Financial Sector)

[A] anyone, discount

[B] corporations, federal funds

[C] individuals, federal funds

[D] banks, federal funds

[E] banks, discount

47. Long-Run Aggregate Supply is:

(National Income and Price Determination)

[A] The same vertical line as NAIRU

[B] The curve showing how much a nation can produce at a given price level at some point in time

[C] The maximum production potential of a nation at any price level

[D] Perfectly price elastic

[E] Representative of actual production rather than full-employment production

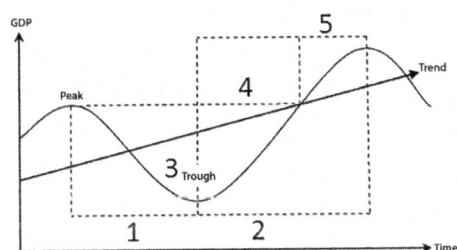

48. A period of _____ is shown at 1:

(National Income and Price Determination)

[A] expansion

[B] contraction

[C] recession

[D] recovery

[E] boom

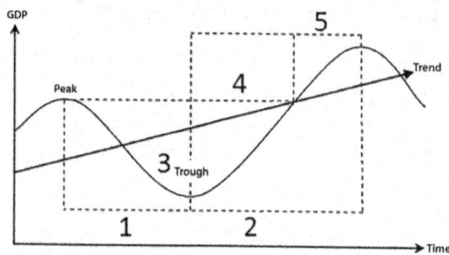

49. A _____ has been reached at 3:

(National Income and Price Determination)

[A] Contraction

[B] Recession

[C] Expansion

[D] Recovery

[E] Boom

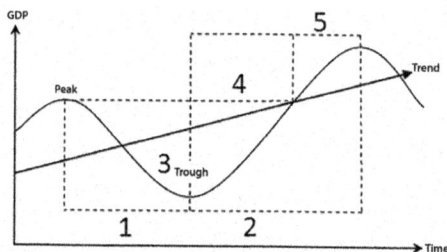

50. At 5, the economy is in a _____:

(National Income and Price Determination)

[A] recession

[B] boom

[C] contraction

[D] recovery

[E] expansion

51. CPI increases from 100 to 150, and GDP increases from $500,000 to $600,000, which means that:

(Measurements of Economic Performance)

[A] GDP grew by 20% which is 30% less than CPI indicating 10% economic contraction

[B] Prices increased by 50% indicating that GDP grew by 10% rather than 20%

[C] Prices increased by 30% more than GDP indicating equivalent economic contraction

[D] GDP grew by 16% but real GDP was only 8% due to 50% inflation

[E] GDP decreased by 70%

52. LRAS increases as:

(National Income and Price Determination)

[A] Prices increases

[B] SRAS responds to deviations from equilibrium

[C] Technology improves

[D] LRAD increases

[E] LRAS never increases

53.

	Fish	Wheat
A	15 labor hr	10 labor hr
B	20 labor hr	60 labor hr

Country A has a __ opportunity cost in its comparative advantage, and Country B has a __ opportunity cost in its comparative advantage:

(Basic Economic Concepts)

[A] 1/4, 2/3

[B] 2/3, 3/4

[C] 1/2, 1/4

[D] 2/3, 1/3

[E] 1/3, 2/3

54. Quantitative easing attempts to do the following:

(Inflation, Unemployment, and Stabilization Policies)

Real Interest Rates, Investment

[A] Decrease, Decrease

[B] Decrease, Increase

[C] No change, Increase

[D] Increase, No Change

[E] No change, Increase

55. Stimulus increase = $500,000

Income increase = $2 million

MPC = __:

(Economic Growth)

[A] 0.25

[B] 0.5

[C] 0.75

[D] 0.33

[E] 0.66

56. If the government increases expenditures and increases taxation by the same amount, AD will increase if:

(Growth Policy)

[A] Taxation is greater than expenditures

[B] Expenditures are greater than taxation

[C] Expenditures stimulate growth greater than the opportunity cost

[D] Expenditures do not rely on increasing national debt

[E] Cannot be determined using the available information

57. Buying government securities on OPO is a method used by the Fed to:

(Inflation, Unemployment, and Stabilization Policies)

[A] Slow GDP growth to sustainable levels

[B] Prevent budget deficits

[C] Strengthen the dollar

[D] Prevent inflation

[E] Alleviate a recession

58. **What effect will an decrease in the global energy production have on CPI and real GDP:**

(National Income and Price Determination)

Real GDP, CPI

[A] Decrease, Decrease

[B] Decrease, Increase

[C] Increase, Increase

[D] Increase, No Change

[E] Decrease, Increase

59. **If both monetary and fiscal policies are contractionary, then the following is guaranteed to happen:**

(Inflation, Unemployment, and Stabilization Policies)

Interest Rates, Unemployment

[A] Increase, Indeterminate

[B] Increase, Decrease

[C] Decrease, Decrease

[D] Indeterminate, Indeterminate

[E] Indeterminate, Increase

60. **___ will cause a decrease in the volume of commercial funds available for loans:**

(Economic Growth)

[A] Increase in sale of federal loans

[B] A decrease in the reserve ratio

[C] An increase in savings

[D] A decrease in investing

[E] An increase in exports

1. National debt stuff

[A] Reinhart and Rogoff showed a correlation between lower GDP growth and national debt levels greater than 90% GDP

   (i)   Explain the conclusion they came to using these results

   (ii)   Explain the causational error they made between these two things

   (iii)   Explain how these two things are related as per time-series analyses contradicting the conclusions of Reinhart and Rogoff

[B] Consider debt and deficit

   (i)   Describe the relationship between national debt and fiscal deficit

   (ii)   Explain the function of a debt ceiling

[C] Choose one model of economic growth and name it

   (i)   What does this model say is the source of economic growth? Why?

   (ii)   What is the role of fiscal policy within the context of this model?

[D] Consider the size and composition of national debt

   (i)   What traits must debt spending exhibit to be considered "good debt"? Why is it beneficial to taxpayers?

   (ii)   What are the traits of "bad debt"? Why is it considered toxic?

   (iii)   How is the interest rate determined on government debt?

2. Nation A and Nation B are trade partners with a 1/1 exchange rate and PPP of 1.

[A] Nation A increases its interest rates 2%, and Nation B does not change

   (i)   According to the International Fisher Effect, what will happen to the exchange rates between these two nations? Why?

   (ii)   Assuming the conditions of the Marshall-Lerner condition are met, what will the impact from your answer in part [A](i) have on the balance of payments

(iii) If Nation B's currency is pegged to Nation A, then given your answer to part [A](i), calculate the difference between exchange rate and purchasing power parity. Is Nation B's currency overvalue, undervalued, or at market equilibrium?

[B] Nation A and Nation B both decide to peg their currencies to gold and have a currency war

    (i)   What will happen between each nation's currencies relative to the other during this time?

    (ii)   How will this differ from a currency war between floating currencies?

    (iii) What is the effect of a currency war on trade between the warring nations? What about the effect on uninvolved nations?

3. **Nation A can produce 75 beer or 35 pizza or any combination of linear opportunity cost. Nation B can produce 50 beer or 70 pizza or any combination of linear opportunity cost.**

[A] Draw the production possibilities curve of each assuming a constant opportunity cost and properly label them

    (i)   In an index, calculate each nation's opportunity cost ratio

    (ii)   In the same index, list which nation has the absolute advantage, and which nation has a comparative advantage in each product

[B] Create a grid demonstrating the maximum total production volume between the two nations without trade, and with trade.

    (i)   How many more of each product can be produced when the two nations trade with each other compared to when they don't trade

    (ii)   How much of either good will each nation import?

    (iii) Using your answer from part [B](ii), quantitatively describe each nation's current and capital accounts in the balance of payments

    (iv) Calculate the terms of trade and explain what it means

[C] Qualitatively explain what will happen to production and trade if Nation A implements a 10% tariff on imports from Nation B.

[D] How do the principles of international trade apply to exchanges in domestic commerce?

    (i)   How does division of labor relate to comparative advantage?

    (ii)   Why does the individual competitive advantages of a nation's firms translate into an international comparative advantage?

    (iii) What does this mean for protectionist trade policy?

AP Macroeconomics: Sample Test 2- Answer Key

Question Number	Correct Answer	Your Answer		Question Number	Correct Answer	Your Answer
1	B			31	B	
2	E			32	C	
3	A			33	A	
4	B			34	B	
5	E			35	D	
6	A			36	C	
7	A			37	B	
8	A			38	A	
9	E			39	C	
10	A			40	B	
11	A			41	A	
12	E			42	A	
13	B			43	D	
14	B			44	A	
15	E			45	A	
16	C			46	D	
17	B			47	C	
18	E			48	B	
19	A			49	B	
20	C			50	B	
21	B			51	C	
22	A			52	C	
23	A			53	D	
24	A			54	C	
25	A			55	C	
26	C			56	E	
27	E			57	E	
28	B			58	E	
29	E			59	D	
30	B			60	A	

Multiple Choice Questions

1. ____ **will not cause an increase to the capital account:**

(Open Economy: International Trade and Finance)

[A] Foreign investment in corporate bonds

[B] Direct investment into foreign nations

[C] Foreign investment in government bonds

[D] Importing consumer goods

[E] Importing agricultural goods

The answer is B

The capital account is sometimes called the financial account, and deals with investments

2. The light-hearted measurement of purchasing power parity is called:

(Open Economy: International Trade and Finance)

[A] Fast Food Index

[B] White Castle Index

[C] Burger Index

[D] Whopper Index

[E] Big Mac Index

The answer is E

The Economist (a magazine) used the price of a Big Mac in every country as a way to assess the purchasing power of that currency; more serious indices use a "basket" of goods

3. **A tax on imported cars that begins after the first 5,000 is an example of:**

   (Open Economy: International Trade and Finance)

   [A] Tariff-rate quota

   [B] Quota by unit

   [C] Quota by weight

   [D] Tariff

   [E] Embargo

The answer is A

Tariff-rate quotas charge a tariff against a type of good only after a threshold volume for that good has been imported

4. **A currency with PPP of 1 and exchange rate of 3/1 is considered:**

   (Open Economy: International Trade and Finance)

   [A] Overvalued

   [B] Undervalued

   [C] In equilibrium

   [D] Appreciated

   [E] Depreciated

The answer is B

The intrinsic value of a currency is based in how much you can buy, so when an exchange rate goes much lower than the relative purchasing power, then it is considered undervalued

5. **Nation B's currency is pegged to Nation A; if Nation A's currency strengthens 10% more than Nation B, then to maintain stability Nation B must:**

   (Open Economy: International Trade and Finance)

   [A] End the peg

   [B] Appreciate

   [C] Depreciate

   [D] Revalue

   [E] Devalue

The answer is E

Without adjusting the pegged rate, the pegged value of the currency will deviate too greatly from the market value, causing problems

6. **The AK model is a simple example of:**
   (*Economic Growth and Productivity*)

   [A] Endogenous growth model

   [B] Solow-Swan model

   [C] Harrod-Domar model

   [D] Exogenous growth model

   [E] Unified growth model

The answer is A

Endogenous models state that growth comes from within

7. **"Growth is a function of capital and labor" is indicative of:**
   (*Economic Growth and Productivity*)

   [A] Solow-Swan model

   [B] Harrod-Domar model

   [C] Endogeous growth model

   [D] Exogenous growth model

   [E] Unified growth model

The answer is A

Solow-Swan expands on the Harrod-Domar model by separating labor from total capital

8. **An increase in supply without an increase in demand will:**
   (Inflation, Unemployment, and Stabilization Policy)

   [A] Increase unemployment until surplus inventories and capacity are absorbed

   [B] Increase unemployment in the short-run

   [C] Decrease unemployment in the long-run

   [D] Decrease unemployment in the short-run

   [E] Increase unemployment until inflation slows

The answer is A

AS>AD results in cyclical unemployment and recessions; growth must be grounded in demand

9. **Technological progress:**

(Economic Growth and Productivity)

[A] Replaces human capital

[B] Shifts the production possibilities curve left

[C] Decreases employment

[D] Increases employment

[E] Increases per capita production potential

The answer is E

Better technology means we can produce more stuff per person

10. **Knowledge Spillover is:**

(Economic Growth and Productivity)

[A] Increased production potential resulting from shared information between non-competitors

[B] Leaked industry secrets

[C] Unemployment from surplus human capital

[D] The result of investing in technology too quickly

[E] Gains from increased competition resulting from expired patents

The answer is A

When a lot of people of the same trade come together to share information, innovation occurs more quickly, hence the popularity of trade shows

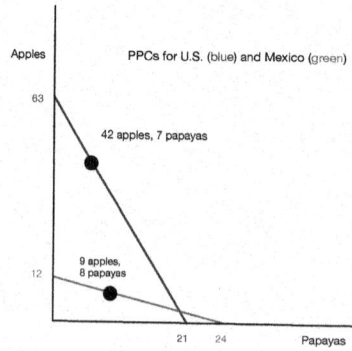

Apples

PPCs for U.S. (blue) and Mexico (green)

63

42 apples, 7 papayas

12

9 apples,
8 papayas

21   24

Papayas

11. What is Mexico's opportunity cost per papaya:

(Basic Economic Concepts)

[A] 0.5

[B] 2

[C] 12

[D] 24

[E] 0.33

The answer is A

The opportunity cost is the volume of good which must be given up to produce a unit of papaya

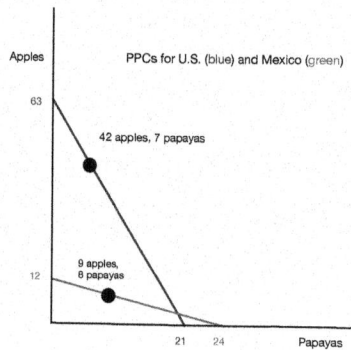

Apples

PPCs for U.S. (blue) and Mexico (green)

63

42 apples, 7 papayas

12

9 apples,
8 papayas

21   24

Papayas

12. What is the maximum combined production without trade:

(Basic Economic Concepts)

[A] 90

[B] 24

[C] 63

[D] 49

[E] 66

The answer is E

Without trade, each nation must produce their own goods, including those which are more expensive to produce than others

13. _____ would cause a demand curve to shift right:

(Basic Economic Concepts)

[A] Drought

[B] Increased median income

[C] Increased unemployment

[D] Inflation

[E] Overproduction

The answer is B

A right-shift in demand means people can afford to buy more stuff

14. Long-run aggregate supply is:

(Basic Economic Concepts)

[A] Increasing with price

[B] The same at all price levels

[C] Decreasing with price

[D] Drops to 0 at any price other than equilibrium

[E] The same as short-run aggregate supply

The answer is B

In the long-run, any price can be adjusted to

15. Economics only matters because of:

(Basic Economic Concepts)

[A] Banks

[B] Government

[C] Trade

[D] Money

[E] Scarcity

The answer is E

Without scarcity, we wouldn't be concerned with the manner in which we distribute resources

16. The New Deal was created to:

(Inflation, Unemployment, and Stabilization Policies)

[A] End the Great Depression through conscripted labor

[B] End the Great Depression by increasing aggregate supply

[C] End the Great Depression by stimulating consumption through social investment

[D] Stimulate competition by providing companies with funds to invest

[E] Stimulate competition by breaking-up large companies called trusts

The answer is C

It was created by Franklin Roosevelt to bolster spending in order to deplete surplus inventories and put people back to work

17. The Square Deal was created to:

(Inflation, Unemployment, and Stabilization Policies)

[A] End the Great Depression

[B] Stimulate competition by breaking-up large companies called trusts

[C] Reduce taxation

[D] Reduce the federal deficit

[E] Fund infrastructure development

The answer is B

It was created by Teddy Roosevelt, giving birth to anti-trust laws

18. Decreased unemployment will:

(Inflation, Unemployment, and Stabilization Policies)

[A] Have no influence on inflation

[B] Decrease inflation

[C] Increase inflation

[D] Decrease the amount of inflationary pressure

[E] Increase the amount of inflationary pressure

The answer is E

Since there are many types of inflation and unemployment, one will have an influence on the other but not cause an immediate, direct change

19. ____ is an example of cost-push inflation:

(Measurement of Economic Performance)

[A] Drought making agricultural production more expensive

[B] Production of new consumer products at higher prices

[C] Increased income driving demand higher

[D] Increased money supply driving money value down

[E] High interest rates reducing demand for money

The answer is A

Base goods like agriculture and energy influence the prices of an entire economy

20. ____ can cause demand-pull inflation:

(Measurement of Economic Performance)

[A] High interest rates

[B] Birth of a natural monopoly

[C] Population boom

[D] Increased taxation

[E] Increased money supply

The answer is C

More people leads to more demand

21. ____ causes cyclical unemployment:

(Measurement of Economic Performance)

[A] Wages below equilibrium

[B] AD<AS

[C] Mismatch of labor demand and skills

[D] Low inflation

[E] People changing jobs

The answer is B

Cyclical unemployment is what leads to recessions

22. Phillips Curve states that:

(Measurement of Economic Performance)

[A] Unemployment and inflation are direct opposites

[B] High unemployment increases inflation

[C] High inflation increases unemployment

[D] Unemployment and inflation put inverse pressure on each other but are not direct opposites

[E] There is no relationship between inflation and unemployment

The answer is A

Phillips was wrong

23. NAIRU states that:

(Measurement of Economic Performance)

[A] In the long-run, the labor markets will adjust to any rate of inflation to return to the natural rate of unemployment

[B] Inflation will accelerate at unemployment levels above natural

[C] Full employment will be reached at 0% inflation

[D] Unemployment and inflation are inversely related

[E] Unemployment and inflation are directly related

The answer is A

NAIRU = Non-accelerating inflationary rate of unemployment, which can make you sound like a genius at parties

24. _____ and _____ unemployment are still seen during full employment:

(Measurement of Economic Performance)

[A] Structural, frictional

[B] Structural, cyclical

[C] Frictional, cyclical

[D] Cyclical, full

[E] No unemployment exists at full unemployment

The answer is A

People still change jobs and need to learn new skills

25. The multiplier effect:

(Inflation, Unemployment, and Stabilization Policy)

[A] The amount of final income created from a stimulus package

[B] The number of times the same money changes hands, contributing to economic growth, within a time period

[C] The amount by which GDP multiplies in response to policy

[D] The amount that employment increases in response to increased spending resulting from initial employment stimulus

[E] The increase in monetary velocity created by monetary inflation

The answer is A

Higher MPC causes elevated monetary velocity, allowing for a higher multiplier, which is why economic stimulus is more effective when directed at the poor

26. Long-term NAIRU stabilization is possible due to:

(Measurement of Economic Performance)

[A] Policies developed to reduce unemployment

[B] Policies developed to reduce inflation

[C] Expectations of inflation allowing a return to the natural rate of unemployment

[D] AS = AD

[E] Price stickiness

The answer is C

When companies and labor account for a given stable inflation rate, then unemployment will also stabilize, all other things being equal

27. A $100,000 economic stimulus package with a multiplier of 5 shows a MPC of _____:

(Inflation, Unemployment, and Stabilization Policy)

[A] 8

[B] 2

[C] 0.5

[D] 0.2

[E] 0.8

The answer is E

Marginal propensity to consume is the ratio of income spent rather than saved

28. A deficit of **$100,000 funded with 20-year bonds at 1% will have a total nominal cost of** _____ **for taxpayers:**

(National Income and Price Determination)

[A] $100,000

[B] $120,000

[C] $1,000

[D] $20,000

[E] $250,000

The answer is B

Taxes pay not only expenditures but also interest costs

29. Which is not a measurement of inflation:

(Measures of Economic Growth and Productivity)

[A] Purchasing power parity

[B] Foreign exchange rates

[C] Producer Price Index

[D] Consumer Price Index

[E] GDP growth

The answer is E

GDP measures growth, real GDP accounts for inflation but still measures growth

30. The components of GDP by expenditure are:

(Measures of Economic Growth and Productivity)

[A] Y+P+R

[B] C+I+G+(X-M)

[C] GNP+NNI

[D] C+I+G+(M-X)

[E] C+I+G+(X+M)

The answer is B

(X-M), exports less imports, is called net exports

31. The process of the state taking over industries and businesses is called:

(Basic Economic Concepts)

[A] Industrialization

[B] Nationalization

[C] Redistribution

[D] Amalgamation

[E] Reclamation

The answer is B

Nationalization is a type of economic seizure

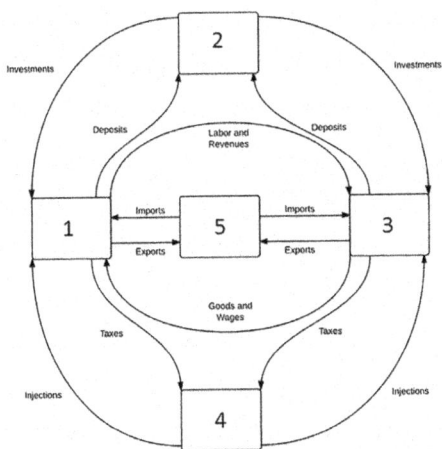

32. Sector 2 is:

(Measurement of Economic Performance)

[A] Households

[B] Foreign

[C] Financial

[D] Government

[E] Companies

The answer is C

Investments and deposits are the domain of the financial sector

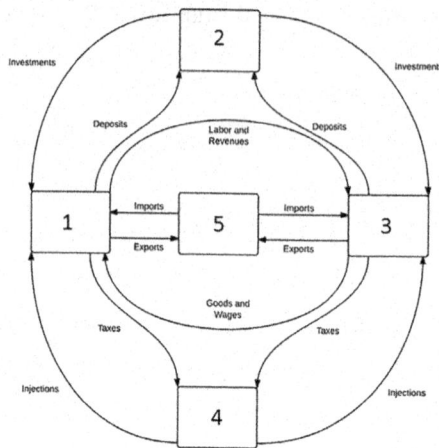

33. Sector 4 is:

(Measurement of Economic Performance)

[A] Government

[B] Financial

[C] Foreign

[D] Companies

[E] Households

The answer is A

Injections and taxes are the realm of the government sector

34. Any period of time in which the economy cannot fully respond to a change, typically determined by the replacement of large capital, is:

(National Income and Price Determination)

[A] Long-term

[B] Short-term

[C] Medium-term

[D] Time value

[E] Business cycle

The answer is B

It's difficult to replace property, plants, or equipment, so any economic response that requires a change to these things will have an extended short-term period

35. When government spending or investment impose-upon or hinder private spending or investment, it is:

(Inflation, Unemployment, and Stabilization Policies)

[A] Multiplier

[B] Privatization

[C] Nationalization

[D] Crowding out

[E] Municipalization

The answer is D

Crowding-out does not mean the government is taking over private industry, but rather replacing it

36. Principle = $100,000

Rate = 0.005

Time = 10 years

Calculate the balance using simple interest:

(Financial Sector)

[A] $5,000,000

[B] $5,000

[C] $105,000

[D] $150,000

[E] $50,000

The answer is C

$P(1+r)^t$

37. Future value = $100,000

Rate = 0.005

Time = 10 years

Calculate present value:

(Financial Sector)

[A] $95,140

[B] $95,135

[C] $95,130

[D] $105,000

[E] $100,000

The answer is B

$C/[(1+r)^t]$

38. Monetary policy includes managing the _____ and _____ of money:

(Financial Sector)

[A] supply and price

[B] supply and velocity

[C] price and multiplier

[D] velocity and multiplier

[E] price and velocity

The answer is A

The price of money refers to interest rates; and the volume is managed by total amount of money created, the amount of liquidity given to banks through operations like quantitative easing, or through bank reserve ratios

39. The Gold Standard:

(Financial Sector)

[A] Was highly successful

[B] Relied on the intrinsic value of gold to define the US economy

[C] Used gold as a fiat currency to which the dollar was pegged

[D] Did not create limitations on monetary policy

[E] Resolved the currency war between European and North American countries

The answer is C

The Gold Standard failed because it limited monetary policy options by failing to recognize that even gold is a fiat currency

40. The value of money is derived from:

(Financial Sector)

[A] The amount of hard assets owned by a country

[B] The ability to purchase things, backed by the production which is measured using that currency

[C] Supply and demand of currency markets

[D] Government promises of debt repayment

[E] Nowhere – it is valueless

The answer is B

It is the things which you can purchase that gives money its value

41. With money supply of $100,000 at equilibrium with production, a $10,000 nominal increase in production with no change in money supply will result in:

(Inflation, Unemployment, and Stabilization Policies)

[A] Deflation of 10%

[B] Inflation of 10%

[C] No inflation

[D] Inflation of 90%

[E] Deflation of 5%

The answer is A

An equivalent volume of money representing a larger value of production causes each dollar to be worth more, which is why monetary policy is so important

42. Aggregate supply, production possibilities curve, and economic growth all share the same:

(National Income and Price Determination)

[A] Factors

[B] Equation

[C] Usage

[D] Graphs

[E] Model

The answer is A

Capital, labor, technology, etc., depending on the model used

43. The market efficiency hypothesis fails as a result of:

(National Income and Price Determination)

[A] Sticky prices and wages

[B] Imperfect information

[C] Fixed nature of large capital

[D] A, B, and C

[E] Nothing, the market is efficient

The answer is D

This lack of efficiency is what allows for investment arbitrage

44. Delayed response to sudden price changes by companies using LIFO inventory management is an example of:

(National Income and Price Determination)

[A] Price stickiness

[B] Price Rigidity

[C] Price flexibility

[D] Imperfect information

[E] Cost stickiness

The answer is A

Companies need time to respond to changes in the market, which is called stickiness

45. A corporation with 10 million shares outstanding with share price of $2 has a total market capitalization of:

(Financial Sector)

[A] $20 million

[B] $10 million

[C] $5 million

[D] $200,000

[E] $15 million

The answer is A

Market capitalization is the total market value of a company's shares, each share representing a piece of ownership in that company

46. The Federal Reserve lends money to _____ at the _____ rate:

(Financial Sector)

[A] anyone, discount

[B] corporations, federal funds

[C] individuals, federal funds

[D] banks, federal funds

[E] banks, discount

The answer is D

The Fed only works with member banks, lending money at the federal funds rate

47. Long-Run Aggregate Supply is:

(National Income and Price Determination)

[A] The same vertical line as NAIRU

[B] The curve showing how much a nation can produce at a given price level at some point in time

[C] The maximum production potential of a nation at any price level

[D] Perfectly price elastic

[E] Representative of actual production rather than full-employment production

The answer is C

LRAS refers to the production level possible after responding to any change in price

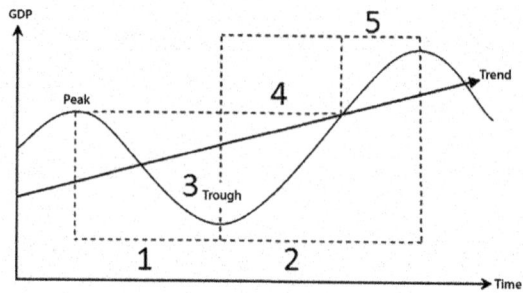

48. A period of _____ is shown at 1:

(National Income and Price Determination)

[A] expansion

[B] contraction

[C] recession

[D] recovery

[E] boom

The answer is B

A contracting economy is one that is shrinking

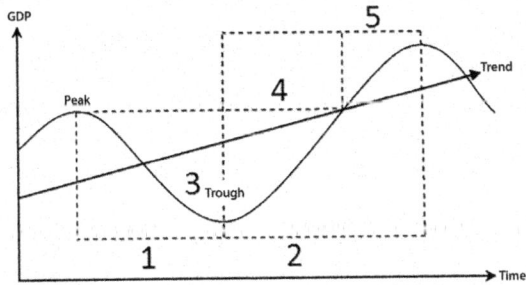

49. A ____ has been reached at 3:

(National Income and Price Determination)

[A] contraction

[B] recession

[C] expansion

[D] recovery

[E] boom

The answer is B

A recession is defined as 2 consecutive quarters of negative growth

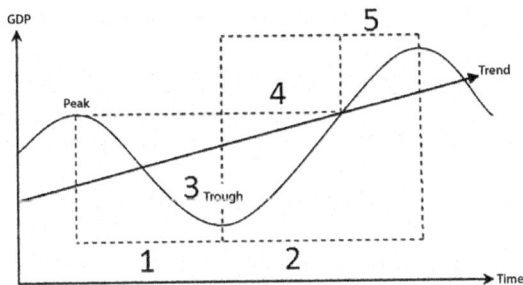

50. At 5, the economy is in a ____:

(National Income and Price Determination)

[A] recession

[B] boom

[C] contraction

[D] recovery

[E] expansion

The answer is B

A boom occurs when the economy reaches record levels of GDP

51. CPI increases from 100 to 150, and GDP increases from $500,000 to $600,000, which means that:

(Measurements of Economic Performance)

[A] GDP grew by 20% which is 30% less than CPI indicating 10% economic contraction

[B] Prices increased by 50% indicating that GDP grew by 10% rather than 20%

[C] Prices increased by 30% more than GDP indicating equivalent economic contraction

[D] GDP grew by 16% but real GDP was only 8% due to 50% inflation

[E] GDP decreased by 70%

The answer is C

Real GDP accounts for GDP growth less inflation

52. LRAS increases as:

(National Income and Price Determination)

[A] Prices increases

[B] SRAS responds to deviations from equilibrium

[C] Technology improves

[D] LRAD increases

[E] LRAS never increases

The answer is C

53.

	Fish	Wheat
Country A	15 labor hours	10 labor-hours
Country B	20 labor-hours 6	0 labor-hours

Country A has a __ opportunity cost in its comparative advantage, and Country B has a __ opportunity cost in its comparative advantage:

(Basic Economic Concepts)

[A] 1/4, 2/3

[B] 2/3, 3/4

[C] 1/2, 1/4

[D] 2/3, 1/3

[E] 1/3, 2/3

The answer is D

Although Country B has an absolute advantage in all things, their comparative advantage is in Country B, which means they will trade wheat for fish

54. Quantitative easing attempts to do the following:

(Inflation, Unemployment, and Stabilization Policies)

Real Interest Rates, Investment

[A] Decrease, Decrease

[B] Decrease, Increase

[C] No change, Increase

[D] Increase, No Change

[E] No change, Increase

The answer is C

The goal of QE is to increase liquidity of loanable funds markets

55. Stimulus increase = $500,000

Income increase = $2 million

MPC = __:

(Economic Growth)

[A] 0.25

[B] 0.5

[C] 0.75

[D] 0.33

[E] 0.66

The answer is C

The stimulus is 25% of the income increase

56. If the government increases expenditures and increases taxation by the same amount, AD will increase if:

(Growth Policy)

[A] Taxation is greater than expenditures

[B] Expenditures are greater than taxation

[C] Expenditures stimulate growth greater than the opportunity cost

[D] Expenditures do not rely on increasing national debt

[E] Cannot be determined using the available information

The answer is E

The amount of change in AD, AS, and price resulting from the increased demand and increased taxation costs depends entirely on the types of taxes and expenditures being made, and the elasticity of both supply and demand in response.

57. Buying government securities on OPO is a method used by the Fed to:

(Inflation, Unemployment, and Stabilization Policies)

[A] Slow GDP growth to sustainable levels

[B] Prevent budget deficits

[C] Strengthen the dollar

[D] Prevent inflation

[E] Alleviate a recession

The answer is E

Buying securities pumps money back into the economy and increases liquidity by limiting the amount of debt held privately

58. What effect will an decrease in the global energy production have on CPI and real GDP:

(National Income and Price Determination)

Real GDP, CPI

[A]   Decrease, Decrease

[B]   Decrease, Increase

[C]   Increase, Increase

[D]   Increase, No Change

[E]   Decrease, Increase

The answer is E

Economic production is heavily dependent on energy production, so shortages of energy result in shortages of most things

59. If both monetary and fiscal policies are contractionary, then the following is guaranteed to happen:

(Inflation, Unemployment, and Stabilization Policies)

Interest Rates, Unemployment

[A]   Increase, Indeterminate

[B]   Increase, Decrease

[C]   Decrease, Decrease

[D]   Indeterminate, Indeterminate

[E]   Indeterminate, Increase

The answer is D

The effects of economic policy is almost entirely dependent upon the context in which they are used, especially the current point in the business cycle

60. ___ will cause a decrease in the volume of commercial funds available for loans:

(Economic Growth)

[A] Increase in sale of federal loans

[B] A decrease in the reserve ratio

[C] An increase in savings

[D] A decrease in investing

[E] An increase in exports

The answer is A

Selling federal loans decreases the total amount of cash available for commercial loans unless you also decrease the reserve ratio

AP
MICROECONOMICS
Sample Test 1

Multiple Choice Questions

1. **The law of increasing opportunity cost results from:**
   (Basic Economic Concepts)

   [A] Increasing price elasticity of supply

   [B] Increasing allocation of resources which are better suited to other production

   [C] Missed investments and the time value of money

   [D] Scarcity of resources

   [E] The marginal rate of substitution

2. **When a peoples' income increases, they will have greater demand for the price/volume of goods as a result of:**
   (The Nature and Functions of Product Markets)

   [A] The substitution effect

   [B] Income elasticity

   [C] The income effect

   [D] Demand elasticity

   [E] Supply elasticity

3. **____ is the shut-down point for a profit-maximizing company:**
   (The Nature and Functions of Product Markets)

   [A] R<AFC

   [B] AVC<ATC

   [C] P<AVC

   [D] ATC<AVC

   [E] AVC<P

4. **A positive externality results in:**
   (Market Failure and the Role of Government)

   [A] Overproduction from a disproportionately high price relative to the benefits

   [B] Overproduction from a disproportionately low price relative to the benefits

   [C] Underproduction from a disproportionately high price relative to the benefits

   [D] Underproduction from a disproportionately low price relative to the benefits

   [E] Efficient production and price

5. **Person A is in an ambulance with a serious injury and will be taken directly to the nearest hospital. The market has failed as a result of:**

(Market Failure and the Role of Government)

[A] Positive externalities

[B] Elimination of consumer choice and competition

[C] Price collusion in an oligopoly

[D] Overpayment to insurance companies

[E] Negative externalities

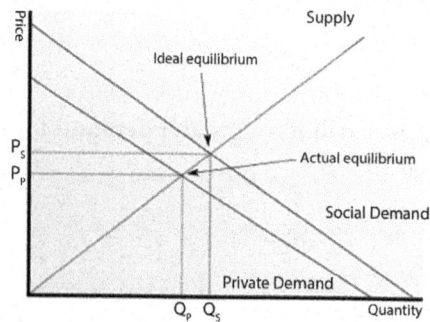

6. **This graph illustrates:**

(Market Failure and the Role of Government)

[A] Negative externality

[B] Positive externality

[C] Increased demand

[D] Increased price

[E] Decreased price

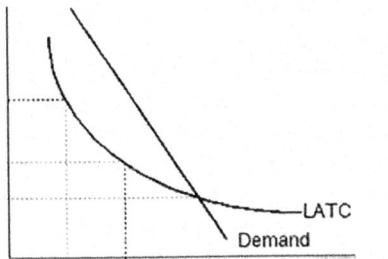

LATC
Demand

7. **This graph illustrates:**

   (Market Failure and the Role of Government)

   [A] Natural Monopoly

   [B] Negative externalities

   [C] Positive externalities

   [D] Competitive monopoly

   [E] Public goods

8. **A loss of market influence in the supply and demand of labor for individual workers results from:**

   (Factor Markets)

   [A] Income dependence and market competition

   [B] Collective bargaining

   [C] Income inequality

   [D] Public goods

   [E] Positive externalities

9. **A Lorenz Curve with a Gini Coefficient of 0 with have a slope of:**

   (Market Failure and the Role of Government)

   [A] 0

   [B] 1

   [C] 1/2

   [D] 2/1

   [E] 1/3

10. **A linear demand curve with m=1/2 has point [q=500, p=$500], what will demand be at p=$1,000:**

(Basic Economic Concepts)

[A] $750

[B] $1,000

[C] $1,500

[D] $2,500

[E] $500

11. **Ceteris paribus, a firm operating at PED = -3/1 will benefit most from a _____ strategy:**

(The Nature and Functions of Product Markets)

[A] revenue maximization

[B] profit maximization

[C] cost reduction

[D] second-mover

[E] niche

12. **A linear supply curve with points [q=10, p=$20] and [q=20, p=$50], what is PES:**

(The Nature and Functions of Product Markets)

[A] 1/3

[B] -1/3

[C] 3/1

[D] -3/1

[E] 1/2

13. **Which of these companies is most likely to thrive during a deep recession:**

(The Nature and Functions of Product Markets)

[A] Dollar Tree

[B] Maserati

[C] Gucci

[D] Rolex

[E] Louis Vuitton

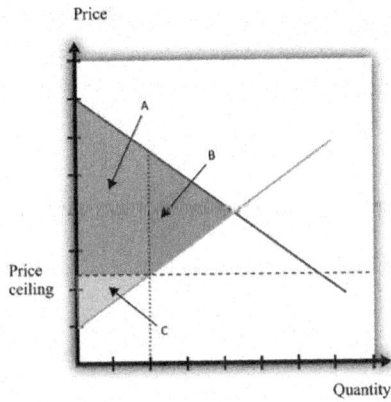

14. Area A is:

(The Nature and Functions of Product Markets)

[A] Consumer surplus

[B] Deadweight loss

[C] Producer surplus

[D] Shortage quantity

[E] Price ceiling

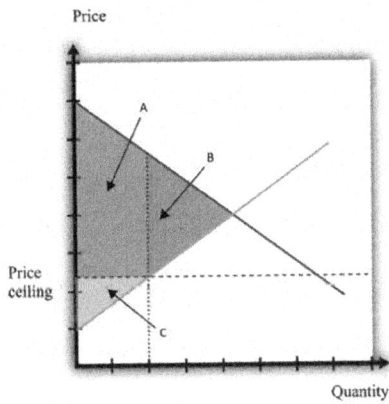

15. Area C is:

(The Nature and Functions of Product Markets)

[A] Consumer surplus

[B] Deadweight loss

[C] Producer surplus

[D] Equilibrium

[E] Minimum wage

16. Company A sells 50 units for $10 each, and their competitor Company B sells 55 units for $10. If they have a CED of 1/2, how will a 10% tax change their relative positions, ceteris paribus:
(The Nature and Functions of Product Markets)

[A] Company A will gain customers

[B] Company B will gain customers

[C] Both companies will gain customers

[D] No effect

[E] Company A will lose customers

17. Two economists are walking down the street when they see $100 on the ground. One stops to pick it up, and the other replies "Don't bother. If it was real someone would have picked it up already". This is a criticism of:
(The Nature and Functions of Product Markets)

[A] Market equilibrium

[B] Efficient market hypothesis

[C] Imperfect information

[D] Price control

[E] Arbitrage

18. Which is not a determinant of demand:
(The Nature and Functions of Product Markets)

[A] Income

[B] Population

[C] Employment

[D] Profitability

[E] Consumer preference

19. _____ **is not an example of the law of diminishing marginal utility:**
(The Nature and Functions of Product Markets)

[A] Getting sick after too many beers

[B] Decreased labor efficiency after scheduling too many people

[C] Increased productivity through specialization of labor

[D] Increasing interest rates with increased borrowing

[E] Increasing risk with higher equity market prices

20. The implications of the income effect on an individual company can be calculated by:

(The Nature and Functions of Product Markets)

[A] $\Delta D/\Delta P$

[B] $\Delta D/\Delta Y$

[C] $\Delta S/\Delta P$

[D] $\Delta I/\Delta D$

[E] $\Delta D/\Delta I$

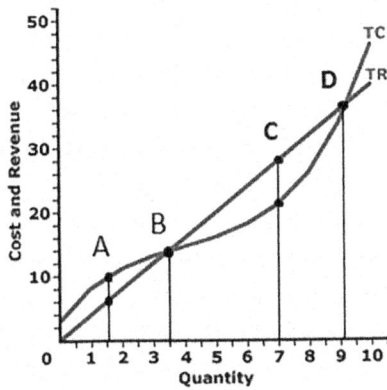

21. Revenue is maximized at:

(The Nature and Functions of Product Markets)

[A] A

[B] B

[C] C

[D] D

[E] 0

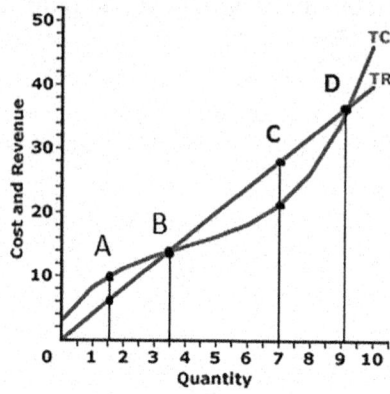

22. Profit is maximized at:

(The Nature and Functions of Product Markets)

[A] A

[B] B

[C] C

[D] D

[E] 0

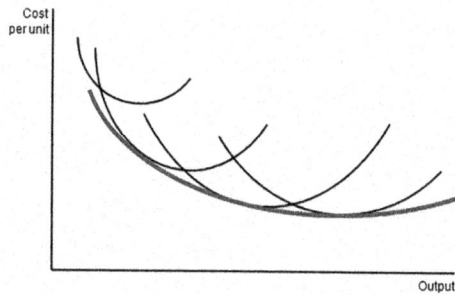

23. The red curve is:

(The Nature and Functions of Product Markets)

[A] LRAC with current capital

[B] SRAC with current capital

[C] SRAC with changes in capital potential

[D] LRAC with changes in capital potential

[E] LRAC using SRAC

24. FC=$100,000

VC = $100

1,000 unit AC =:

(The Nature and Functions of Product Markets)

[A] $1,000

[B] $1,100

[C] $100

[D] $110,000

[E] $110

25. Basic cost minimization combination is modeled as:

(The Nature and Functions of Product Markets)

[A] $MP_L/w = MP_K/r$

[B] $MP_L/r = MP_K/w$

[C] $MP_L\text{-}w = MP_K\text{-}r$

[D] $MP_L\text{-}r = MP_K\text{-}w$

[E] $MP_r\text{-}L = MP_w\text{-}k$

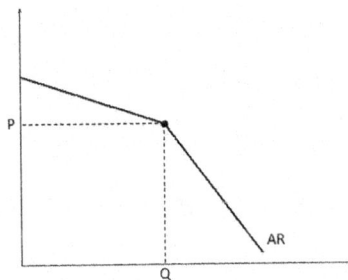

26. The kink in this curve occurs because:

(The Nature and Functions of Product Markets)

[A] A decrease in price is more elastic than an increase, leading to collusion

[B] An increase in price is more elastic than a decrease, leading to competition

[C] A decrease in price is less elastic than an increase, leading to collusion

[D] It's supposed to be curvilinear but differential calculus is too hard

[E] The kink doesn't occur at all

27. **In perfect competition, producers are _____ and consumers are _____:**
(The Nature and Functions of Product Markets)

[A]   price makers, price takers

[B]   price takers, price makers

[C]   price takers, price takers

[D]   price makers, price makers

[E]   consumers, producers

28. **In perfect competition there are _____ producers with _____ market influence :**
(The Nature and Functions of Product Markets)

[A]   few, high

[B]   many, low

[C]   infinite, none

[D]   one, full

[E]   one, none

29. **Can monopolistic profits be sustained indefinitely:**
(The Nature and Functions of Product Markets)

[A]   Yes because MR=MC

[B]   Yes because a monopoly has no competition

[C]   No because competitors will take customers

[D]   No because of the threat of new entrants

[E]   No because MR=MC

30. **Market exit occurs at:**
(The Nature and Functions of Product Markets)

[A]   MR<LRAC

[B]   P<LRAC

[C]   MR<SRAC

[D]   P<SRAC

[E]   LRAC<P

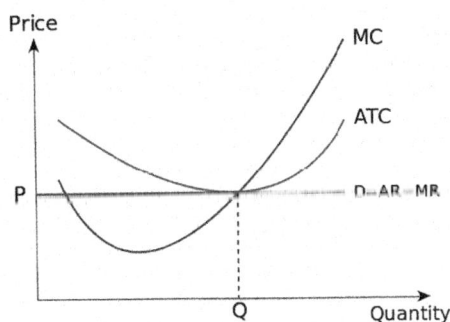

Price (y-axis), Quantity (x-axis). Curves labeled MC, ATC, and horizontal line D=AR=MR at level P. Vertical dashed line at Q.

31. Firms in perfect competition will produce at MC=ATC=MR because:

(The Nature and Functions of Product Markets)

[A] Producers are price takers

[B] Firms must continue to MR=MC to break-even

[C] Marginal profits are maximized when ATC is at its lowest point

[D] Q>MC would create per unit losses and market efficiency prevents greater profits by limiting Q

[E] MC>Q would create per unit losses and market efficiency prevents greater profits

32. Monopsony markets are not found in:

(The Nature and Functions of Product Markets)

[A] Defense

[B] Utilities

[C] Labor

[D] Agriculture

[E] Infrastructure

33. Lower wages do not lead to higher employment because:

(The Nature and Functions of Product Markets)

[A] Fewer people are willing to work at a given price level despite their need to survive

[B] Companies will never hire more people than they need to meet production demand, regardless of wage level

[C] Lower wages cause greater per-person output

[D] Higher employment requires higher price levels to increase supply

[E] Unions prevent labor negotiations

34. Suppliers that set price and consumers that set quantity are indicative of:
(The Nature and Functions of Product Markets)

[A] Cournot competition

[B] Stackelberg competition

[C] Bertrand competition

[D] Nash equilibrium

[E] Perfect competition

35. Antitrust laws do everything except:
(The Nature and Functions of Product Markets)

[A] Limit the power of unions

[B] Increase free market competition by breaking-up monopolies

[C] Protect against bid rigging

[D] Prevent collusion in oligopolies

[E] Protect against price gouging

36. Intellectual property rights give incentive to _____ but _____ prices:
(Basic Economic Concepts)

[A] hire, increases

[B] innovate, increases

[C] increase supply, decreases

[D] invest, decreases

[E] invest, increases

37. "It is not from the benevolence of the butcher, the brewer, or the baker that we expect our dinner, but from their regard to _____":
(Basic Economic Concepts)

[A] demonstrate superior morals

[B] earn receivables

[C] develop social capital

[D] their own interest

[E] government regulations

38. The factors of production do not include:
(Factor Markets)

[A] Labor

[B] Producers

[C] Land

[D] Entrepreneurship

[E] None of these

39. A competitive advantage requires an activity to be everything except:

(Basic Economic Concepts)

[A] Rare

[B] Unsubstitutable

[C] Imitable

[D] Valuable

[E] Inimitable

40. A company whose competitive advantage is in managing supply chain will benefit most from a _____ strategy:

(Basic Economic Concepts)

[A] first mover

[B] price leader

[C] niche

[D] differentiation

[E] second mover

41. Profit = $1 million

Cost = $125,000

The ROI is:

(Basic Economic Concepts)

[A] 7

[B] 10

[C] 8

[D] 5

[E] 6

42. The point at which it is impossible to allocate resources to one activity without taking them away from another is called:

(The Nature and Functions of Product Markets)

[A] Productive efficiency

[B] Allocative efficiency

[C] Pareto efficiency

[D] Kaldor-Hicks efficiency

[E] Market efficiency

43. The marginal rate of substitution calculates:
(The Nature and Functions of Product Markets)

[A] The changing amount of one product it requires to equal the utility of a substitute product

[B] The rate at which PED changes along a demand curve

[C] The rate at which labor is substituted for capital over time

[D] The rate of production required of workers to remain competitive against improving technological capital

[E] The substitution effect

44. If Company A acquires a competitor, it is an example of _____ integration:
(Factor Markets)

[A] Horizontal

[B] Vertical

[C] Diagonal

[D] Orthogonal

[E] Inverse

45. Pat builds a website which requires $10,000 worth of construction. Pat will do $6,000 of it, but needs someone to build $4,000 of economic models for the back-end. What is the derived factor demand:
(Factor Markets)

[A] $4,000

[B] $6,000

[C] $10,000

[D] $2,000

[E] $3,000

46. At L=100, R=$10,000
At L=500, R=$100,000

MRP is:
(Factor Markets)

[A] 2

[B] 10

[C] 5

[D] 1/2

[E] 1

47. Cost = $10,000

Revenue = $20,000

Revenue from 2nd Choice = $15,000

The opportunity cost is:

(Factor Markets)

[A] $20,000

[B] $35,000

[C] $10,000

[D] $15,000

[E] $5,000

48. For a person or firm to contribute to supply or demand, they must have:

(Basic Economic Concepts)

[A] Willingness but not ability

[B] Willingness and ability

[C] Ability but not willingness

[D] Already participated in an exchange

[E] Income

49. That a firm is a collection of resources and the activities which utilize those resources comes from:

(Factor Markets)

[A] Knowledge-based view of the firm

[B] Resource-based view of the firm

[C] Factor-based view of the firm

[D] Asset-based view of the firm

[E] Capital-based view of the firm

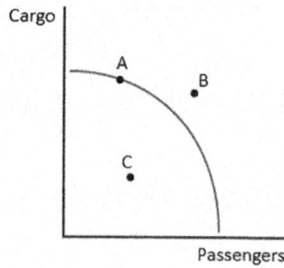

50. The efficient frontier is:

(Basic Economic Concepts)

[A] B

[B] A

[C] C

[D] Min cargo or min passengers

[E] 0

51. Which of the following situations would necessarily lead to an increase in the price of cherries:

(Factor Markets)

[A] The minimum wage to farm workers is raised at the same time that El Nino weather patterns cause production shortages

[B] The minimum wage to farm workers is raised at the same time that record volume is produced

[C] Demand for cherries increases as a result of a breakthrough in pie technology

[D] Price for pie crust increases

[E] None of the above

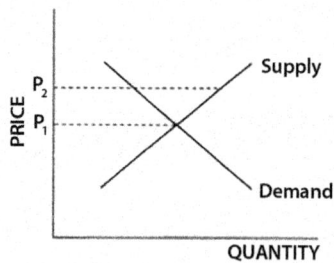

52. _____ will cause prices to rise from P_1 to P_2 if:

(The Nature and Function of Product Markets)

[A] Higher incomes cause greater demand

[B] A price ceiling is passed

[C] Unemployment increases

[D] A subsidy is issued

[E] Inflation is negative

53. **If two products from the same company sell for the same price and use the same factors of production, then how should factors of production be distributed between them:**

(Factor Markets)

[A] Until demand for at least one is fully met

[B] Until the marginal product of each factor is equal for both products

[C] Until they are in equal volume

[D] B and C

[E] A and C

54. **If the price of a good declines but total revenues remains the same, then:**

(The Nature and Functions of Product Markets)

[A] PED=Undefined

[B] PED=0

[C] PED<1

[D] PED>1

[E] PED=1

55. **The law of diminishing returns causes:**

(The Nature and Functions of Product Markets)

[A] Diseconomies of scale

[B] Economies of scale

[C] Increases in long-run average cost

[D] Increasing marginal cost

[E] Increases in fixed cost

56. **The amount of contribution to total cost created by a single factor of marginal product is known as:**

(Factor Markets)

[A] Marginal product

[B] Marginal factor cost

[C] Marginal cost

[D] Marginal production

[E] Profit margin

57. Which is true:

(The Nature and Function of Product Markets)

[A] ATC increases as MC increases

[B] MC increases when AVC is higher than MC

[C] AVC increases as MC increases

[D] AVC increases when MC is higher than AVC

[E] ATC is constant when MC is constant

58. In the short run a firm will stop production when:

(The Nature and Functions of Product Markets)

[A] R<ATC

[B] P<ATC

[C] R<AVC

[D] P<AVC

[E] R<AFC

59. In response to an increase in a firm's MC, _____ will happen in monopolistic competition:

(The Nature and Functions of Product Markets)

Price, Output

[A] Decrease, Increase

[B] Decrease, Decrease

[C] Increase, Decrease

[D] Increase, Increase

[E] No change, No change

60. If a firm dumps their waste into public waterways and no fees are issued, who incurs the cost burden:

(Market Failure and the Role of Government)

[A] Government

[B] Public

[C] Company

[D] Industry

[E] Workforce

Free-Response Questions

1. Company A is deciding whether to upgrade a piece of capital to one which has greater production potential.

Expected Life of Capital = 10 years

Depreciation = Straight Line

Scrap Value = $10,000

Initial Investment = $1 million

Operating Cost = $5,000 annually

Annual Production = 10,000 units

Price of Goods Sold = $50,000 per unit

Cash Flows = Once per year

[A] Model the conundrum

    (i)   Draw and label a graph of short-term and long-term average cost

    (ii) Explain the difference in market responsiveness between short-term and long-term, including a description of the point that distinguishes the two time periods and economic stickiness.

    (iii) Explain the difference in average costs between short-term and long-term, including economies of scale

    (iv) Why does Company A believe demand will increase to meet their new production potential, even though current demand does not?

[B] Financially assess the decision using the following calculations

    (i)   Future value

    (ii) Net Present value

    (iii) Depreciation and scrap value

    (iv) ROI

    (v) Can you calculate net revenue product from the information given? Why or why not? If so, calculate it.

2. You are hired to perform efficiency consulting for Company A.

    (i)   Allocative efficiency

    (ii) Productive efficiency

    (iii) Dynamic efficiency

(iv) X-efficiency

(v) Social efficiency

(vi) Difference between Pareto efficiency and Kaldor-Hicks efficiency

[B] Identify problems

(i) What process should be used to identify problems within a Six Sigma framework? Identify and describe 4 types of waste to look for during this process.

(ii) What process should be used to identify problems within a transfer pricing framework? Identify the role of cost and revenue centers.

[C] Decide whether to outsource

(i) When should a company outsource operations based on financial considerations?

(ii) Should the degree of strategic importance of an operations be considered in the decision to outsource? Why or why not?

3. Describe the games of oligopoly markets

[A] Draw a graph demonstrating the kinked demand curve

(i) Label AR, D, P, Q, and equilibrium

(ii) Label the graph with notation of PED above and below the kink

[B] Explain why competitors collude in oligopoly markets

(i) List the characteristics of an oligopoly market and its goods

(ii) Create a game matrix demonstrating the 4 possible strategy combinations and their general outcomes between two competitors

(iii) Describe the role of PED and game theory in the decision to collude

[C] Compare and contrast oligopolies to monopolies

(i) Do the cost, revenue, and profit curves differ between them at equilibrium? Why or why not?

(ii) When do antitrust laws apply to collusion in an oligopoly market?

[D] Provide 3 examples of oligopoly markets and defend your choices

AP Microeconomics: Sample Test 1- Answer Key

Question Number	Correct Answer	Your Answer		Question Number	Correct Answer	Your Answer
1	B			31	D	
2	C			32	B	
3	C			33	B	
4	D			34	C	
5	B			35	A	
6	B			36	B	
7	A			37	D	
8	A			38	B	
9	B			39	C	
10	A			40	B	
11	A			41	A	
12	A			42	C	
13	A			43	A	
14	A			44	A	
15	C			45	A	
16	D			46	A	
17	B			47	D	
18	D			48	B	
19	C			49	B	
20	B			50	B	
21	D			51	A	
22	C			52	A	
23	D			53	B	
24	B			54	E	
25	A			55	D	
26	A			56	A	
27	A			57	D	
28	C			58	D	
29	D			59	E	
30	B			60	B	

AP Microeconomics: Sample Test 1- Explanations

1. The law of increasing opportunity cost results from:
(Basic Economic Concepts)

[A] Increasing price elasticity of supply

[B] Increasing allocation of resources which are better suited to other production

[C] Missed investments and the time value of money

[D] Scarcity of resources

[E] The marginal rate of substitution

The answer is B

After allocating those resources most efficient in a given activity, you need to start allocating less efficient resources.

2. When a peoples' income increases, they will have greater demand for the price/volume of goods as a result of:
(The Nature and Functions of Product Markets)

[A] The substitution effect

[B] Income elasticity

[C] The income effect

[D] Demand elasticity

[E] Supply elasticity

The answer is C

The income effect means that an increase in income increases demand, and vice versa.

3. _____ is the shut-down point for a profit-maximizing company:
(The Nature and Functions of Product Markets)

[A] R<AFC

[B] AVC<ATC

[C] P<AVC

[D] ATC<AVC

[E] AVC<P

The answer is C

If price drops below average variable cost, then a company will lose money for each unit produced.

4. **A positive externality results in:**

(Market Failure and the Role of Government)

[A] Overproduction from a disproportionately high price relative to the benefits

[B] Overproduction from a disproportionately low price relative to the benefits

[C] Underproduction from a disproportionately high price relative to the benefits

[D] Underproduction from a disproportionately low price relative to the benefits

[E] Efficient production and price

The answer is D

A positive externality means that a social benefit is being produced that isn't accounted for in the price.

5. **Person A is in an ambulance with a serious injury and will be taken directly to the nearest hospital. The market has failed as a result of:**

(Market Failure and the Role of Government)

[A] Positive externalities

[B] Elimination of consumer choice and competition

[C] Price collusion in an oligopoly

[D] Overpayment to insurance companies

[E] Negative externalities

The answer is B

Without consumer choice or competition, the free-market breaks-down

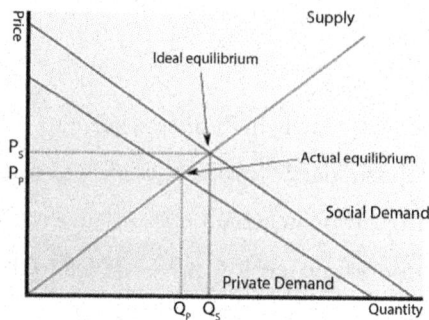

6. This graph illustrates:

(Market Failure and the Role of Government)

[A] Negative externality

[B] Positive externality

[C] Increased demand

[D] Increased price

[E] Decreased price

The answer is B

The ideal equilibrium for production with a positive externality is greater than the actual equilibrium.

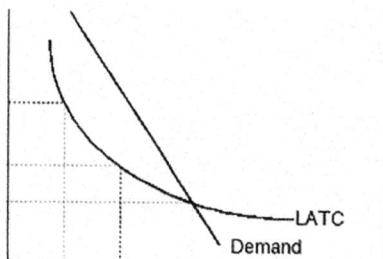

7. This graph illustrates:

(Market Failure and the Role of Government)

[A] Natural Monopoly

[B] Negative externalities

[C] Positive externalities

[D] Competitive monopoly

[E] Public goods

The answer is A

A natural monopoly occurs from inordinately high entry costs and extremely low variable cost

8. A loss of market influence in the supply and demand of labor for individual workers results from:

(Factor Markets)

[A] Income dependence and market competition

[B] Collective bargaining

[C] Income inequality

[D] Public goods

[E] Positive externalities

The answer is A

People with extremely high MPC do not have the luxury of a strong negotiating position.

9. A Lorenz Curve with a Gini Coefficient of 0 with have a slope of:

(Market Failure and the Role of Government)

[A] 0

[B] 1

[C] 1/2

[D] 2/1

[E] 1/3

The answer is B

The Gini Coefficient can be any value between 0 and 1, with 1 having a 1/1 slope, and 0 having a slope of 0 except for the richest person who has a vertical slope with a value of "undefined" since its calculation requires dividing by 0.

10. A linear demand curve with m=1/2 has point [q=500, p=$500], what will demand be at p=$1,000:

(Basic Economic Concepts)

[A] $750

[B] $1,000

[C] $1,500

[D] $2,500

[E] $500

The answer is A

"Rise over run"; for each increase of 1 in q there will be an increase of 2 in price.

11. Ceteris paribus, a firm operating at PED = -3/1 will benefit most from a _____ strategy:

(The Nature and Functions of Product Markets)

[A] revenue maximization

[B] profit maximization

[C] cost reduction

[D] second-mover

[E] niche

The answer is A

A PED of -3/1 means that customer volume will increase faster than the drop in their per-unit profits, so they can make-up for lower profits with higher volume, like Wal-Mart.

12. A linear supply curve with points [q=10, p=$20] and [q=20, p=$50], what is PES:

(The Nature and Functions of Product Markets)

[A] 1/3

[B] -1/3

[C] 3/1

[D] -3/1

[E] 1/2

The answer is A

"Rise over run"; $(y_2-y_1)/(x_2-x_1)$

13. Which of these companies is most likely to thrive during a deep recession:

(The Nature and Functions of Product Markets)

[A] Dollar Tree

[B] Maserati

[C] Gucci

[D] Rolex

[E] Louis Vuitton

The answer is A

Dollar Tree thrived during the 2008 financial collapse as people sought to save money

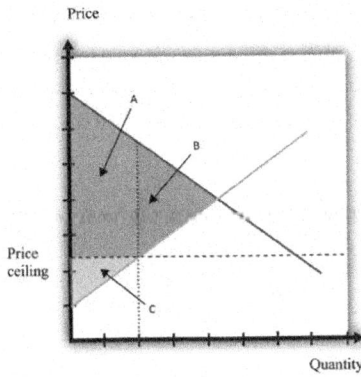

14. Area A is:

(The Nature and Functions of Product Markets)

[A] Consumer surplus

[B] Deadweight loss

[C] Producer surplus

[D] Shortage quantity

[E] Price ceiling

The answer is A

The consumer surplus is the benefit over price received by consumers

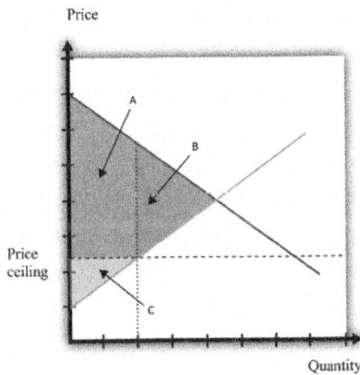

15. Area C is:

(The Nature and Functions of Product Markets)

[A] Consumer surplus

[B] Deadweight loss

[C] Producer surplus

[D] Equilibrium

[E] Minimum wage

The answer is C

The producer surplus is the value received by producers above price by selling you products

16. Company A sells 50 units for $10 each, and their competitor Company B sells 55 units for $10. If they have a CED of 1/2, how will a 10% tax change their relative positions, ceteris paribus:

(The Nature and Functions of Product Markets)

[A] Company A will gain customers

[B] Company B will gain customers

[C] Both companies will gain customers

[D] No effect

[E] Company A will lose customers

The answer is D

A tax will effect both companies equally, so that their price and demand relative to the other is left unchanged.

17. Two economists are walking down the street when they see $100 on the ground. One stops to pick it up, and the other replies "Don't bother. If it was real someone would have picked it up already". This is a criticism of:

(The Nature and Functions of Product Markets)

[A] Market equilibrium

[B] Efficient market hypothesis

[C] Imperfect information

[D] Price control

[E] Arbitrage

The answer is B

The efficient market hypothesis states that the market responds perfectly and immediately to any change, which is preposterous.

18. Which is not a determinant of demand:

(The Nature and Functions of Product Markets)

[A] Income

[B] Population

[C] Employment

[D] Profitability

[E] Consumer preference

The answer is D

The level of company profitability has no influence on a person's decision of whether to purchase something.

19. _____ is not an example of the law of diminishing marginal utility:

(The Nature and Functions of Product Markets)

[A] Getting sick after too many beers

[B] Decreased labor efficiency after scheduling too many people

[C] Increased productivity through specialization of labor

[D] Increasing interest rates with increased borrowing

[E] Increasing risk with higher equity market prices

The answer is C

Diminishing marginal utility states that each additional unit will increase total utility, but at a decreasing rate, until you reach the apex at which point your total utility actually starts to decrease.

20. The implications of the income effect on an individual company can be calculated by:

(The Nature and Functions of Product Markets)

[A] $\Delta D/\Delta P$

[B] $\Delta D/\Delta Y$

[C] $\Delta S/\Delta P$

[D] $\Delta I/\Delta D$

[E] $\Delta D/\Delta I$

The answer is B

The income effect refers to the amount that demand [D] changes in response to a change in income (Y).

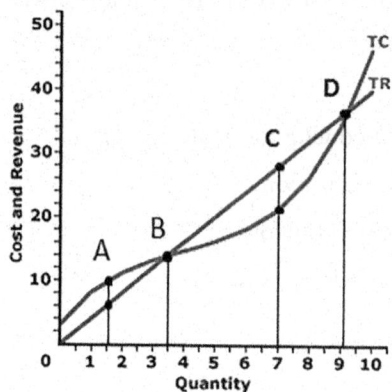

21. Revenue is maximized at:

(The Nature and Functions of Product Markets)

[A] A

[B] B

[C] C

[D] D

[E] 0

The answer is D

The profit margin is lower, but a revenue-maximizing company will still earn money until TC = TR

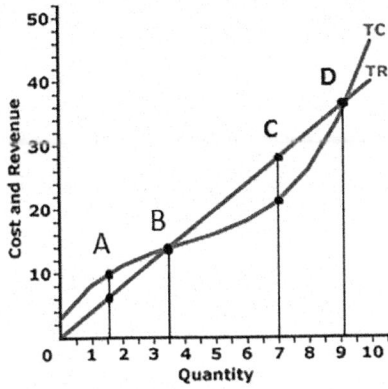

22. Profit is maximized at:

(The Nature and Functions of Product Markets)

[A] A

[B] B

[C] C

[D] D

[E] 0

The answer is C

The biggest difference in TC and TR is the largest profit.

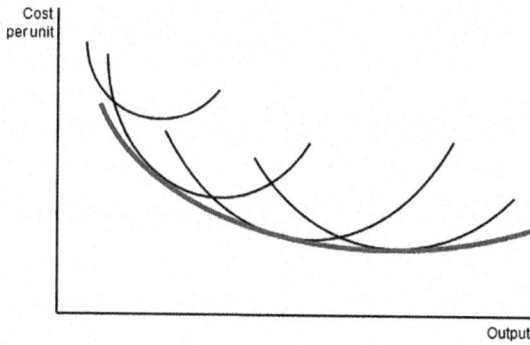

23. The red curve is:

(The Nature and Functions of Product Markets)

[A] LRAC with current capital

[B] SRAC with current capital

[C] SRAC with changes in capital potential

[D] LRAC with changes in capital potential

[E] LRAC using SRAC

The answer is D

In the long-run, any piece of equipment can be replaced

24. FC=$100,000
VC = $100
1,000 unit AC =:

(The Nature and Functions of Product Markets)

[A] $1,000

[B] $1,100

[C] $100

[D] $110,000

[E] $110

The answer is B

$AC = (FC+VCx)/x$

25. Basic cost minimization combination is modeled as:

(The Nature and Functions of Product Markets)

[A] $MP_L/w = MP_K/r$

[B] $MP_L/r = MP_K/w$

[C] $MP_L \cdot w = MP_K \cdot r$

[D] $MP_L - r = MP_K - w$

[E] $MP_r - L = MP_w - k$

The answer is A

A company will utilize the lower cost of capital or labor until the two are equal

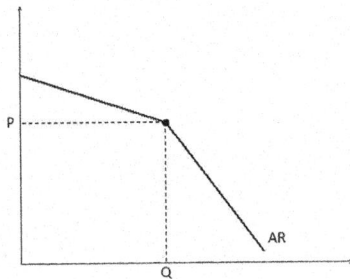

26. The kink in this curve occurs because:

(The Nature and Functions of Product Markets)

[A] A decrease in price is more elastic than an increase, leading to collusion

[B] An increase in price is more elastic than a decrease, leading to competition

[C] A decrease in price is less elastic than an increase, leading to collusion

[D] It's supposed to be curvilinear but differential calculus is too hard

[E] The kink doesn't occur at all

The answer is A

An increase in price by one firm will just lower their volume, but a decrease in price will raise volume, causing others to follow-suit. Either they compete, or they collude.

27. In perfect competition, producers are _____ and consumers are _____:
(The Nature and Functions of Product Markets)

[A] price makers, price takers

[B] price takers, price makers

[C] price takers, price takers

[D] price makers, price makers

[E] consumers, producers

The answer is A

There are many sellers producing a homogeneous product, so that each cannot influence price without either losing all their customers or forcing other sellers to follow-suit.

28. In perfect competition there are _____ producers with _____ market influence :
(The Nature and Functions of Product Markets)

[A] few, high

[B] many, low

[C] infinite, none

[D] one, full

[E] one, none

The answer is C

High competition and an efficient market decreases individual influence over the market.

29. Can monopolistic profits be sustained indefinitely:
(The Nature and Functions of Product Markets)

[A] Yes because MR=MC

[B] Yes because a monopoly has no competition

[C] No because competitors will take customers

[D] No because of the threat of new entrants

[E] No because MR=MC

The answer is D

Market structures are not static, even monopolies can be competed against through new innovations or new entrants during a period of abnormal profits.

30. Market exit occurs at:

(The Nature and Functions of Product Markets)

[A] MR<LRAC

[B] P<LRAC

[C] MR<SRAC

[D] P<SRAC

[E] LRAC<P

The answer is B

If P is less than LRAC, then there is no way to avoid losing money so the firm will exit the market entirely – they will cease to exist.

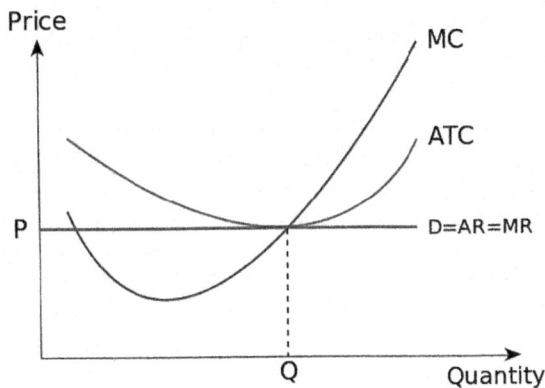

31. Firms in perfect competition will produce at MC=ATC=MR because:

(The Nature and Functions of Product Markets)

[A] Producers are price takers

[B] Firms must continue to MR=MC to break-even

[C] Marginal profits are maximized when ATC is at its lowest point

[D] Q>MC would create per unit losses and market efficiency prevents greater profits by limiting Q

[E] MC>Q would create per unit losses and market efficiency prevents greater profits

The answer is D

Once MC surpasses MR, each unit of production will lose money, but limiting supply will not increase price due to the nature of perfect competition.

32. Monopsony markets are not found in:
(The Nature and Functions of Product Markets)

[A] Defense

[B] Utilities

[C] Labor

[D] Agriculture

[E] Infrastructure

The answer is B

Utilities are generally monopolies.

33. Lower wages do not lead to higher employment because:
(The Nature and Functions of Product Markets)

[A] Fewer people are willing to work at a given price level despite their need to survive

[B] Companies will never hire more people than they need to meet production demand, regardless of wage level

[C] Lower wages cause greater per-person output

[D] Higher employment requires higher price levels to increase supply

[E] Unions prevent labor negotiations

The answer is B

Conversely, a gradual increase in wages does not decrease employment – the company will still hire only as many people as needed to meet production demands.

34. Suppliers that set price and consumers that set quantity are indicative of:
(The Nature and Functions of Product Markets)

[A] Cournot competition

[B] Stackelberg competition

[C] Bertrand competition

[D] Nash equilibrium

[E] Perfect competition

The answer is C

Bertrand competition is heavily criticized for requiring a lot of assumptions, putting into question whether such a market is realistic.

35. Antitrust laws do everything except:

(The Nature and Functions of Product Markets)

[A] Limit the power of unions

[B] Increase free market competition by breaking-up monopolies

[C] Protect against bid rigging

[D] Prevent collusion in oligopolies

[E] Protect against price gouging

The answer is A

Antitrust laws were developed to prevent monopolies, and de facto monopolies wherein companies create collective monopolistic conditions by colluding.

36. Intellectual property rights give incentive to _____ but _____ prices:

(Basic Economic Concepts)

[A] hire, increases

[B] innovate, increases

[C] increase supply, decreases

[D] invest, decreases

[E] invest, increases

The answer is B

When a company can guarantee a higher profit margin by protecting its exclusive rights to a product, it can invest more in the overhead of research and development, but this causes higher market prices, particularly as companies slightly tweak their intellectual property to artificially extend the duration. This is particularly problematic for pharmaceuticals used in 3rd world nations.

37. "It is not from the benevolence of the butcher, the brewer, or the baker that we expect our dinner, but from their regard to _____":

(Basic Economic Concepts)

[A] demonstrate superior morals

[B] earn receivables

[C] develop social capital

[D] their own interest

[E] government regulations

The answer is D

This passage in *The Wealth of Nations* clinched the end of mercantilism and the start of free markets in the West.

38. The factors of production do not include:

(Factor Markets)

[A] Labor

[B] Producers

[C] Land

[D] Entrepreneurship

[E] None of these

The answer is B

Producers use factors, but they are not considered a factor.

39. A competitive advantage requires an activity to be everything except:

(Basic Economic Concepts)

[A] Rare

[B] Unsubstitutable

[C] Imitable

[D] Valuable

[E] Inimitable

The answer is C

To maintain a competitive advantage, it must be inimitable, so that others can't copy it.

40. A company whose competitive advantage is in managing supply chain will benefit most from a ___ strategy:

(Basic Economic Concepts)

[A] first mover

[B] price leader

[C] niche

[D] differentiation

[E] second mover

The answer is B

Effective supply chain management is what allows Wal-Mart to operate on razor-thin profit margins.

41. Profit = $1 million

Cost = $125,000

The ROI is:

(Basic Economic Concepts)

[A] 7

[B] 10

[C] 8

[D] 5

[E] 6

The answer is A

(P-C)/C

42. **The point at which it is impossible to allocate resources to one activity without taking them away from another is called:**

(The Nature and Functions of Product Markets)

[A] Productive efficiency

[B] Allocative efficiency

[C] Pareto efficiency

[D] Kaldor-Hicks efficiency

[E] Market efficiency

The answer is C

Kaldor-Hicks expands on Pareto by calculating whether the gains from reallocating assets away from a particular activity are great enough to account for the opportunity cost of those assets plus more.

43. **The marginal rate of substitution calculates:**

(The Nature and Functions of Product Markets)

[A] The changing amount of one product it requires to equal the utility of a substitute product

[B] The rate at which PED changes along a demand curve

[C] The rate at which labor is substituted for capital over time

[D] The rate of production required of workers to remain competitive against improving technological capital

[E] The substitution effect

The answer is A

Beer and water will both quench your thirst, but as you drink more and more beer, that water starts to seem like a good idea.

44. If Company A acquires a competitor, it is an example of _____ integration:

(Factor Markets)

[A] Horizontal

[B] Vertical

[C] Diagonal

[D] Orthogonal

[E] Inverse

The answer is A

Horizontal, across to a different supply chain but at an equivalent point within that chain.

45. Pat builds a website which requires $10,000 worth of construction. Pat will do $6,000 of it, but needs someone to build $4,000 of economic models for the back-end. What is the derived factor demand:

(Factor Markets)

[A] $4,000

[B] $6,000

[C] $10,000

[D] $2,000

[E] $3,000

The answer is A

Derived demand is created when you need to buy a complementary factor to properly utilize the intended factor.

46. At L=100, R=$10,000

At L=500, R=$100,000

MRP is:

(Factor Markets)

[A] 2

[B] 10

[C] 5

[D] 1/2

[E] 1

The answer is A

The rate at which revenues increase in response to an increase in a given factor (in this case, labor) is the marginal revenue product.

47. Cost = $10,000

Revenue = $20,000

Revenue from 2nd Choice = $15,000

The opportunity cost is:

(Factor Markets)

[A] $20,000

[B] $35,000

[C] $10,000

[D] $15,000

[E] $5,000

The answer is D

Opportunity cost is the value of the forgone opportunity.

48. **For a person or firm to contribute to supply or demand, they must have:**

(Basic Economic Concepts)

[A] Willingness but not ability

[B] Willingness and ability

[C] Ability but not willingness

[D] Already participated in an exchange

[E] Income

The answer is B

If they've already participated in the exchange, then they no longer have demand or supply because it's already been met.

49. **That a firm is a collection of resources and the activities which utilize those resources comes from:**

(Factor Markets)

[A] Knowledge-based view of the firm

[B] Resource-based view of the firm

[C] Factor-based view of the firm

[D] Asset-based view of the firm

[E] Capital-based view of the firm

The answer is B

RBV is the standard approach for company economic and financial analysis.

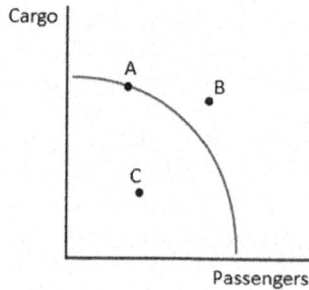

Cargo / Passengers

50. The efficient frontier is:

(Basic Economic Concepts)

[A] B

[B] A

[C] C

[D] Min cargo or min passengers

[E] 0

The answer is B

The efficient frontier is the maximum amount of output possible, at any balance of different possible outputs.

51. Which of the following situations would necessarily lead to an increase in the price of cherries:

(Factor Markets)

[A] The minimum wage to farm workers is raised at the same time that El Nino weather patterns cause production shortages

[B] The minimum wage to farm workers is raised at the same time that record volume is produced

[C] Demand for cherries increases as a result of a breakthrough in pie technology

[D] Price for pie crust increases

[E] None of the above

The answer is A

An increase in minimum wage won't necessarily increase prices by itself, but an unexpected shortage will prevent suppliers from absorbing the increased cost causing market shocks

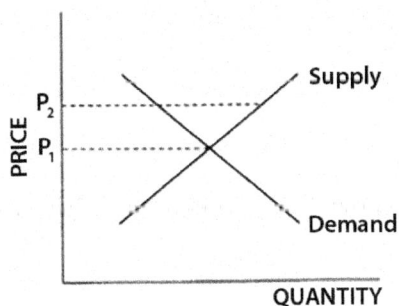

52. _____ will cause prices to rise from P$_1$ to P$_2$ if:

(The Nature and Function of Product Markets)

[A] Higher incomes cause greater demand

[B] A price ceiling is passed

[C] Unemployment increases

[D] A subsidy is issued

[E] Inflation is negative

The answer is A

The income effect states that as incomes increase so does demand. The amount of change in response to a given income change is calculated using Income Elasticity of Demand.

53. If two products from the same company sell for the same price and use the same factors of production, then how should factors of production be distributed between them:

(Factor Markets)

[A] Until demand for at least one is fully met

[B] Until the marginal product of each factor is equal for both products

[C] Until they are in equal volume

[D] B and C

[E] A and C

The answer is B

If price and cost are equal, then factors of production should be distributed to whichever can produce the most volume with a fixed volume of resources until the point that the other product becomes more efficient to produce.

54. If the price of a good declines but total revenues remains the same, then:

(The Nature and Functions of Product Markets)

[A] PED=Undefined

[B] PED=0

[C] PED<1

[D] PED>1

[E] PED=1

The answer is E

If prices decline, causing sales volume to increase in the proportion which maintains constant expenditures, then demand is unit elastic

55. The law of diminishing returns causes:

(The Nature and Functions of Product Markets)

[A] Diseconomies of scale

[B] Economies of scale

[C] Increases in long-run average cost

[D] Increasing marginal cost

[E] Increases in fixed cost

The answer is D

Each additional unit is slightly more expensive to produce; even if average cost decreases through economies of scale, the rate of decrease diminishes with higher marginal cost.

56. The amount of contribution to total cost created by a single factor of marginal product is known as:

(Factor Markets)

[A] Marginal product

[B] Marginal factor cost

[C] Marginal cost

[D] Marginal production

[E] Profit margin

The answer is A

If it takes $100 to produce the next unit, and $10 is composed of labor, then $10 is the marginal factor cost of labor.

57. Which is true:

(The Nature and Function of Product Markets)

[A] ATC increases as MC increases

[B] MC increases when AVC is higher than MC

[C] AVC increases as MC increases

[D] AVC increases when MC is higher than AVC

[E] ATC is constant when MC is constant

The answer is D

Only once the cost of producing each unit is higher than average will the average start to increase

58. In the short run a firm will stop production when:

(The Nature and Functions of Product Markets)

[A] R<ATC

[B] P<ATC

[C] R<AVC

[D] P<AVC

[E] R<AFC

The answer is D

When price drops below average variable cost, then a firm will lose money for each unit of production.

59. In response to an increase in a firm's MC, _____ will happen in monopolistic competition:

(The Nature and Functions of Product Markets)

Price, Output

[A]   Decrease, Increase

[B]   Decrease, Decrease

[C]   Increase, Decrease

[D]   Increase, Increase

[E]   No change, No change

The answer is E

If marginal cost for one firm increases, then it will not necessarily be representative of a change in price for the whole industry

60. If a firm dumps their waste into public waterways and no fees are issued, who incurs the cost burden:

(Market Failure and the Role of Government)

[A] Government

[B] Public

[C] Company

[D] Industry

[E] Workforce

The answer is B

"There is no such thing as a free lunch", so if a company consumes a resource without paying for it then it is the public which will incur the cost of this inefficiency

AP
MICROECONOMICS
Sample Test 2

Multiple Choice Questions

1. A price in decrease for Coke will cause demand do _____ and will force Pepsi to _____ their price:
   (The Nature and Functions of Product Markets)

   Coke, Pepsi

   [A] increase, increase

   [B] increase, decrease

   [C] decrease, decrease

   [D] no change, increase

   [E] increase, no change

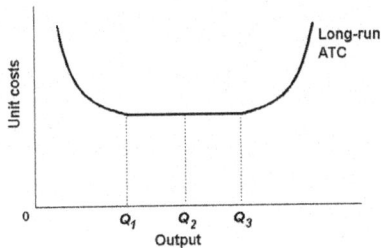

2. The long-run average total cost curve above shows:
   (The Nature and Functions of Product Markets)

   [A] Decreasing returns to scale from 0-Q1

   [B] Constant returns to scale from Q1 – Q3

   [C] Increasing returns to scale from 0-Q1

   [D] Constant returns to scale after Q3

   [E] Decreasing returns to scale after Q3

3. In perfect competition, the marginal cost of labor:
   (The Nature and Functions of Product Markets)

   [A] Increases more quickly than in oligopoly

   [B] Increases more quickly than in monopolistic competition

   [C] Remains constant at any volume

   [D] Increases with higher demand for labor

   [E] Decreases with higher demand for labor

4. **Antitrust laws were passed by Teddy Roosevelt as part of "The Square Deal" in order to:**

   (Market Failure and the Role of Government)

   [A] Protect the rights of large companies

   [B] Facilitate market competition

   [C] Formally recognize organized labor

   [D] Privatize utilities

   [E] Reform subsidies spending

5. **Military is a market failure as a result of:**

   (Market Failure and the Role of Government)

   [A] Non-excludability

   [B] Public goods

   [C] Negative externalities

   [D] National income misallocation

   [E] Off-balance sheet expenses

6. **The economy is currently at a rate of static-state consumption. What must happen for the economy to grow without entering degradation levels of consumption:**

   (Market Failure and the Role of Government)

   [A] Decreased consumption of resources through lower production

   [B] Decreased efficiency of the resources consumed

   [C] Increased efficiency of the resources consumed

   [D] Restoration levels of consumption

   [E] Decreased efficiency of the resources produced

7. **MPC elasticity of income resulting in investment differentials in a
    non-regulated market naturally causes:**
    (Market Failure and the Role of Government)

    [A] Decreasing income inequality

    [B] Increasing income inequality

    [C] Higher economic growth

    [D] Lower savings rates

    [E] Monopolies

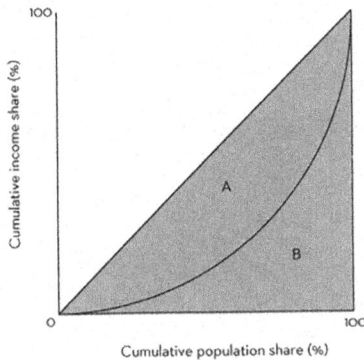

Cumulative income share (%)

Cumulative population share (%)

8. **The Gini Coefficient measuring national income inequality is calculated as:**
    (Market Failure and the Role of Government)

    [A] A/B

    [B] B/A

    [C] B-A

    [D] 2A+B

    [E] A+2B

9. **Free-riding of public goods causes constantly increasing air and water
    pollution in an unregulated market because:**
    (Market Failure and the Role of Government)

    [A] Public goods cannot be freely consumed, so only those who use them must pay
    for their cost

    [B] Public goods are controlled by the government, preventing the market from
    reaching equilibrium

    [C] Public goods are sold to producers

    [D] Public goods can be consumed without paying directly for their cost, placing the
    burden on taxpayers

    [E] Public goods are natural monopolies

10. Ceteris paribus, a firm operating at PED = -1/2 will benefit most from a _____ strategy:

(The Nature and Functions of Product Markets)

[A] revenue maximization

[B] profit maximization

[C] price competition

[D] cost reduction

[E] niche

11. Company A has CED = 2/1 relative to Company B, what is Company A likely to do to their price relative to Company B, ceteris paribus:

(The Nature and Functions of Product Markets)

[A] Decrease price because Company B will lose customers faster than Company A lowers price

[B] Increase price because Company A will increase profitability faster than Company B will gain customers

[C] Increase price because Company A will increase profitability faster than Company B will lose customers

[D] Decrease price because Company B will lose customers faster than Company A raises price

[E] Decrease price because Company B will increase costs faster than Company A will lose customers

12. A linear demand curve for a superior good will be _____ and for an inferior good it will be _____:

(The Nature and Functions of Product Markets)

[A] positive, positive

[B] positive, negative

[C] negative, negative

[D] negative, positive

[E] none of these

13. **An increase in minimum wage will cause:**

(The Nature and Functions of Product Markets)

[A] A short-run reduction in producer surplus, and long-run cost-push inflationary pressure

[B] A short-run shortage of jobs, and long-run cost-push inflationary pressure

[C] A short-run reduction in producer surplus, and long-run shortage of jobs

[D] A short-run reduction in producer surplus, and long-run increase in deadweight loss

[E] A long-run reduction in consumer surplus, and a short run increase in producer surplus

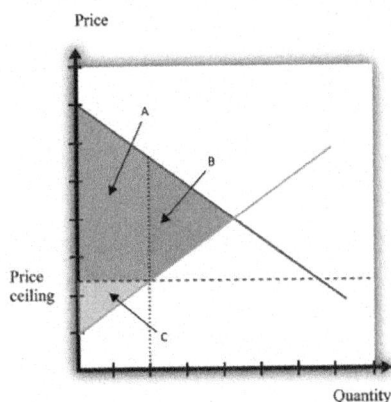

14. **Area B is:**

(The Nature and Functions of Product Markets)

[A] Consumer surplus

[B] Deadweight loss

[C] Producer surplus

[D] Surplus quantity

[E] Price floor

15. **Subsidies contribute most to:**

(The Nature and Functions of Product Markets)

[A] Price reductions

[B] Recipient profitability

[C] Decreased consumer surplus

[D] Increased deadweight loss

[E] Decreased costs

16. A consumer tax refund increases short-term demand 5%. This is an example of:

(The Nature and Functions of Product Markets)

[A] Income elasticity of supply

[B] The substitution effect

[C] The income effect

[D] Deadweight loss

[E] Price elasticity of supply

17. Which is not a determinant of supply:

(The Nature and Functions of Product Markets)

[A] Capital gains tax

[B] Equity markets

[C] Bond prices

[D] Quantity demanded

[E] Degree of trade barriers

18. Money = $25

$5 Pizza = 10U-2n

$5 Beer = 20U-5n

Maximize total U:

(The Nature and Functions of Product Markets)

[A] 50

[B] 55

[C] 60

[D] 100

[E] 120

19. Increased demand as a result of changes in consumer preferences after repeated exposure through advertising is an example of:

(The Nature and Functions of Product Markets)

[A] Mere-exposure effect

[B] Substitution effect

[C] Income effect

[D] Marginal utility optimization

[E] Marketing effect

20. ΔU/ΔQ calculates:

(The Nature and Functions of Product Markets)

[A] The rate of increase in nominal utility

[B] The rate of decrease in marginal utility

[C] The rate of decrease in quantity demanded with price increases

[D] The rate of increase in quantity supplied with price decreases

[E] The rate of increase in utility resulting from increasing quantity

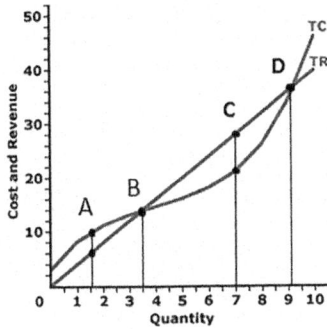

21. The breakeven point is at:

(The Nature and Functions of Product Markets)

[A] A

[B] B

[C] C

[D] D

[E] 0

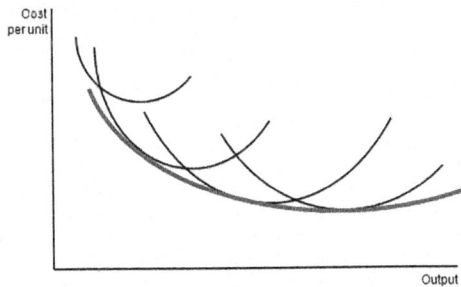

22. The black curves are:

(The Nature and Functions of Product Markets)

[A] LRAC with changes in capital potential

[B] SRAC with changes in capital potential

[C] LRAC using current capital

[D] SRAC using current capital

[E] LRAC using SRAC

23. Why do SRAC and LRAC decrease:

(The Nature and Functions of Product Markets)

[A] Increases in current capital productivity decrease AFC until capacity then more productive capital is purchased

[B] Decreases in current capital productivity increase AFC until capacity then more productive capital is purchased

[C] Increases in current capital productivity increase SRAC until capacity then more productive capital is purchased

[D] Decreases in current capital productivity decrease SRAC until capacity then more productive capital is purchased

[E] Economies of scale only cause average costs to increase

24. Decreased costs resulting from being in close proximity to suppliers, partners, and customers is called:

(The Nature and Functions of Product Markets)

[A] Economies of agglomeration

[B] Economies of scale

[C] Diseconomies of agglomeration

[D] Diseconomies of scale

[E] Economies of proximity

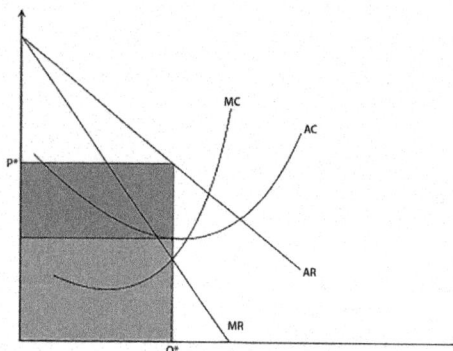

25. Monopolistic profits are maximized at the point:

(The Nature and Functions of Product Markets)

[A] MR = MC

[B] AR = Q

[C] MC = AR

[D] AC = AR

[E] MC>MR

26.

	Price 1	Price 2
Price 1	50, 50	75, 25
Price 2	25, 75	25, 25

This game is typical of:

(The Nature and Functions of Product Markets)

[A] Differentiation in monopolistic competition

[B] Price elasticity of demand in perfect competition

[C] Monopolistic profit maximization

[D] Oligopoly market collusion incentive

[E] Prisoner's dilemma

27. In oligopoly, producers are _____ and consumers are _____:

(The Nature and Functions of Product Markets)

[A] price takers, price takers

[B] price takers, price makers

[C] price makers, price takers

[D] price makers, price makers

[E] consumers, producers

28. Monopolistic competition relies on _____ firms with _____ products:

(The Nature and Functions of Product Markets)

[A] many, differentiated

[B] many, homogeneous

[C] few, differentiated

[D] few, homogeneous

[E] one, differentiated

29. Shutdown occurs at:

(The Nature and Functions of Product Markets)

[A] MR<FC

[B] MR<MC

[C] MR<AVC

[D] MR<ATC

[E] AVC<MR

30. Does ATC decrease until MC>ATC:
(The Nature and Functions of Product Markets)

[A] No because decreasing AFC will always lower MC with higher quantity

[B] Yes because AFC increases with higher quantity

[C] Yes because each unit with MC>ATC will raise ATC

[D] No because ATC will always be the lowest as FC is distributed over higher quantity

[E] No because each unit with ATC>MC will raise ATC

31. Abnormal profits can be earned in monopolistic competition?
(The Nature and Functions of Product Markets)

[A] Only in the short-run due threats from competitors

[B] Only in the long-run after the years to break-even

[C] In both the short- and long-run due to continuous development of new differentiations

[D] In neither the short- or long-run because firms of price takers

[E] In both the short- and long-run due to new entrants

32. Monopsony and monopsonistic competition contribute to:
(The Nature and Functions of Product Markets)

[A] Greater output per capita through lower employment levels

[B] Greater innovation through intense labor competition

[C] Lower levels of unemployment as a single company hires everyone

[D] Higher income disparity through lower competitive strength by workers in labor markets

[E] Lower levels of inflation

33. Leader and follower competitive games are indicative of:
(The Nature and Functions of Product Markets)

[A] Nash equilibrium

[B] Bertrand competition

[C] Cournot competition

[D] Stackelberg competition

[E] Perfect competition

34. Coercive monopolies use all of these methods to prevent new entrants, except:

(The Nature and Functions of Product Markets)

[A] Predatory pricing

[B] Competitive wages

[C] Expensive lawsuits

[D] Acquisitions

[E] Intellectual property rights

35. Antitrust laws were established by Teddy Roosevelt as part of the _____ Deal:

(The Nature and Functions of Product Markets)

[A] square

[B] new

[C] good

[D] slick

[E] hot

36. Money facilitates transactions due to the trait of:

(Basic Economic Concepts)

[A] Spendability

[B] Convertibility

[C] Transferability

[D] Exchangeability

[E] Flexibility

37. A person who makes pins can make 1 million per day, but if they also tried to smelt their own metal that number would drop to 100 per day. This is a result of:

(Basic Economic Concepts)

[A] Transfer pricing in multi-step production

[B] Longer production cycles

[C] Trade between specialists in the division of labor

[D] Labor burnout

[E] Overtime

38. An entrepreneur is deciding on a venture to purchase. Which do they choose:

(Factor Markets)

[A] P=1 million, r=.16, t=3

[B] P=$2 million, r=.05, t=10

[C] P=$500,000, r=.17, t=7

[D] P=$1 million, r=.15, t=5

[E] P=$2 million, r=.15, t=5

39. A company whose competitive advantage is innovation would benefit most from a _____ strategy:

(Basic Economic Concepts)

[A] price leader

[B] differentiation

[C] first mover

[D] niche

[E] second mover

40. The PED of emergency healthcare is:

(Market Failure and the Role of Government)

[A] -1/2

[B] 1

[C] 0

[D] ∞

[E] Undefined

41. MR=MC is:

(The Nature and Functions of Product Markets)

[A] Productive efficiency

[B] Allocative efficiency

[C] Pareto efficiency

[D] Kaldor-Hicks efficiency

[E] Market efficiency

42. **That we put more value on the things we own than the exact same things owned by others is a result of:**

(The Nature and Functions of Product Markets)

[A] Disposition effect

[B] Endowment effect

[C] Substitution effect

[D] Observation effect

[E] Income Effect

43. **The relationship between the marginal rate of substitution and the law of decreasing marginal utility is:**

(The Nature and Functions of Product Markets)

[A] They are competing measures of consumer utility

[B] Diminishing utility means it takes marginally less of Product A to create the same utility as 1 unit of Product B

[C] Diminishing utility means it takes marginally more of Product A to create the same utility as 1 unit of Product B

[D] There is no relationship

[E] Marginal rate of substitution measures the law of decreasing marginal utility

44. **If Company A acquires a supplier, it is an example of _____ integration:**

(Factor Markets)

[A] diagonal

[B] horizontal

[C] orthogonal

[D] vertical

[E] inverse

45. Cost = $10,000

Revenue = $20,000

Revenue from 2nd Choice = $15,000

The accounting profit is _____ and the economic profit is _____:

(The Nature and Functions of Product Markets)

[A] $10,000, $25,000

[B] $5,000, $10,000

[C] $10,000, $5,000

[D] $10,000, -$5,000

[E] -$10,000, -$5,000

46. A labor supply curve will sometimes bend backwards at higher wage rates due to the following possibilities except:

(Factor Markets)

[A] Unreasonably long work hours

[B] Lack of skill level required at that wage

[C] Forgoing other benefits for higher wages

[D] Unsafe types of work

[E] Undesirable types of work

47. The principle of scarcity states that:

(Basic Economic Concepts)

[A] In times of shortage, price increases

[B] There are not enough resources for everyone to have a comfortable life

[C] It is not possible to produce enough to meet the wants and needs of everyone

[D] There are not enough resources for everyone to survive

[E] We will eventually run-out of resources

48. "Firms" include everything except:

(Basic Economic Concepts)

[A] Households

[B] Businesses

[C] Industries

[D] Governments

[E] Non-profits

49. That a firm is a collection of ideas, policies, knowledge, and expertise comes from:

(Factor Markets)

[A] Resource-based view of the firm

[B] Factor-based view of the firm

[C] Knowledge-based view of the firm

[D] Asset-based view of the firm

[E] Ideal-based view of the firm

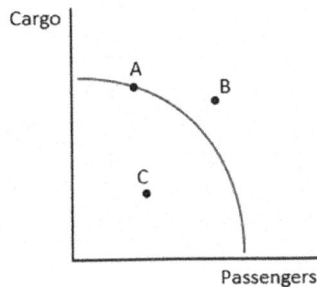

50. Production is possible at:

(Basic Economic Concepts)

[A] B and C

[B] A, B, and C

[C] A and B

[D] A and C

[E] None of these

51. Which of the following is not true of a perfectly competitive market:

(The Nature and Functions of Product Markets)

[A] P>ATC in the long run

[B] P>MC in the short run

[C] MR>ATC in the short run

[D] MR>MC in the short run

[E] ATC>MC in the long run

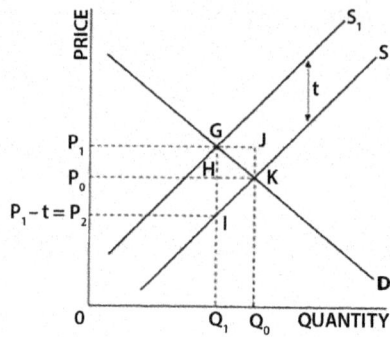

52. Taxes are found in the area:

(The Nature and Function of Product Markets)

[A] P_1GHP_0

[B] P_1GIP_2

[C] P_2IHP_1

[D] P_1JKP_0

[E] P_0KJG

53. Which of the following bears the burden of taxation:

(The Nature and Function of Product Markets)

[A] The consumer

[B] The producer

[C] The consumer and producer

[D] The group which pays the tax bears it

[E] It cannot be determined based on the information available

54. The shutdown point for monopolies is:

(The Nature and Function of Product Markets)

[A] MR<MC at all price levels

[B] AR<TC at all price levels

[C] AR<ATC at profit maximization

[D] AR<AVC at profit maximization

[E] MR<MC at profit maximization

55. **A monopolist in the long-run:**

(The Nature and Functions of Product Markets)

[A] Are earning a return on investments equal to opportunity cost

[B] Will collude with competitors

[C] Will lose economic profits

[D] Will adapt to rapidly-changing market trends

[E] There is no difference between short-run and long-run monopolistic markets

56. **A monopolist price is too _____ and quantity too _____:**

(The Nature and Functions of Product Markets)

[A] low, low

[B] high, High

[C] low, high

[D] high, low

[E] perfectly efficient price and quantity

	Strategy 1	Strategy 2
Strategy 1	**A** $1,000 / $1,000	**B** $1,200 / $600
Strategy 2	**C** $600 / $1,200	**D** $800 / $800

57. Company A and Company B can each choose a single strategy. In the first-round game (i.e., before collusion), they will pick:

(The Nature and Functions of Product Markets)

	Company A	**Company B**
[A]	Strategy 1	Strategy 1
[B]	Strategy 1	Strategy 2
[C]	Strategy 2	Strategy 1
[D]	Strategy 2	Strategy 2
[E]	None	None

Output	Total Cost
0	$13
1	20
2	25
3	28
4	32
5	43
6	60

58. MC of the 5th unit is:

(The Nature and Functions of Product Markets)

[A] $11

[B] $17

[C] $4

[D] $7

[E] Cannot be determined

59. Information about US tariffs and rates a firm must pay is found in:

(The Nature and Functions of Product Markets)

[A] Harmonized tariff schedule

[B] US Tariff guidebook

[C] Federal Trade Commission compendium

[D] Customs and Border Patrol tariff index

[E] The official Congressional tariff herald

60. The factors used to calculate HDI include:

(Market Failure and the Role of Government)

[A] Health, happiness, and education

[B] Health, wealth, and happiness

[C] Health, wealth, and equality

[D] Health, wealth, and education

[E] Equality, wealth, and education

Free-Response Questions

1. Company A operates in a perfectly competitive market for beef.

   [A] Draw and label graphs

   (i) Industry graph with S, D, P, Q, and equilibrium

   (ii) Long-run firm graph with MC, ATC, MR, AR, P, Q, and equilibriu

   (iii) Short-run firm graph with MC, ATC, MR, AR, P, Q, profit maximization point, and equilibrium

   [B] Describe why firms in perfect competition advertise collectively for the industry, rather than individually

   (i) Include the traits of perfectly competitive markets

   [C] The beef industry also has differentiation from Kobe and Wagyu beef

   (i) Does company A compete directly with these specialty beefs? Why or why not?

2. Address the matter of monopolization

   [A] Create a graph of monopolistic price and output, including

   (i) Marginal revenue

   (ii) Demand

   (iii) Marginal cost

   (iv) Average total cost

   (v) Monopoly profit

   (vi) Consumer surplus

   (vii) Producer surplus

   (viii) Deadweight loss

   [B] Compare and contrast monopolies and natural monopolies, including the differences in cost and revenue curves

[C] Describe several measures intended to prevent monopolistic abuses

    (i)   Sherman Antitrust Act

    (ii)   Elkins Act

    (iii) Clayton Antitrust Act

3.   **You are hired to develop market strategy for Company A, which operates in a market of monopolistic competition.**

[A] Use RBV to assess firm

    (i)   What factors of production are likely to lead to a differentiation strategy?

    (ii)   In what areas of a standard value chain might a company maintain a competitive advantage if they are to pursue a price leader strategy?

    (iii) If a company chooses a first-mover strategy, resources must be allocated to what types of capabilities? Why?

[B] Assess price positioning

    (i)   Draw a graph with standard, generic supply and demand curves

    (ii)   Label the range where it PED is elastic, where it is inelastic, and where it is unit elastic

    (iii) Consider your answer to part [B](iii) and do the same for PES

    (iv) In terms of PED, define when profit optimization or revenue optimization is recommended

    (v)   Write the formula for CED, and describe its role in price positioning, ensuring to make note of inferior and superior goods

[C] Draw a graph illustrating points of profit maximization and revenue maximization through a relationship between TR and TC

    (i)   Include labels for price and quantity for the points of break-even, profit maximization, and revenue maximization

[D] Identify and describe the types of goods which violate the law of demand

    (i)   Giffen goods.

    (ii)   Veblen goods.

    (iii) Investments. What differentiates investing from purchasing?

AP Microeconomics: Sample Test 2- Answer Key

Question Number	Correct Answer	Your Answer		Question Number	Correct Answer	Your Answer
1	C			31	C	
2	B			32	D	
3	C			33	D	
4	B			34	B	
5	A			35	A	
6	C			36	C	
7	B			37	C	
8	A			38	D	
9	D			39	C	
10	B			40	D	
11	A			41	B	
12	D			42	B	
13	A			43	C	
14	B			44	D	
15	B			45	C	
16	C			46	B	
17	A			47	C	
18	C			48	C	
19	A			49	C	
20	B			50	D	
21	B			51	A	
22	D			52	B	
23	A			53	E	
24	A			54	D	
25	A			55	E	
26	D			56	D	
27	C			57	D	
28	A			58	A	
29	C			59	A	
30	C			60	D	

1. A price in decrease for Coke will cause demand do _____ and will force Pepsi to _____ their price:

    (The Nature and Functions of Product Markets)

    Coke, Pepsi

    [A] increase, increase

    [B] increase, decrease

    [C] decrease, decrease

    [D] no change, increase

    [E] increase, no change

    The answer is C

    A price decrease will either decrease demand for competitors and substitutes, or force them to lower price in response.

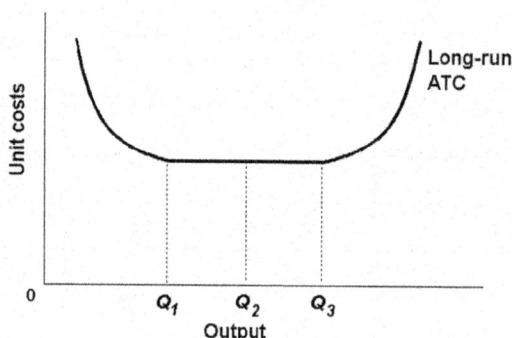

2. The long-run average total cost curve above shows:

    (The Nature and Functions of Product Markets)

    [A] Decreasing returns to scale from 0-Q1

    [B] Constant returns to scale from Q1 – Q3

    [C] Increasing returns to scale from 0-Q1

    [D] Constant returns to scale after Q3

    [E] Decreasing returns to scale after Q3

    The answer is B

    Q1-Q3 demonstrates constant returns to scale.

3. **In perfect competition, the marginal cost of labor:**

   (The Nature and Functions of Product Markets)

   [A] Increases more quickly than in oligopoly

   [B] Increases more quickly than in monopolistic competition

   [C] Remains constant at any volume

   [D] Increases with higher demand for labor

   [E] Decreases with higher demand for labor

The answer is C

Perfect competition prevents producer price influence, ensuring that P=MR=AR.

4. **Antitrust laws were passed by Teddy Roosevelt as part of "The Square Deal" in order to:**

   (Market Failure and the Role of Government)

   [A] Protect the rights of large companies

   [B] Facilitate market competition

   [C] Formally recognize organized labor

   [D] Privatize utilities

   [E] Reform subsidies spending

The answer is B

Breaking-up monopolies stimulates market competition by increasing the number of firms in the market.

5. **Military is a market failure as a result of:**

   (Market Failure and the Role of Government)

   [A] Nonexcludability

   [B] Public goods

   [C] Negative externalities

   [D] National income misallocation

   [E] Off-balance sheet expenses

The answer is A

You cannot control who benefits from a standing military

6. **The economy is currently at a rate of static-state consumption. What must happen for the economy to grow without entering degradation levels of consumption:**

(Market Failure and the Role of Government)

[A] Decreased consumption of resources through lower production

[B] Decreased efficiency of the resources consumed

[C] Increased efficiency of the resources consumed

[D] Restoration levels of consumption

[E] Decreased efficiency of the resources produced

The answer is C

Static-state consumption means that total resource consumption is equal to the rate of resource restoration, so the only way to increase growth while remaining static-state is to increase the output using an equal volume of resources.

7. **MPC elasticity of income resulting in investment differentials in a non-regulated market naturally causes:**

(Market Failure and the Role of Government)

[A] Decreasing income inequality

[B] Increasing income inequality

[C] Higher economic growth

[D] Lower savings rates

[E] Monopolies

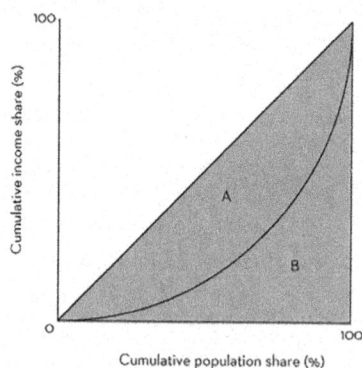

Cumulative population share (%)

The answer is B

If you spend all you income on subsistence, then you have none to invest, so you never have a chance to get your money working for you.

8. **The Gini Coefficient measuring national income inequality is calculated as:**
   (Market Failure and the Role of Government)

   [A] A/B

   [B] B/A

   [C] B-A

   [D] 2A+B

   [E] A+2B

The answer is A

The Gini Coefficient is calculated by diving the area between perfect equality and the Lorenz Curve, by the area between the Lorenz Curve and perfect inequality.

9. **Free-riding of public goods causes constantly increasing air and water pollution in an unregulated market because:**
   (Market Failure and the Role of Government)

   [A] Public goods cannot be freely consumed, so only those who use them must pay for their cost

   [B] Public goods are controlled by the government, preventing the market from reaching equilibrium

   [C] Public goods are sold to producers

   [D] Public goods can be consumed without paying directly for their cost, placing the burden on taxpayers

   [E] Public goods are natural monopolies

The answer is D

There is no way for the market to control the consumption of freely-available things like air, but the emergence of problems like "black lung" prompted government intervention.

10. Ceteris paribus, a firm operating at PED = -1/2 will benefit most from a _____ strategy:

(The Nature and Functions of Product Markets)

[A] revenue maximization

[B] profit maximization

[C] price competition

[D] cost reduction

[E] niche

The answer is B

A PED of -1/2 means that profits will increase more quickly than the company will lose customers for an increase in price, like Apple.

11. Company A has CED = 2/1 relative to Company B, what is Company A likely to do to their price relative to Company B, ceteris paribus:

(The Nature and Functions of Product Markets)

[A] Decrease price because Company B will lose customers faster than Company A lowers price

[B] Increase price because Company A will increase profitability faster than Company B will gain customers

[C] Increase price because Company A will increase profitability faster than Company B will lose customers

[D] Decrease price because Company B will lose customers faster than Company A raises price

[E] Decrease price because Company B will increase costs faster than Company A will lose customers

The answer is A

$\Delta D_B / \Delta P_A$

12. A linear demand curve for a superior good will be _____ and for an inferior good it will be _____:

(The Nature and Functions of Product Markets)

[A] positive, positive

[B] positive, negative

[C] negative, negative

[D] negative, positive

[E] none of these

The answer is D

Higher prices leads people to seek value brands.

13. An increase in minimum wage will cause:

(The Nature and Functions of Product Markets)

[A] A short-run reduction in producer surplus, and long-run cost-push inflationary pressure

[B] A short-run shortage of jobs, and long-run cost-push inflationary pressure

[C] A short-run reduction in producer surplus, and long-run shortage of jobs

[D] A short-run reduction in producer surplus, and long-run increase in deadweight loss

[E] A long-run reduction in consumer surplus, and a short run increase in producer surplus

The answer is A

Prices are sticky, forcing company to reduce their profit margins to adhere to the new wage laws. Prices will not increase until increased demand resulting from the income effect starts to drive increased sales.

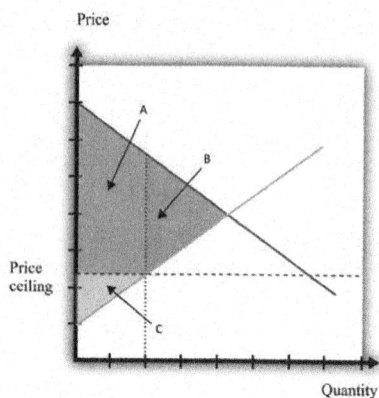

14. Area B is:

(The Nature and Functions of Product Markets)

[A] Consumer surplus

[B] Deadweight loss

[C] Producer surplus

[D] Surplus quantity

[E] Price floor

The answer is B

Deadweight loss occurs when there is lost potential value

15. Subsidies contribute most to:

(The Nature and Functions of Product Markets)

[A] Price reductions

[B] Recipient profitability

[C] Decreased consumer surplus

[D] Increased deadweight loss

[E] Decreased costs

The answer is B

Prices typically only decrease as a result of price competition, or surplus inventory.

16. A consumer tax refund increases short-term demand 5%. This is an example of:

(The Nature and Functions of Product Markets)

[A] Income elasticity of supply

[B] The substitution effect

[C] The income effect

[D] Deadweight loss

[E] Price elasticity of supply

The answer is C

When people have more money, they spend more money, which turns into company revenues, which depletes inventories, forcing companies into production, which drives employment up, causing investors to become more confident and invest more money.

17. Which is not a determinant of supply:

(The Nature and Functions of Product Markets)

[A] Capital gains tax

[B] Equity markets

[C] Bond prices

[D] Quantity demanded

[E] Degree of trade barriers

The answer is A

Equity and bond markets influence the cost of capital, and demand drive the incentive to produce.

18. Money = $25

$5 Pizza = 10U-2n

$5 Beer = 20U-5n

Maximize total U:

(The Nature and Functions of Product Markets)

[A] 50

[B] 55

[C] 60

[D] 100

[E] 120

The answer is C

Pizza decreases in utility by 2 for each marginal unit, while beer decreases by 5. With $25 you'll get 4 beers and 1 pizza. Your next purchase would be another pizza, but you spent almost all your money on beer.

19. **Increased demand as a result of changes in consumer preferences after repeated exposure through advertising is an example of:**

(The Nature and Functions of Product Markets)

[A] Mere-exposure effect

[B] Substitution effect

[C] Income effect

[D] Marginal utility optimization

[E] Marketing effect

The answer is A

Songs will "start to grow on you", many foods and drinks are "acquired tastes", and so forth. These are all the result of the mere-exposure effect.

20. ΔU/ΔQ calculates:

(The Nature and Functions of Product Markets)

[A] The rate of increase in nominal utility

[B] The rate of decrease in marginal utility

[C] The rate of decrease in quantity demanded with price increases

[D] The rate of increase in quantity supplied with price decreases

[E] The rate of increase in utility resulting from increasing quantity

The answer is B

An increase in quantity will result in a decrease in marginal utility

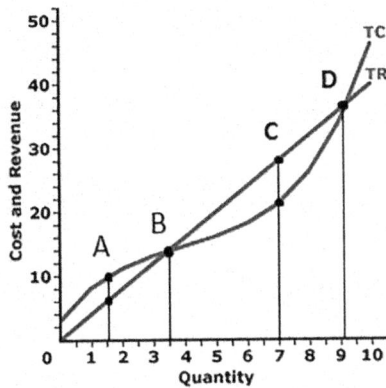

21. The breakeven point is at:

(The Nature and Functions of Product Markets)

[A] A

[B] B

[C] C

[D] D

[E] 0

The answer is B

Fixed cost ensures that a minimum quantity must be sold to avoid losing money

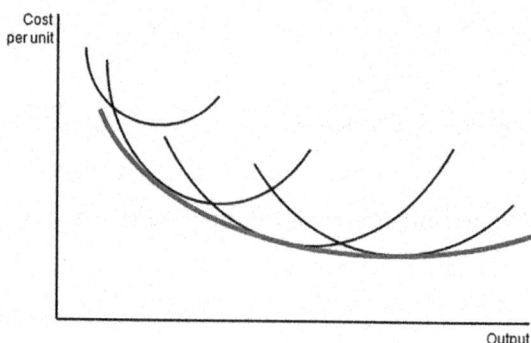

Cost per unit / Output

22. The black curves are:

(The Nature and Functions of Product Markets)

[A] LRAC with changes in capital potential

[B] SRAC with changes in capital potential

[C] LRAC using current capital

[D] SRAC using current capital

[E] LRAC using SRAC

The answer is D

A given piece of equipment has limited minimum AC, but higher-volume equipment can be bought.

23. Why do SRAC and LRAC decrease:

(The Nature and Functions of Product Markets)

[A] Increases in current capital productivity decrease AFC until capacity then more productive capital is purchased

[B] Decreases in current capital productivity increase AFC until capacity then more productive capital is purchased

[C] Increases in current capital productivity increase SRAC until capacity then more productive capital is purchased

[D] Decreases in current capital productivity decrease SRAC until capacity then more productive capital is purchased

[E] Economies of scale only cause average costs to increase

The answer is A

Distributing fixed-cost over more volume decreases per-unit cost, then once the current equipment reaches full capacity it will be replaced by something bigger.

24. Decreased costs resulting from being in close proximity to suppliers, partners, and customers is called:

(The Nature and Functions of Product Markets)

[A] Economies of agglomeration

[B] Economies of scale

[C] Diseconomies of agglomeration

[D] Diseconomies of scale

[E] Economies of proximity

The answer is A

Closer proximity results in lower costs of logistics, plus improved knowledge spillover

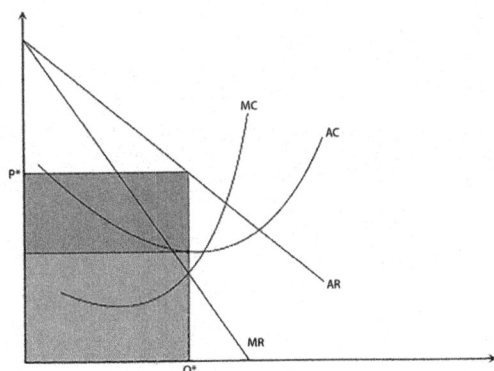

25. Monopolistic profits are maximized at the point:

(The Nature and Functions of Product Markets)

[A] MR = MC

[B] AR = Q

[C] MC = AR

[D] AC = AR

[E] MC>MR

The answer is A

MR=MC is the maximization point for monopolies, but their profit level extends all the way to AR.

26.

	Price 1	Price 2
Price 1	50, 50	75, 25
Price 2	25, 75	25, 25

This game is typical of:

(The Nature and Functions of Product Markets)

[A] Differentiation in monopolistic competition

[B] Price elasticity of demand in perfect competition

[C] Monopolistic profit maximization

[D] Oligopoly market collusion incentive

[E] Prisoner's dilemma

The answer is D

One company can choose price 2 to maximize their profits, but that will only work in the short-run until both companies are competing at lower profits, leading them to collude.

27. In oligopoly, producers are _____ and consumers are _____:

(The Nature and Functions of Product Markets)

[A] price takers, price takers

[B] price takers, price makers

[C] price makers, price takers

[D] price makers, price makers

[E] consumers, producers

The answer is C

Price-fixing is typical of collusion

28. Monopolistic competition relies on _____ firms with _____ products:

(The Nature and Functions of Product Markets)

[A] many, differentiated

[B] many, homogeneous

[C] few, differentiated

[D] few, homogeneous

[E] one, differentiated

The answer is A

Price positioning and market strategy is most pronounced in monopolistic competition.

29. Shutdown occurs at:

(The Nature and Functions of Product Markets)

[A] MR<FC

[B] MR<MC

[C] MR<AVC

[D] MR<ATC

[E] AVC<MR

The answer is C

If MR is less than AVC, a firm will lose money for each unit of production, so they will stop operating until they can respond to the problem.

30. Does ATC decrease until MC>ATC:

(The Nature and Functions of Product Markets)

[A] No because decreasing AFC will always lower MC with higher quantity

[B] Yes because AFC increases with higher quantity

[C] Yes because each unit with MC>ATC will raise ATC

[D] No because ATC will always be the lowest as FC is distributed over higher quantity

[E] No because each unit with ATC>MC will raise ATC

The answer is C

ATC starts high due to FC, but a low MC gradually brings it down, but at the point that MC>ATC, the average will start to increase again.

31. Abnormal profits can be earned in monopolistic competition?

(The Nature and Functions of Product Markets)

[A] Only in the short-run due threats from competitors

[B] Only in the long-run after the years to break-even

[C] In both the short- and long-run due to continuous development of new differentiations

[D] In neither the short- or long-run because firms of price takers

[E] In both the short- and long-run due to new entrants

The answer is C

Companies don't wait for their abnormal profits to disappear, they develop new products, new strategies, new markets, and new advertising.

32. Monopsony and monopsonistic competition contribute to:

(The Nature and Functions of Product Markets)

[A] Greater output per capita through lower employment levels

[B] Greater innovation through intense labor competition

[C] Lower levels of unemployment as a single company hires everyone

[D] Higher income disparity through lower competitive strength by workers in labor markets

[E] Lower levels of inflation

The answer is D

When all market influence is removed from labor supply, firms will lower wages to its bare minimum.

33. Leader and follower competitive games are indicative of:

(The Nature and Functions of Product Markets)

[A] Nash equilibrium

[B] Bertrand competition

[C] Cournot competition

[D] Stackelberg competition

[E] Perfect competition

The answer is D

Stackelberg competition assess markets with two or more producers of unequal market influence, so that they maintain a first-mover, second-mover strategy.

34. Coercive monopolies use all of these methods to prevent new entrants, except:

(The Nature and Functions of Product Markets)

[A] Predatory pricing

[B] Competitive wages

[C] Expensive lawsuits

[D] Acquisitions

[E] Intellectual property rights

The answer is B

Coercive monopolies will temporarily shift their market to push-out new entrants so that they can then maintain monopolistic profits.

35. Antitrust laws were established by Teddy Roosevelt as part of the _____ Deal:

(The Nature and Functions of Product Markets)

[A] square

[B] new

[C] good

[D] slick

[E] hot

The answer is A

The "New Deal" was Franklin Roosevelt.

36. Money facilitates transactions due to the trait of:

(Basic Economic Concepts)

[A] Spendability

[B] Convertibility

[C] Transferability

[D] Exchangeability

[E] Flexibility

The answer is C

Without transferability, we would all be using individualized IOUs or loans from the individual suppliers.

37. A person who makes pins can make 1 million per day, but if they also tried to smelt their own metal that number would drop to 100 per day. This is a result of:

(Basic Economic Concepts)

[A] Transfer pricing in multi-step production

[B] Longer production cycles

[C] Trade between specialists in the division of labor

[D] Labor burnout

[E] Overtime

The answer is C

You can get more done at work than you could if you also tried to make all the tools you use at your job. That's why gains from trade are possible, and why division of labor is no different than international trade

38. An entrepreneur is deciding on a venture to purchase. Which do they choose:

(Factor Markets)

[A] P=1 million, r=.16, t=3

[B] P=$2 million, r=.05, t=10

[C] P=$500,000, r=.17, t=7

[D] P=$1 million, r=.15, t=5

[E] P=$2 million, r=.15, t=5

The answer is D

$P(1+r)^t$

39. A company whose competitive advantage is innovation would benefit most from a _____ strategy:

(Basic Economic Concepts)

[A] price leader

[B] differentiation

[C] first mover

[D] niche

[E] second mover

The answer is C

An innovative company will consistently be able to produce the next big thing before anyone else can offer it.

40. The PED of emergency healthcare is:

(Market Failure and the Role of Government)

[A] -1/2

[B] 1

[C] 0

[D] ∞

[E] Undefined

The answer is D

No matter how much it costs, if you're seriously wounded then it's unlikely you'll refuse treatment, even if given the option to refuse.

41. MR=MC is:

(The Nature and Functions of Product Markets)

[A] Productive efficiency

[B] Allocative efficiency

[C] Pareto efficiency

[D] Kaldor-Hicks efficiency

[E] Market efficiency

The answer is B

Allocative efficiency refers to the allocation of the factors of production within a firm, so that they maximize revenues.

42. That we put more value on the things we own than the exact same things owned by others is a result of:
(The Nature and Functions of Product Markets)

[A] Disposition effect

[B] Endowment effect

[C] Substitution effect

[D] Observation effect

[E] Income Effect

The answer is B

The endowment effect is universal not just in humans, but in primates, too.

43. The relationship between the marginal rate of substitution and the law of decreasing marginal utility is:
(The Nature and Functions of Product Markets)

[A] They are competing measures of consumer utility

[B] Diminishing utility means it takes marginally less of Product A to create the same utility as 1 unit of Product B

[C] Diminishing utility means it takes marginally more of Product A to create the same utility as 1 unit of Product B

[D] There is no relationship

[E] Marginal rate of substitution measures the law of decreasing marginal utility

The answer is C

The law of diminishing marginal utility is what defines that shape and rate of the marginal rate of substitution.

44. If Company A acquires a supplier, it is an example of _____ integration:
(Factor Markets)

[A] Diagonal

[B] Horizontal

[C] Orthogonal

[D] Vertical

[E] Inverse

The answer is D

Vertical, meaning up or down your own supply chain.

45. Cost = $10,000

Revenue = $20,000

Revenue from 2nd Choice = $15,000

The accounting profit is _____ and the economic profit is _____:

(The Nature and Functions of Product Markets)

[A] $10,000, $25,000

[B] $5,000, $10,000

[C] $10,000, $5,000

[D] $10,000, -$5,000

[E] -$10,000, -$5,000

The answer is C

Accounting profit refers to the financial gain only, while economic profit also considers the opportunity cost.

46. A labor supply curve will sometimes bend backwards at higher wage rates due to the following possibilities except:

(Factor Markets)

[A] Unreasonably long work hours

[B] Lack of skill level required at that wage

[C] Forgoing other benefits for higher wages

[D] Unsafe types of work

[E] Undesirable types of work

The answer is B

Some things are just more important than money, particularly when you're already making enough money to satisfy your need for it.

47. The principle of scarcity states that:

(Basic Economic Concepts)

[A] In times of shortage, price increases

[B] There are not enough resources for everyone to have a comfortable life

[C] It is not possible to produce enough to meet the wants and needs of everyone

[D] There are not enough resources for everyone to survive

[E] We will eventually run-out of resources

The answer is C

The needs of people can be met, but the wants are limitless.

48. "Firms" include everything except:

(Basic Economic Concepts)

[A] Households

[B] Businesses

[C] Industries

[D] Governments

[E] Non-profits

The answer is C

A firm is any unified collection of people and resources working toward a single purpose.

49. That a firm is a collection of ideas, policies, knowledge, and expertise comes from:

(Factor Markets)

[A] Resource-based view of the firm

[B] Factor-based view of the firm

[C] Knowledge-based view of the firm

[D] Asset-based view of the firm

[E] Ideal-based view of the firm

The answer is C

Operating strategies are often developed using KBV in industries that include a lot of specialized skills, information, or intellectual property.

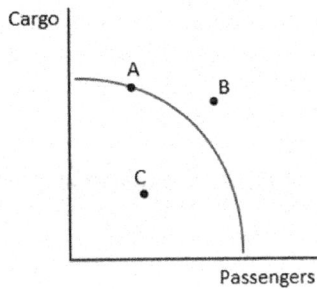

50. Production is possible at:

(Basic Economic Concepts)

[A] B and C

[B] A, B, and C

[C] A and B

[D] A and C

[E] None of these

The answer is D

Although point C is an inefficient utilization of resources, it is possible. Point B is impossible.

51. Which of the following is not true of a perfectly competitive market:

(The Nature and Functions of Product Markets)

[A] P>ATC in the long run

[B] P>MC in the short run

[C] MR>ATC in the short run

[D] MR>MC in the short run

[E] ATC>MC in the long run

The answer is A

In perfect competition, economic profits can only be sustained in the short-run

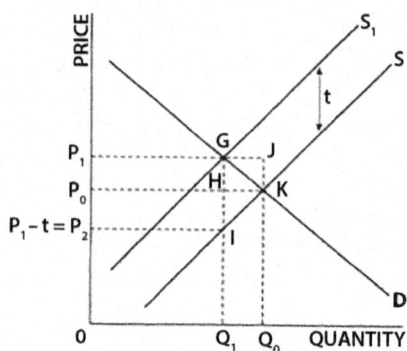

52. Taxes are found in the area:

(The Nature and Function of Product Markets)

[A] P_1GHP_0

[B] P_1GIP_2

[C] P_2IHP_1

[D] P_1JKP_0

[E] P_0KJG

The answer is B

The difference in the equilibrium at S and S_1 is representative of the tax rate, t, which is applied to Q_1

53. Which of the following bears the burden of taxation:

(The Nature and Function of Product Markets)

[A] The consumer

[B] The producer

[C] The consumer and producer

[D] The group which pays the tax bears it

[E] It cannot be determined based on the information available

The answer is E

There are many types of taxes, despite the tendency to think of "taxes" as a collective whole

54. The shutdown point for monopolies is:

(The Nature and Function of Product Markets)

[A] MR<MC at all price levels

[B] AR<TC at all price levels

[C] AR<ATC at profit maximization

[D] AR<AVC at profit maximization

[E] MR<MC at profit maximization

The answer is D

If a monopoly is earning revenues lower than their variable cost, then even at their profit maximization point they are merely minimizing losses.

55. A monopolist in the long-run:

(The Nature and Functions of Product Markets)

[A] Are earning a return on investments equal to opportunity cost

[B] Will collude with competitors

[C] Will lose economic profits

[D] Will adapt to rapidly-changing market trends

[E] There is no difference between short-run and long-run monopolistic markets

The answer is E

56. A monopolist price is too _____ and quantity too _____:

(The Nature and Functions of Product Markets)

[A] low, low

[B] high, high

[C] low, high

[D] high, low

[E] perfectly efficient price and quantity

The answer is D

Monopolistic profits represent the value of social inefficiency

	Strategy 1	Strategy 2
Strategy 1	**A** $1,000 / $1,000	**B** $1,200 / $600
Strategy 2	**C** $600 / $1,200	**D** $800 / $800

57. Company A and Company B can each choose a single strategy. In the first-round game (i.e.: before collusion), they will pick:
(The Nature and Functions of Product Markets)

Company A, Company B

[A] Strategy 1, Strategy 1

[B] Strategy 1, Strategy 2

[C] Strategy 2, Strategy 1

[D] Strategy 2, Strategy 2

[E] None, None

The answer is D

Before either company knows anything about the other, they will each pursue the strategy which benefits them most, and only choose the strategy that is most collectively beneficial upon collusion. It is the consumer which loses this game, as the collusion strategy has the highest price, by far.

Output	Total Cost
0	$13
1	20
2	25
3	28
4	32
5	43
6	60

58. MC of the 5th unit is:

(The Nature and Functions of Product Markets)

[A] $11

[B] $17

[C] $4

[D] $7

[E] Cannot be determined

The answer is A

The 5th unit requires $11 to produce, bringing total cost to $43

59. Information about US tariffs and rates a firm must pay is found in:

(The Nature and Functions of Product Markets)

[A] Harmonized tariff schedule

[B] US Tariff guidebook

[C] Federal Trade Commission compendium

[D] Customs and Border Patrol tariff index

[E] The official Congressional tariff herald

The answer is A

The Official Harmonized Tariff Schedule is updated and republished every year by the US Trade Commission and can be found easily online

60. The factors used to calculate HDI include:

(Market Failure and the Role of Government)

[A] Health, happiness, and education

[B] Health, wealth, and happiness

[C] Health, wealth, and equality

[D] Health, wealth, and education

[E] Equality, wealth, and education

The answer is D

Life expectancy at birth (health), GNI per capita (wealth), and years of schooling (education)

CPSIA information can be obtained
at www.ICGtesting.com
Printed in the USA
BVOW04s0001140817
491837BV00048B/359/P

9 781607 876335